Offshore Outsourcing

Business Models, ROI
and Best Practices

Marcia Robinson
Ravi Kalakota

Mivar Press, Inc.

Publisher's Cataloging-in-Publication Data

Robinson, Marcia.
    Offshore outsourcing : business models, roi, and best practices / Marcia Robinson and
Ravi Kalakota — 1ˢᵗ ed.
    p. cm.
    Includes bibliographical references and index.
    ISBN 0-9748270-0-2
    1.   Management. 2. Performance. 3. Business process outsourcing. 4. Re-engineering—
        Management. 5. Information technology. I. Robinson, Marcia. II. Kalakota, Ravi. III.
        Title.

    HD31.B626 2004
    658—dc21
        2003116223

Mivar Press

Published by Mivar Press, Inc.
4080 McGinnis Ferry Road, Suite 603
Alpharetta, GA 30005

Cover design by Graphix Works.

The publisher offers discounts on this book when ordered in quantity for bulk purchases and
special sales. For more information, please contact Corporate and Government Sales at
Mivar Press at sales@mivarpress.com or (678) 339 1236 x207.

Visit Mivar Press, Inc. on the Web: www.mivarpress.com

Printed in the United States of America.
First Printing

Contents

Preface

Why are corporations such as General Electric, HSBC, IBM, Oracle, and Deutsche Bank transforming their internal services and administrative operations using offshore outsourcing? Can companies that have focused on outsourcing manufacturing for so many years replicate similar cost and productivity improvements by offshoring business processes such as IT, finance and accounting, human resources, customer care, and transaction processing? What can others learn from the market leaders? Is offshore outsourcing a temporary management fad or a long-term business trend?

These are some of the questions that led us to write *Offshore Outsourcing*. In this book, we introduce readers to offshore strategy creation and implementation. We hope to help managers of all levels tap into the power of the offshore outsourcing trend that is transforming the cost structures and competitive dynamics of several industries.

Slowly but surely, offshore initiatives are resulting in millions of dollars in operational cost savings for corporations like Citigroup, Ford, and American Express. Can your business achieve the same results? The answer is yes. Contrary to many people's fear, you do not have to be a multinational company to reap the benefits of offshore outsourcing. If done well, offshore outsourcing can improve your bottom line and streamline the structure of your organization.

Offshore Outsourcing — Where Do You Start?

When building something innovative, one needs a clear blueprint. Unfortunately, while there is a lot of general discussion about offshore outsourcing, almost all of it is either anecdotal or simplistic. In order to help you unlock the value of offshore outsourcing, we decode some of the core concepts behind this trend in *Offshore Outsourcing*. In particular, we illustrate five areas.

1. **Best Practices.** Offshore outsourcing encompasses a broad array of business best practices and skills that are essential ingredients for success. Throughout this book, we use best-practice case studies to show you how to apply offshore outsourcing to many different processes and tasks and maximize the impact of your efforts.

2. **Business Models.** There are many business models for offshore outsourcing. This book gives you customizable guidelines that take into account your business needs and readiness for change.

3. **Process Focus.** Whether you decide on information technology outsourcing or business process outsourcing, the potential gains from each are equally impressive Our priority is to explain how to make offshore outsourcing work in administrative, customer-facing, and transactional areas that are relatively untapped in the quest for cost reduction.

4. **Creating Your Roadmap.** Offshore outsourcing is as much about people, vendor selection, country selection, and project management as it is about cost reduction. Our goal is to show you how to achieve a balance between managing people and improving performance.

5. **Assessing ROI and Business Risks.** Done right, offshore outsourcing can deliver sizable bottom-line impact, but it's a lot of work, and it's not without risks. *Offshore Outsourcing* sheds light on the dangers and mistakes that can derail an offshore initiative.

It doesn't take a genius to realize that the companies that successfully implement offshore outsourcing are going to put a lot of pressure on their competitors to follow suit. Obtaining even a small cost advantage in today's brutally competitive market place can mean the difference between market leadership and failure.

The Organization of This Book

When we wrote this book we tried to structure it so that a variety of readers, from offshore outsourcing novices to managers in the midst of offshore projects, would find it easy to navigate. While you may prefer to read it cover to cover, the content is organized in three parts to help you learn about offshore outsourcing at the level of depth you choose. Following is a quick guide to the content.

- Part One of the book provides a thorough overview of the offshore outsourcing landscape. We begin by defining key concepts and trends (Chapter 1), business models (Chapter 2), and the process landscape (Chapter 3). We also explain how three best-practice firms — General Electric, Dell, and American Express — are capitalizing on the offshore outsourcing trend.

- Part Two of the book provides a detailed overview of the different business processes — information technology (Chapter 4), customer care (Chapter 5), finance and accounting (Chapter 6), human resources (Chapter 7), and transaction processing (Chapter 8) — that companies are sending offshore. Throughout these chapters, we have included many case studies because they allow you to see the key business processes being transformed, the implementation challenges that companies and third-party providers struggle with, and the ROI that results from resolving them.

- Part Three of the book focuses on the "how-to." We discuss how you can create, implement, and benefit from an offshore outsourcing strategy. We present the steps that are normally included when companies create clear, focused offshore strategies (Chapter 9), decide on vendors (Chapter 10), and select countries (Chapter 11).

At the end of this book, we hope that readers will return to their organizations with new ideas and an understanding that offshore outsourcing is a journey, not a one-time event with a quick payoff. Agree or disagree — offshore outsourcing is changing the business landscape.

Acknowledgements

We were very fortunate to have the participation of many people who took the time to discuss offshoring with us. To each of these people, we would like to express thanks for the ideas, insights, and experiences they shared with us: Shirish Netke, Ananthan Thandri, Raman Roy, Somshankar Das, Ilya Billig, Tim Lavin, Venu Vaishya, Krishnaswamy Subrahmaniam, Michael Gantt, Anshuman "Andy" Kankan, Derek Holley, Phaneesh Murthy, Tim Barry, Richard Swanson, Bob Evans, Abhay Chauhan, Eric Paljug, Sanjay Kumar, Supriyo Sanyal, Richard Welke, S. Parathasarathy, Charina Quizon, Alison Jones, Ashish Kumar, Vellayan Subbiah, Stephen Wong, Madhu Ankarath, Robert Green, Vinod Keni, Kent Webb, and Randall McCroskey.

Several individuals were extremely helpful in arranging interviews and providing information on offshore outsourcing. In particular, we would like to thank Donna Candelori, Tony Viola, Natalie Fischer, Laura Livingstone, Denise Nelson, Ericka Loften, Rahul Gaur, Prasanna Satpathy, Puja Karki, Joe Peterson, and Glen Wendt.

We also would like to thank the staff at E-Business Strategies who helped shape our ideas and research into a book. The team included Pavan Gundepudi, Allison Loudermilk, and Brandon Doty. Their energy and persistence are especially appreciated.

Finally, thank you to our family and friends who continue to support us book after book. And to Lynn Lorenc, for her encouragement and graphic expertise.

Marcia Robinson

marcia@ebstrategy.com

Ravi Kalakota

ravi@ebstrategy.com

Chapter One

Offshore Outsourcing: The Next Wave

"If you do not develop a strategy of your own, you become part of someone else's strategy."

— Alfred Toffler

Introduction

Consider the following headlines:

- In the airline industry, Delta Air Lines offshore outsourced some of its worldwide reservation services to India–based Wipro Spectramind. This third-party vendor manages Delta's reservations from it Mumbai call center; a move that Delta expects will save $26 million in 2003 alone.

- In the aerospace industry, Boeing is reported to have saved at least 50% on the cost of developing an Internet-based system for creating and distributing engineering schematics by outsourcing to Russia-based LUXOFT.

- In the Internet services industry, America Online (AOL) has a large call center facility in Subic, the Philippines, handling all e-mail queries from the company's 35 million subscribers. AOL operates a 24-hour customer service facility, staffed by 500 Filipino employees.

- In the telecommunications industry, BellSouth Corporation is outsourcing IT work to a facility run by Accenture in India. The business case suggests moving one-third to one-half of BellSouth's IT application work offshore. The plan is expected to save BellSouth $275 million over five years.

- In the software industry, Microsoft announced a $100-million investment to scale up its Indian product development and R&D center. Oracle announced plans to double its software development workforce in India to 6,000 people.

- In the retail industry, The Home Depot sent some of its IT application development offshore to India-based Wipro. Starting with the development of a comprehensive security system, the relationship has spanned a wide range of projects — from globalization of store applications to developing point-of-sale and merchandise systems.

- In the financial services industry, the investment bank Goldman Sachs is tightening its belt and relocating part of its IT, equity research, and administrative operations to an Indian center that should begin operations by year-end 2004 and employ around 250 IT and administrative staff.

- In the private equity sector, General Atlantic announced a $100 million investment in India's sixth-largest software services exporter, Patni Computer Systems, while private equity firm Oak Hill Capital acquired ExlService, an offshore BPO services firm with 1,700 employees previously owned by Conseco.

Why are so many market leaders in a variety of industries rapidly formulating and executing offshore outsourcing strategies? Do they see a trend that others do not? What strategic advantages are the early adopters of the offshore outsourcing model receiving? Are we beginning to see the same trends in back-office services that happened in manufacturing? Is this a long-term trend or a short-term fad?

Before we answer these questions, let's define offshoring. Broadly speaking, offshoring is the migration of part or all of the value chain to a low-cost location. Offshoring hinges on cost management through labor and skill arbitrage. It is dependent on the dramatic advances in telecommunications technology that have made it possible to locate back-office operations in a variety of locations and to benefit from significantly lower labor costs.

Customer Pressure: Do More but Charge Less

More than anything else, the driving force of offshore outsourcing are customers who want more of everything for less money. If they value low cost, they want it lower. If they value service, convenience, or speed, they want it even easier, faster, and all the time. If they value innovation, they want to see state-of-the-art gadgets and features. The companies that don't meet these customer demands quickly fall by the wayside.

Increasing customer value creation is precisely why companies like Ford, IBM, Siemens, Oracle, Sun Microsystems, Kodak, Microsoft, and Accenture are transforming themselves. One or more competitors in their markets are constantly increasing the value offered to customers by improving products, cutting prices, or enhancing service. For instance, Indian firms Wipro and Infosys, with their low prices, caused their competitors Accenture and IBM to follow suit. By raising the level of value that customers expect, some leading firms are driving the market and their competition downhill. Companies that cannot hold their own in their ability to cut costs will slip off the radar screen.

Most market leaders understand the "more value for less" battle in which they are engaged. They know that customers will not pay higher prices, so they have to squeeze their cost structure. This means that they have to drive margin improvement by reducing sales, general, and administrative (SG&A) costs.

Most large corporations have reached (or are quickly reaching) the limits of cost-cutting using traditional methods. These firms realize that to drive even more costs out of their operations they have to go offshore. However, before they can identify and execute offshore opportunities that give them operating leverage, three elements are crucial:

1. The skills and management practices required to seamlessly integrate both individual projects and large-scale process offshore outsourcing activities into the overall company strategy.

2. Leadership that defines and communicates a unifying vision, together with a strategy for achieving it.

3. For long-term effectiveness, an organizational culture that encourages and supports offshoring.

In this book, we explain how companies can develop and strengthen all three elements, with particular emphasis on the skills, knowledge, and management methods needed to control individual and large-scale business process outsourcing (BPO) projects.

Offshore Outsourcing: What Is It? Why Do It?

Every ten years or so there is a surge of interest in cutting operating costs. The previous wave of cost-cutting occurred in the early 1990s under the guise of re-engineering. The side effect of this wave was corporate downsizing. In the early 2000s, after a multiyear economic downturn, we are seeing a similar trend of reshaping business processes with the goal of reducing costs. Now, however, the trend is called business process outsourcing (BPO) and offshore outsourcing.

In this section, we define offshore outsourcing and provide a variety of examples to illustrate the trend. We then consider some basic premises or assumptions that are shaping offshore outsourcing decisions.

What Is Offshore Outsourcing?

Offshore outsourcing is the delegation of administrative, engineering, research, development, or technical support processes to a third-party vendor in a lower-cost location. It can also include the re-engineering of processes. The term "re-engineering" in the context of offshore outsourcing refers to a strategy of developing new process designs and solutions in order to eliminate business performance problems.

Before we delve deeper into the offshoring trend, it is important to differentiate offshoring from business process outsourcing (BPO), which involves the migration of services to an external provider. A common misconception is that all offshoring involves outsourcing. This is not true. While outsourced processes are handed off to third-party vendors, offshored processes can be handed off to third-party vendors *or* remain in-house. The definition of offshoring includes organizations that build dedicated captive centers of their own in remote, lower-cost locations.

Offshore outsourcing encompasses manufacturing, IT, and back-office services. Manufacturing outsourcing began in the 1970s and 1980s when U.S. jobs in steel and textiles shifted from the northern states to the southern states. In the 1990s, manufacturing facilities in Mexico, Puerto Rico, Canada, South Korea, and Taiwan began to proliferate and absorb much of consumer electronics and personal computer production. In the late 1990s, Southeast Asian countries like Malaysia became key areas for manufacturing. In the 2000s, China has become the favored destination with unbeatable labor costs.

Information technology outsourcing has followed a similar pattern. In the 1990s, companies began offshoring application development and maintenance, especially Y2K work. With the urgency surrounding Y2K, companies could not find enough IT resources onshore, so they hired offshore firms. The Y2K work soon grew to include mainframe, e-commerce, and ERP programming. In the early 2000s, IT outsourcing expanded to other processes such as help desks and technical support. Originally, companies headed for Ireland, but as Ireland became more costly, they changed course and went to India.

Business process outsourcing — call centers, finance and accounting, human resources, and transaction processing — has followed a different pattern. In the 1990s, there was a tremendous movement in corporations to consolidate various fragmented divisional activities and create shared services centers (SSCs). An SSC is essentially a "do-it-yourself" insourcing model in which a large firm sets up its own captive operation. Some of these SSCs began to migrate offshore. The companies that pioneered the offshore SSC model, such as American Express, understood that they could realize more value if they based these centers in foreign countries. As a result of their early hard work, we are seeing a steady rise in the number of large corporations establishing back-office processing centers in India, the Philippines, South Africa, and Russia.

The emerging trend of offshoring business processes (or white-collar work) represents a fundamental structural adjustment, not a short-term business cycle phenomenon. The experience of manufacturing illustrates that when it is possible to do things cheaper elsewhere in the world, the work will migrate there. For instance, tough-to-beat labor and overhead costs have made China a top choice for almost all types of manufacturing.

With the relentless pursuit of the lowest global costs, offshoring is becoming institutionalized at many companies. A new job title, global sourcing officer, has been created to describe the cadre of managers responsible for figuring out how best to move certain business processes to overseas locations and how to manage them once there. Table 1.1 summarizes some of the drivers for rapid offshore outsourcing growth.

- Continuous cost pressure on U.S. and European companies
- Rapid declines in communication and computing costs
- Dramatic improvements in Internet reliability and functionality
- More offshore suppliers with better capabilities
- High-quality onshore suppliers offering offshore services
- Access to low-cost, high-quality employees, especially for labor-intensive tasks
- A business model for offshoring that has been proven by successful pioneers such GE and American Express

Table 1.1: Drivers for Rapid Offshore Outsourcing Growth

Examples of Offshore Outsourcing

The practice of offshore outsourcing is slowly but surely becoming an entrenched part of modern management. In fact, it would be hard to find a senior management team in any large corporation that is not currently investigating or prototyping an offshore project to see whether it is right for them.

In this subsection, we describe a variety of offshoring endeavors. The companies executing them range from high-tech to insurance, and the processes include finance and accounting, IT, and customer service. All — HSBC Holdings, Amazon.com, Cadence Design Systems, General Motors, and Fluor Corporation — highlight the basic tenet that business flows to the areas with the lowest cost.

Back-Office Outsourcing at HSBC Holdings

HSBC Holdings, the world's second-largest bank, has over 9,500 offices in 80 countries in Europe, Asia Pacific, the Americas, the Middle East, and Africa. HSBC offers financial services to personal, commercial, corporate, institutional, investment, and private banking clients.

As a global bank, HSBC is under increasing pressure from Citigroup, the top global bank, to remain competitive on cost. HSBC already runs a number of global processing hubs in India and Malaysia. Recently, it announced plans to migrate certain business tasks — mainly processing work and call center inquires — to India, Malaysia, and China.

Accompanying the migration of these tasks is the relocation of 4,000 jobs, considered one of the largest overseas transfers of British jobs. HSBC's decision mirrors similar offshore outsourcing moves by other British companies such as British Telecom and Prudential.

In the world of financial services, offshore outsourcing was once regarded as a short-term solution for problems such as sharp or unexpected rises in demand or shortages in programmers. Modern companies now view offshore outsourcing as a key element of their overall corporate strategies.

Customer Service Offshore Outsourcing at Amazon.com

Amazon.com commenced operations on the Web in July 1995. Since then, the online retailer has accumulated approximately 45 million customers across a variety of sites. As Amazon.com continues to attract new customers from all over the world, it has become important to have trained support staff ready to respond to the many customer questions and inquiries no matter what time of day or night.

To reply to customer e-mails faster, Amazon.com selected Daksh in June 2000 to provide e-mail customer service from India. Amazon.com expects Daksh to respond to 95% of e-mails received in 24 hours and 100% within 48 hours. Several hundred Daksh professionals work exclusively for the retailing giant. Amazon.com also bought a 10% equity stake in the company.

The rationale for this e-mail offshoring decision: Amazon.com pays a full-time customer service rep based in the United States an average of $2,000 per month whereas an equivalent rep in India costs $150–$200 per month. Although companies cite multiple reasons in their decisions to offshore, cost remains a major driver.

IT Offshore Outsourcing at Cadence Design Systems

As the world's largest provider of electronic design automation products, Cadence Design Systems helps companies bring their ideas for electronic products to life. It does the bulk of its design work for businesses that manufacture items such as semiconductors, computer systems, telecommunications and networking equipment, mobile and wireless devices, and other advanced electronics.

With almost all of its customer base adversely affected by an economic downturn, Cadence had to work much harder to sell its products. To reduce IT costs, Cadence outsourced some of its application development to Aztec Software. When the project began, Aztec sent between eight and ten software engineers to Cadence's California location to support its design team. The two groups worked to pinpoint what would make the project a success and to get comfortable with each other's work styles. Aztec had to understand Cadence's processes, infrastructure, and reporting before it could move any work to headquarters in India.

Eventually, Aztec began moving the work to Bangalore piece by piece, and the Aztec group dedicated to the project increased from eight to 38 people. Currently, two Aztec staffers remain in California and 35 work offshore from India. Faced with economic slowdowns and an urgent need to enhance competitiveness, more technology companies are choosing the path Cadence chose — to offshore.

Finance and Accounting Offshore Outsourcing at General Motors

General Motors (GM) has outsourced several finance and accounting (F&A) processes from its North American and European operations. In 2001, Affiliated Computer Services (ACS) signed a ten-year outsourcing contract with GM, agreeing to take over and execute the automaker's accounts payable (AP), accounts receivable (AR), payroll, travel and expense, and cash management processes.

GM's goal: achieve considerable cost reductions and improve quality and control. The company is leveraging ACS's capability to perform transactional activities. ACS provides its services from centers in Arizona, Jamaica, and Spain. GM monitors the quality of ACS's work with the aid of numerous controls: service level agreements, desk procedures, internal and external audits, onsite quality assurance teams, segregation of duties, delegation of authority, and process risk validations.

GM was not the first to blaze this path, and it definitely will not be the last. Other leading organizations such as British Airways and Ford have seized the F&A outsourcing opportunity as a method for saving money, substantially improving service levels, and redeploying resources to initiatives that generate profitable growth. Faced with high internal F&A costs, more and more companies are looking at offshoring as a way to free up staff to focus on strategic aspects of operations.

Architecture Offshore Outsourcing at Fluor Corporation

Fluor Corporation, headquartered in California, is one of the world's largest engineering, construction, and business services companies. Fluor provides services worldwide to the energy, chemicals, industrial, government services, and power industries.

Fluor is offshoring architectural design work. The company employs more than 1,200 engineers and draftsmen in the Philippines, Poland, and India to turn layouts of giant, multibillion-dollar industrial projects into detailed blueprints. Some of these construction projects, such as a petrochemical plant in Saudi Arabia, require nearly 50,000 separate construction plans. To develop these plans, Fluor has offshore engineers collaborate in real time with U.S. and British engineers via Web portals.

When Fluor CEO Alan Boeckmann was asked why he has sent high paying jobs offshore, he responded, "The Manila operation knocks up to 15% off Fluor's project prices. We have developed this into a core competitive advantage."[1] Fluor's competitors are responding with similar strategies. Bechtel Group, a large engineering-construction firm, employs 400 engineers in New Delhi, India. The average starting salary of a Bechtel engineer in India is $4,000 per year compared to $70,000 in the United States. With salary differentials that large, it isn't hard to see why Fluor and Bechtel are outsourcing architectural and design work.

Six Themes in Offshore Outsourcing

Why do companies pursue offshore outsourcing? The following six themes — globalization, evolution, deflation, demographics, competition, and politics — form the cornerstone of the offshoring wave.

Theme 1: Globalization — The inevitable transition to an offshore economy represents a new form of Internet-enabled globalization, the impact of which will dwarf prior globalization efforts.

Companies are rapidly shifting resources, both proactively and reactively, to address the opportunity and threat created by global competition. This shift of resources is fueling the significant market opportunity for forward-thinking companies and their vendors.

Consider the case of the financial services industry, a leader in offshoring business processes. Companies such as GE Finance, American Express, HSBC, and Lehman Brothers are early adopters of the offshore model. Operating offshore is particularly attractive to the financial services industry because its operations depend primarily on data, which is becoming more expensive to process in the United States. If moved offshore, the leading financial services firms are projecting that costs can be reduced by 30%–60%.

The economics of offshoring are too powerful for businesses to ignore. Consider the case of the Procter & Gamble Company (P&G), the consumer products giant. P&G sends payroll, travel, benefits, accounts payable, invoice processing, and other work to its offices in Costa Rica, the Philippines, and the United Kingdom. More than 7,000 people work in these offshore service centers, which began operations in 1999. The business logic behind the decision: P&G gains the benefits of low cost and quality through its offshoring strategy.

Many companies are pushing the concept of virtual corporations to new limits. They outsource most of their back offices to offshore providers, which enables them to focus only on what they do best, be it basic research, brand management, or sales.

Theme 2: Evolution — Offshore outsourcing is a steady evolution rather than a revolution. It will take many years before the true magnitude of the structural impact is understood.

In the past, work was completed where the company was physically located. As travel and communication became easier in the 1970s and 1980s, manufacturing started moving offshore.

The evolution of manufacturing has been steady. A case in point is the U.S. textile industry, which faced unprecedented increases in global manufacturing capacity combined with softening demand in a tough retail environment. For almost two decades, the textile industry was under pressure to restructure while facing fierce competition from overseas manufacturers. Cheap imports flooded the U.S. market and drove prices down. Global sourcing created a new operating model for textile companies that forced many firms to either adapt or exit the industry. The result: an industry no longer able to provide customers the merchandise they wanted at prices that were profitable.

The evolution in manufacturing is called product cycling — when U.S. firms exit labor-intensive commodity products such as textiles, steel, and electronics while lower-cost developing countries move in. Given high relative wages, it is very difficult for the United States to survive head-to-head competition with the world's most labor-abundant countries in the labor-intensive manufacturing industry.

We expect a similar evolutionary trend in services. With an increasingly interlinked global economy and reduced international trade barriers, what happened to blue-collar manufacturing jobs is beginning to happen to white-collar service jobs. In the age of the Internet, a company's location hardly matters. With the improving Internet infrastructure, companies now can send knowledge work anywhere, which means places like India, China, or the Philippines, where, for about $2–$3 per hour, companies can hire college graduates for jobs that cost about $12–$18 per hour in the United States. Ultimately, economies with production capacity (low costs but well-educated workers) are most likely to benefit.

Theme 3: Deflation — Mounting customer demands (faster, cheaper, better) are driving firms offshore.

It would be hard to find a company that remains unaffected by low-cost Chinese labor in manufacturing or low-cost Indian labor in back-office services and IT application development. Their impact is apparent in the declining prices of various commodity products and services.

To combat price deflation, firms are forced to adopt the offshore model in order to aggressively lower costs and thereby set lower prices for their products. These lower prices set in motion a deflationary cycle that plays havoc with the weak companies. While customers may love the lower prices, small and midsized companies don't, as they are hard-pressed to match prices below their costs. We call this the Wal-Mart syndrome. Wal-Mart, the world's number-one retailer, operates on an "Every Day Low Price" philosophy and through this strategy continuously reduces prices, which forces competitors to keep up or get out.

Look at what happened to Cap Gemini, a leading provider of consulting, technology, and outsourcing services, and its relationship with Sony. Although Sony was happy with the services provided by Cap Gemini, it switched to India's Wipro in 2002. By signing a $5 million contract with Wipro for writing information technology applications for Sony's TV and computer assembly plants in the United States, Sony expects to save 30%. Cap Gemini could not compete with Wipro's low-priced offshore resources. How do companies like Wipro do more for less? The trick, other than offering low-cost labor, lies in building up expertise or economies of scale that a single company cannot match.

The quest for continual cost reduction with reasonable quality forces firms to embrace the offshore outsourcing model. In doing so, they have to get over two offshore outsourcing myths: 1) foreign work lacks quality and 2) offshore outsourcing is hard to supervise. These two myths, although true in some circumstances, are becoming less relevant as the developing countries gain experience and expertise. For instance, the quality at India-based providers has steadily improved in the last decade. With the abundance of well-educated and now well-trained middle management talent in many foreign countries and the availability of technology to help monitor the performance of these employees, the expectations of service quality for offshored operations will be raised.

Theme 4: Demographics — The aging population and declining birth rates in developed countries will fuel the offshore fire.

The demographics of the United States and European countries are changing. Despite immigration, the average age in these countries continues to increase as baby boomers enter their 50s and 60s. It is the older countries, such as India and China, rather than the younger countries, such as the United States, that have younger populations.

If India, China, and the Philippines can create the right environment for offshoring (tax incentives, sound infrastructure) as Taiwan, South Korea, and Hong Kong did for manufacturing, their countries' sizable educated populations will be advantageous. According to *BusinessWeek*, 53% of

India's population is considered to be the MTV generation (under the age of 25), versus 45% in China. By 2020, 47% of Indians are going to be between 15 and 59, compared with 35% now.[2]

The changing demographics create several interesting dynamics: 1) with the retirement of experienced employees, firms are choosing to hire offshore replacements versus local replacements primarily due to compensation and rising healthcare benefit costs; 2) growing immigrant populations make it easier for firms to offshore operations as they can use expatriates to bootstrap operations; and 3) the growth of many multinational companies is coming from emerging markets, which forces them to establish an offshore presence to attract workers and consumers.

Theme 5: Competition — Offshore outsourcing is reshaping the service provider landscape in several business process categories.

The service provider landscape is undergoing dramatic competitive changes as the playing field is leveled for U.S. outsourcers and offshore outsourcers. Three general types of service providers exist:

1. Offshore companies such as Wipro, Infosys, and LUXOFT that are based in developing countries such as India or Russia and try to expand outward.

2. Traditional IT consulting and business process outsourcing (BPO) companies such as Accenture, Cap Gemini, BearingPoint, or ADP that are based in the United States or Europe and are establishing their own offshore centers in India, China, or the Czech Republic.

3. Hybrid companies, such as Covansys or Patni Computers, which split their head count almost fifty-fifty between North America and India or another viable offshore destination.

Initially, the traditional consulting firms didn't pay much attention to the offshore threat. They portrayed themselves as high-value service providers and their upstart competitors as low-cost providers. But as the economy cooled rapidly after its torrid pace of the late 1990s, customers naturally gravitated to a low-cost model. The market shift caught the traditional players flatfooted, and they were saddled with high-cost workforces and overcapacity due to the sluggish market demand.

The traditional firms have taken drastic action to compete against the lower-cost providers. Accenture is a good example. Since 2001, Accenture has tripled its workforce in India. By year-end 2003, it will have about 4,300 people in India and 10,000 people by 2005. According to Martin Cole, global managing partner, "We expect all segments to grow as we go forward, but the business process outsourcing sector is growing more rapidly."[3] To compete, vendors like EDS, IBM, and Cap Gemini are racing to build their own branded offerings in India and other countries.

The more value an offshore outsourcer brings to the table, the more pressure it puts on the onshore vendors. We can see this quite clearly in the IT sector. The IT service provider sector is in the midst of a large shakeup as the key players adjust their game plans and better align with the market place. We anticipate a period of consolidation ahead for the IT service provider industry as its pace of growth slows. We expect a similar trend to begin occurring in BPO by 2006.

Theme 6: Politics — Offshoring is an unstoppable mega-trend.

Offshore outsourcing is attracting enormous political attention for good reason. It is profoundly affecting the competitive capabilities and hence the labor structures of all multinational corporations. Anything that has negative implications for employment is a political lightening rod.

There will be a period of public outcry and backlash as the structure of the economy changes. Take, for instance, the situation in New Jersey. The state's social services department hired eFunds to provide food stamp and welfare electronic benefits processing through 2004. In 2002, eFunds moved the call center from Wisconsin to Mumbai, India. The change angered politicians who said moving jobs out of the country undermines efforts to get U.S. citizens off of welfare. In 2003, New Jersey demanded that eFunds move the call center back to the United States, a move that is costing an additional $900,000 per year.[4] A similar outcry in Indiana prompted the state to cancel a $15 million IT contract with India's Tata Consultancy Services. The question to ask is: What are the right offshoring policies for state governments?

Backlash or no backlash, the bigger long-term political issue is the decline in wages. In the IT sector in 2000, U.S. programming jobs were in the $70,000–$100,000 per year range with a sizable signing bonus and extravagant benefits. With increasing offshore competition, the range has shrunk to \$40,000–\$50,000. This wage deflation poses serious problems in an economy that has high levels of consumer debt.

At the same time, the rise in displaced workers necessitates very effective retraining strategies. This presents a thorny problem: In what areas should these workers be retrained? For instance, if call centers move offshore, what new skills should the displaced call center agents have? Retraining workers requires a significant amount of time and money. Clearly, the social impact of offshore outsourcing will be felt for several years.

Decreasing Transaction Costs Driving Offshoring

Why has offshoring become more prevalent? Why now? The reduction of transaction costs associated with finding vendors, monitoring their work, and sending work overseas is helping to reshape the modern company. In an effort to shed light on where the entire offshore trend is heading, we need to examine some fundamental questions: What are the boundaries of the modern firm, and how permeable should they be? Should firms build, buy, or lease? What affects this decision?

In 1932, Ronald Coase gave a lecture to students at the School of Economics and Commerce in Dundee, Scotland. He explained why businesses exist as they do — why, for instance, they choose to produce some goods themselves and contract with outside companies to provide the rest. In 1937, Coase turned the lecture into a paper in the journal *Economica* titled "The Nature of the Firm." Coase's insights were not widely accepted until the 1970s when the transaction cost economics school of thought emerged.[5] In 1991, nearly sixty years after he gave his famous lecture, Coase was awarded the Nobel Prize in economic science for his seminal work.

Transaction cost theory helps managers think about things such as whether to buy, build, or partner. At the core of transaction cost theory is this notion: When a company tries to determine whether to outsource or to produce goods or services on its own, market prices are not the sole factor. Rather, there are significant transaction costs, search costs, contracting costs (for example, legal), and coordination costs. Those costs, Coase theorized, frequently determine whether a company uses internal or external resources for products or services. This is the essence of the make-versus-buy decision.

At the time Coase wrote his theory, transaction costs were very high. Because information flowed at a glacial pace and supplies moved only slightly faster, companies strove to manage the entire chain of production within the walls of their own corporations. For instance, the Ford Motor Company, a shining example of the vertically integrated corporation of the early 1900s, bought a rubber plantation rather than cede control of that part of tire manufacturing. At that time, Ford's River Rouge plant made steel, glass, and tires, and then assembled the parts all at one site. River Rouge absorbed the industries around it or recreated them under its own roof.

Ford is a classic example of insourcing, or when a company keeps all of its processing in-house. Over time, insourcing has given way to outsourcing. For instance, many parts that carmakers once made internally are now manufactured by independent, first-tier suppliers. Vertical integration has given way to horizontal integration across firms, facilitated by lower transaction costs.

As transaction costs plunge, thanks to the Internet, and as barriers between firms are breached, information is moving at the speed of a broadband connection to an offshore location. With literally a desk and an Internet connection, an employee in India can process transactions or write code. As figure 1.1 shows, the economics of offshoring are extremely attractive even after factoring in the additional costs.

With diminishing transaction costs and continued globalization, offshoring will grow steadily. We anticipate that with lower offshore transaction costs, companies will be able to focus on narrow product slivers or business activities and have external parties complete the rest.

The Offshore Adoption Curve: How Big? How Fast?

Offshore outsourcing, especially in information technology or manufacturing, is not new. Companies in these industries have been outsourcing offsite or offshore for at least two decades. What's new is the rapid growth in services offshore outsourcing. Plotting the trajectory of market adoption helps us to understand where we are in the services offshore outsourcing cycle.

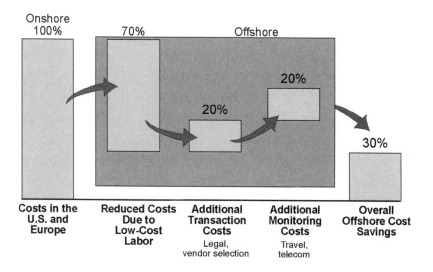

Figure 1.1: The Economics of Offshore Outsourcing

Years of research in the well-established area of diffusion theory tells us that anytime you have a change or a pickup in the market, it follows a pattern known as the S-curve. After about 10%–20% of a population adopts an innovation, we see a relatively rapid adoption by the remaining population, and then a period in which the holdout companies finally cave in or exit that business.

Offshore outsourcing in services follows a similar pattern. For instance, in the area of IT offshore outsourcing, during most of the 1980s and 1990s the offshore market was at the bottom of the S-curve. In the last three years, we have hit the steep part of that S-curve where across multiple industries, particularly in North America, companies are aggressively moving up that adoption curve (see figure 1.2). We think that this trend will continue for many years until the market matures considerably, hits the top end of that curve, and levels off.

Many people consider the economic downturn that followed the bursting of the Internet bubble to be business process offshore outsourcing's tipping point. The notion of a tipping point, the point at which a trend catches fire and spreads exponentially through the population, was made popular by Malcolm Gladwell in his book *The Tipping Point*. The idea suggests that, whether good or bad, change can be promoted easily in a social system through a domino effect. The tipping point concept has its origins in diffusion theory, which is a set of generalizations regarding the typical spread of innovations within a social system.[6]

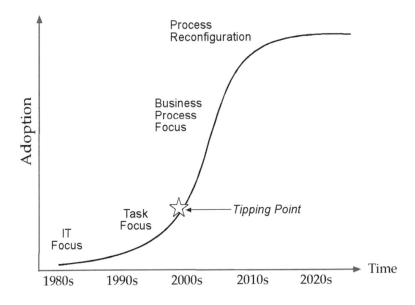

Figure 1.2: The Offshore Outsourcing S-Curve

The tipping point usually occurs around the time when the uncertainty of the innovation is reduced and the cost-benefit analysis is very clear. Companies will adopt an innovation en masse only when they believe that it will enhance their profitability with minimal risk.

We believe that the market is reaching the tipping point with offshore outsourcing. However, in some offshore markets like India, there is a BPO bubble forming with too many early-stage companies. The venture capitalists, to some extent, are causing this BPO bubble as they rush to invest even in marginal ideas. We expect to see a massive shakeout and consolidation beginning in 2005, but we think, despite some growing pains, that the long-term trajectory of exponential growth for offshore outsourcing will remain intact.

Types of Companies Venturing Offshore

If offshore outsourcing is a business model innovation, how will it spread through the different categories of firms that make up the economic ecosystem? Figure 1.3 illustrates the typical categorization of firms in an ecosystem. Based on revenue, we categorized these groups into Global 1000, large, mid-market, small business, and small office/home office.

For the last two decades, the Global 1000 or the big manufacturing multinationals like GE adopted offshore outsourcing. These firms have learned from their many years of offshore manufacturing experience. Now, many years after they ventured into offshore outsourcing, these corporate giants are seeing rising productivity. They are making many more goods with fewer workers.

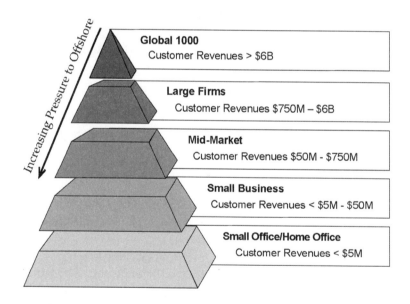

Figure 1.3: Market Segmentation

For proof, look at the numbers. According to the Federal Reserve Bank of Chicago, in the early 1950s the size of the workforce engaged in manufacturing was 35% in the United States. By 2001, that figure had dwindled to 12% relative to overall U.S. employment. Automation is one of the big reasons productivity increased (manufacturing output grew almost 600%). The same trend is evident in agriculture. Only 2.4% of the total workforce is devoted to farming. Technology slowly but surely replaced labor in both agriculture and manufacturing. In contrast, the service sector grew more than fivefold to almost 80% during this period averaging 2.6% growth per year since 1947.[7]

Over time, the managers of some leading multinationals realized that whatever productivity improvements they achieved in manufacturing they could replicate in back-office processing work, a sizable chunk of the services industry. As a result, the game plan for services offshoring is looking more like the one being played out in manufacturing: automate the processes with technology and offshore the parts that require human touch to low-cost locales like China.

The Global 1000 are putting tremendous pressure on their competitors and suppliers. The reason for this pressure is simple: If one company has a 10%–15% cost advantage in any industry, the other players have to follow suit. This "follow the market leader" phenomenon was quite apparent in IT and manufacturing outsourcing in the late 1990s. Currently, a similar pattern is evident in services offshore outsourcing, which is migrating to encompass the large and mid-market segments.

However, it is important to note that not all of the Global 1000 companies are offshoring. Even in this segment we are seeing the classic pattern of technology adoption:[8]

- **Innovators.** These are firms like GE and American Express that pioneered the outsourcing model and are sophisticated in exploiting the offshore economics. Based on a normal statistical distribution, less than 2.5% of the Global 1000 make up this segment.[9]

- **Early Adopters.** These are firms like Siemens and Deutsche Bank that followed the innovators in order to compete against the cost advantage the innovators achieved through offshore outsourcing. Only 13.5% of the Global 1000 make up this segment.

- **Early Majority.** These companies are more cautious. They are pragmatists that want proof from the market leaders in their industries before they move offshore. Their modus operandi is to make incremental steps to remain competitive. Less than 34% of the Global 1000 are designated early majority.

- **Late Majority.** These conservative firms do not like any form of risk — the "if it ain't broke, don't fix it" mind-set. They are more bound by tradition than led by innovation. Less than 34% of the Global 1000 are categorized late majority.

- **Laggards.** Last are the skeptics. Despite the pressure to jump on the offshore bandwagon, these firms are staying put. They are perfectly happy being bystanders rather than changing the way they do things. About 16% of the Global 1000 fall in this segment.

The different groups are distinguished from each other based on their ability to absorb risk. The innovators are very entrepreneurial in their ability to adopt new ways of conducting business. Their willingness to tolerate glitches and change the status quo differentiates them.

The innovators tend to view offshore outsourcing as a continuous process rather than a single project or event. This distinction is critical for successful execution. What, precisely, does the offshore outsourcing process consist of? The basic steps are universal: An offshore opportunity must be identified; evaluated; a solution must be found; resources must be acquired or transitioned; managed; and outcomes measured. When viewed as a process with several stages, it becomes abundantly clear that you don't wake up one day, lay off everyone, and send it all to a low-cost supplier. Management has to gradually get comfortable with offshore outsourcing, find the right partners, and evolve in a way that makes sense for the overall business.

We expect the early adopters and early majority to increasingly adopt the offshore model in the next three years. In the case of IT outsourcing, the model is proven and is becoming mainstream. This implies that the early majority is beginning to embrace the offshore model.

The separation between best-practice firms and the followers will grow. The ability to reduce operating costs and pass gains along to customers is the new competitive game. The impacts of offshore outsourcing are rippling through the entire industrial economy, upsetting not only how business processes are done but also where they are done.

Summary

Strategic and often gut-wrenching changes are taking place in corporations as offshore outsourcing becomes a viable alternative. Smart companies realize that if they don't keep hunting for breakthrough cost innovations, some other organization will.

Advances in the practice of offshore outsourcing are upending the competitive balance across the corporate spectrum and are forcing companies to re-examine their basic ways of doing business. The results are impressive: Firms like Citibank, which took advantage of offshore outsourcing, are reducing their costs in ways that provide competitive advantage.

Embarking on an offshore outsourcing initiative begins with a decision to change — to embrace methods that can boost the performance of your organization. The starting point of offshore outsourcing is verifying that you're ready to learn and to adapt to changes by asking: "Can we reduce our costs considerably?" This need not be a purely quantitative decision.

But CEOs and senior management need to understand the implications of offshore outsourcing. Our research indicates that many firms that fail at offshore outsourcing do so because they are:

- Vague about their goals, which results in strategy changes after investments have been made.

- Inattentive to the difficulties of integrating an offshore operation within the firm.

- Insufficient in their due diligence in choosing the right partners, locations, or expansion plans.

- Unwilling to make the necessary hard, often unpopular decisions.

- Ignorant of the strategies available to mitigate the inherent risk in a significant offshore strategy.

Offshore outsourcing is a major opportunity for those who acknowledge its complexities. It will remain inscrutable — and unprofitable — for the rest. There goes the status quo.

Chapter Two

Offshore Outsourcing
Business Models

"The winds and waves are always on the side of the ablest navigators."

— Edward Gibbon

Introduction

Today's market leaders understand the battle in which they are engaged: to constantly redefine value by reducing costs and raising service quality. They are well aware of the urgent need to create capabilities that make their rivals' positions obsolete.

Some companies have aggressively adopted offshore outsourcing as a core tenet of their operating strategies. In the early 1990s, former General Electric (GE) chief executive Jack Welch declared that "70-70-70" would be his company's rule for sending technology work offsite: 70% would be done by outside suppliers, 70% of that overseas, and 70% of that in India. Welch's vision was to recreate the company using Indian resources.

GE was no stranger to operating in India. In fact, GE has been in India since 1902 when it installed the country's first hydropower plant. In 1930, the multinational set up IGE (International General Electric) to sell GE products and services that were not represented in the region.[1]

GE's growth in India began in earnest in 1992 when the company's medical systems, appliances, plastics, and lighting units all formed joint ventures with local companies. In 1993, GE Capital gained approval for a wholly owned, non-banking financial services company in India.

Between 1992 and 1995, the company focused on growth and acquisitions. By the close of 1998, most of GE's major businesses — aircraft engines, broadcasting, capital services, lighting, medical systems, industrial systems, plastics, power systems, and transportation systems — had a presence in India.

As of 2003, GE has 20,000-plus employees in India, 70% of whom support GE globally. The company's activities in India can be grouped into six categories: 1) local market sales and services, 2) sourced software in Global Development Centers and Global Engineering Centers, 3) GE-owned technology and software operations, 4) back-room services such as call centers and legal and accounting processes 5) exports of components and products made by GE, and 6) sourcing of components from key suppliers for export to GE's global manufacturing locations. In 2001, GE India's revenues and orders exceeded $1 billion.[2]

Each of these six businesses helps drive GE's four corporate initiatives — globalization, services, Six Sigma quality, and e-business. For example, the company's globalization initiative centers on a high-quality labor pool, low-cost suppliers, and engineering and manufacturing plants in less expensive countries such as Mexico, China, India, and Russia. Through globalization, GE hopes to:

1. Generate cost efficiencies in its back-office business processes,

2. Upgrade business processes and provide flexibility to respond to changing business needs, and

3. Create new capabilities and apply them to achieve new strategic objectives.

The results of GE's offshore strategy have been remarkable. According to a 2002 NASSCOM-McKinsey report, the multinational has achieved an annual savings of $340 million from its Indian operations.[3]

GE is a high-profile offshore outsourcing success story. It has brought to back-office services the kind of cost deflation previously seen in manufacturing. However, while we use GE as a poster child for offshoring, it is by no means the only one. Similar stories are emerging in other industries as corporations integrate global sourcing into their overall business strategy to achieve a low-cost advantage. In consulting circles, this is called a "total cost strategy."

Offshore outsourcing has surfaced as both a strategic and tactical method of meeting new business demands. Similar to most business ventures, the challenge of offshore outsourcing lies not in envisioning it but in executing it. GE has multiple delivery models for executing offshore outsourcing: external contractors, joint ventures, and insourced shared services centers. Each of these approaches has advantages and disadvantages, which we discuss in this chapter.

The Three Phases of Offshore Execution

As the pressure on firms to lower costs and maintain or improve quality continues unabated, offshoring strategies are steadily moving away from the label of "something to consider" to "something that must be done." Establishing offshore operations has become a business imperative. Once viewed as a cost-cutting option, offshoring is fast becoming a new frontier in competitive strategy.

What happens if your competitor achieves a lower cost structure? How will your firm respond to this threat? The pressure to migrate offshore is most acute among the larger service firms (Accenture, EDS, ACS, or IBM) and the major outsourcing companies (Exult, ADP, and Sykes).

To combat continued pricing pressure and to win deals, these firms are scaling up in India and other locations. Their logic is quite clear. Let's assume that offshore rates on average are 30%–40% below onsite rates. If you assume that 65%–70% of the work is done offshore, this would imply that the overall pricing structure of a global service provider like Accenture is roughly 20%–30% below its competitors that lack an offshore presence.

The economics leave companies little choice but to make their way offshore. So what is the right way to migrate operations offshore? After examining the approaches of numerous companies with offshore operations, we found that a successful strategy typically moves through three broad phases:

1. Offshore entry,

2. Offshore development, and

3. Offshore integration.

The primary goals of the offshore entry phase are to establish a presence and gain experience with the offshore model. That is, take what your organization does today and do it for less money. The choices for establishing an offshore presence have largely been limited to do-it-yourself, in-house initiatives and outsourcing arrangements. In-house initiatives require substantial management resources. Mistakes can easily nullify the cost savings in the early years. In selecting an entry model, operational risk must be weighed against potential cost savings.

During the second phase, offshore development, the main objectives are increasing your presence and integrating core or mission-critical business initiatives with your offshore operations. You can accomplish these tasks by transferring more management authority and value-added production to the offshore affiliates. However, the process of integrating an offshore delivery model is more difficult than hiring several hundred foreign employees. It requires a more fundamental organizational restructuring to rebalance the processes in the firm.

In the third phase, offshore integration, your mission is to integrate your offshore plan with regional and global efforts. The operational risk is deemed minimal, and your firm moves from a noncore cost focus to a core value strategy. Offshore becomes a normal way of doing business.

Table 2.1 illustrates the key goals, the roles of the offshore and corporate offices, and the ideal manager profile for each of these phases. Because most firms find themselves at the entry phase of offshore outsourcing, the discussion that follows focuses on issues salient to that phase such as ownership and location decisions.

	Offshore Entry	Offshore Development	Offshore Integration
Key Goals	▪ Determine the business model ▪ Select the location ▪ Define expected results ▪ Establish a presence	▪ Expand operation to several initiatives ▪ Migrate from a cost center to a profit center mind-set ▪ Seek positive P&L results	▪ Expand scope and capabilities
Role of the Corporate Office	▪ Get the right people on the team and set clear objectives ▪ Hire experts in key offshore countries ▪ Identify cultural differences ▪ Understand the legal framework	▪ Develop a phased approach for building an onshore presence ▪ Improve processes by setting aggressive goals ▪ Remain ready for a disaster with contingency plans	▪ Establish full integration of offshore center into regional and global operations
Ideal Offshore Manager Profile	▪ Entrepreneurial managers who are creative and flexible ▪ Managers experienced in starting operations in developing countries with numerous hurdles	▪ Senior manager with strong ties to leadership at corporate headquarters ▪ Managers skilled at communicating across a complex corporate matrix	▪ Senior manager able to work with several business divisions
Role of the Local Managers	▪ Establish local brand to attract talent ▪ Provide services to business units to migrate operations	▪ Manage awareness at corporate headquarters ▪ Coordinate activities of the business unitss	▪ Further integrate offshore operations into regional and global strategy

Table 2.1: The Three Phases of an Offshore Migration Strategy

Dimensions of the Offshore Business Model

The number, size, and diversity of organizations offshoring business processes is great. To better understand the business and revenue models, it is important to familiarize yourself with the two dimensions of every business model:

1. Ownership or relationship structure (subsidiary, joint venture, or external vendor), and

2. Geographic location of the work (onsite, offsite onshore, or offshore).

Figure 2.1 illustrates the decision matrix when you put the two together. In the next section, we explore the various business models that emerge from the different combinations of relationship structure and geographic location.

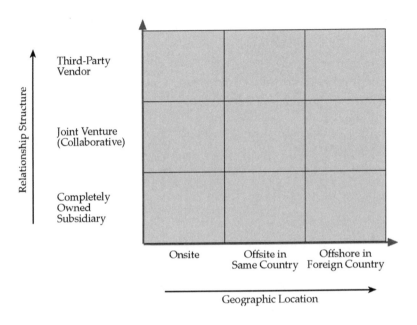

Figure 2.1: The Two Dimensions of Outsourcing Business Models

Ownership Structure: Subsidiary, JV, or External Vendor?

A crucial issue in ensuring future offshoring success involves selecting the most appropriate ownership model. There are three different general relationship structures for outsourcing engagements:

1. Pure contract offshore outsourcing (buy or third-party),

2. Joint ventures (partnership agreement), or

3. Fully owned captive subsidiary (build it or insource).

Clearly, there is a varied and complex spectrum of ownership structures available with particular advantages and disadvantages for each. Let's look at them in more detail.

Pure Contract Offshore Outsourcing

Pure contract offshore outsourcing is the phrase used to describe a company that relinquishes control of a function to an external service provider in a foreign country. The external service provider takes over the function and does much of the work offshore using cheaper labor. Contract outsourcing can lead to three different models:

1. Selective outsourcing in which firms only send out a small subset of their business process activities. The Delta Air Lines/Wipro Spectramind relationship provides a good example of pure contract offshore outsourcing. Delta elected to offshore select reservation services to Wipro Spectramind.

2. Transitional outsourcing occurs when firms temporarily hand over a function to a third-party vendor and bring it back in-house later. An example of transitional offshoring is GE and Satyam Computers.

3. Total outsourcing in which external vendors take over the business process and do whatever the organization was doing at 20%–30% less. The BellSouth/Accenture agreement exemplifies this last model. BellSouth outsourced IT work to a facility run by Accenture in India.

Pure contract offshore outsourcing is a make-versus-buy decision. Its chief advantages are limited operational risk, a potential for cost savings, and the rapid speed at which it can be executed. Typically, it is faster to implement an outsourced project than it is to implement a joint venture or captive center.

Joint Venture

A joint venture (JV) is the product of two or more companies pooling their combined resources to create a new entity to perform a business project together for a set period of time. JVs attempt to create common goals through joint equity ownership. JVs can save both parties money because expenses, resources, and workload are shared.

GE and Satyam Computers formed a joint venture in December 1998. The GE/Satyam company provided a GE industrial systems affiliate with engineering design, software development, and system maintenance services. In 2003, Satyam sold its interest in the JV after GE exercised its option to purchase Satyam's interest for $4 million.

Captive Offshore Subsidiary

In the past, companies pursued the offshore path via joint ventures. These traditional ways were initially satisfactory, but as business evolved, companies eventually discovered that it was better to build their own subsidiaries. Firms began to establish captive offshore subsidiaries or foreign subsidiaries that completed all the BPO work. Some of the companies that have captive subsidiaries in India include HSBC (Hyderabad), American Express (Delhi), British Airways (Mumbai), Citibank (Chennai), and Dell (Bangalore).

Companies that select this ownership model tend to cite reasons of more control and flexibility and lower prices on a long-term basis. Another major reason is cultural issues. In some instances, firms may wish to maintain control of the output by using a model that is more aligned with their internal culture.

Location of Work: Onsite, Offsite, or Offshore?

In March 2003, Electronic Data Systems (EDS) fired its CEO, Richard H. Brown, after disastrous third-quarter results. Upon his arrival, the new CEO, Michael Jordan, immediately began to take steps to make EDS more competitive against the low-cost outsourcing competition.

EDS, which makes the bulk of its revenues by running the back-office operations of big corporations, was losing ground to lower-cost outsourcing firms such as Wipro and Infosys. In July 2003, Jordan told employees "the concepts of low cost and high value must be present in every action we take, in every service we provide, in every piece of new business we pursue."[4]

To improve its competitiveness, EDS moved quickly to lower its cost structure. It increased its head count in India, Argentina, Malaysia, Hungary, and Mexico, the countries in which it expects to have more than 10% of its workforce of 137,000 employees by year-end 2004.

EDS is also hard at work creating a global delivery model that increases customer choice. EDS's Best Shore initiative encompasses a seamless onshore, nearshore, or offshore model. Clients can choose to have their work done in three different ways: onsite, offsite onshore, or offshore.

EDS predicts that it will employ around 7,200 individuals in 16 centers in 12 countries around the world in its Best Shore solution centers.

Onsite Outsourcing

This location model mandates that all processes, starting with information gathering and ending with implementation, be carried out at the client's premises. The third-party provider utilizes its own workforce to service clients on their premises. This model ensures clients a greater degree of project control. It is also suitable for those projects that are mission-critical, location sensitive, and require constant attention.

Offsite Outsourcing

This location model hinges on the service provider having an office onshore. The project or work may be done offsite, but it's still in the same country as the client. Not only is the offsite center close to the client, it may be used to provide support to an onsite team. Thus, the experts at the offsite center work in tandem with the corresponding onsite team to ensure timely, quality service.

Nearshore or Offshore Outsourcing

This location model dictates that the project-related activity is done at the vendor's premises nearshore or offshore. For U.S.-based companies, nearshore is countries such as Canada or Mexico while offshore is countries such as India or the Philippines. The outsourcing service provider may not have any presence at the client's location. This model is best suited when the project plan is well defined and the development team has a clear understanding of client requirements.

The team members at the offshore location interact with the client through various communication means such as telephone, fax, or e-mail. The high level of risk associated with this model becomes an issue for some clients. One risk associated with this model is the communication gap between the vendor and client, which may result in the client's requirements not being captured accurately. Some analysts are of the opinion that a 100% offshore model is not workable.

The bottom line: A range of ownership and location options are available. Executives can use supplemental staff, temporary workforces, consultants, or contractors. They can outsource — hire external contractors to do all or some of the work. They can pool resources through strategic alliances and share in the results. Or they can meet their needs by creating entirely new entities through joint ventures with one or more partners. Because offshoring of services is only in its earliest stages, it is difficult to predict which organizational forms will become dominant. Moreover, it is not clear whether the captives or independents will dominate.

The First Generation of Offshore Business Models

The many combinations of locations and ownership structures that exist give rise to several distinct business models (see figure 2.2). In each model, the relationship between the client and provider is structured uniquely.

As you look at figure 2.2, you will notice that some of the cells represent business models while others are more like delivery models. Taking a moment to point out the differences might be useful. A business model typically illustrates how a firm makes money. This is relevant and pertinent for third-party vendors. However, for companies that are building captive centers, offshore is part of their overall strategy. Offshore is seen more as a delivery mechanism than a new business model. Different models are appropriate at different levels of organizational maturity and complexity.

Internal Delivery (Department-Based Model)

This is a delivery model with which every manager is familiar. In this model, an internal department provides services — finance and accounting, human resources, or information technology support — to other business units and implements new services through internal projects. The internal department and business unit involved manage the relationship directly. Internal delivery is the most flexible model because the unit manager may change the rules and the processes as much and as often as needed. Nevertheless, it is also the most limited sourcing model with regard to scale (dimension of operations) and knowledge (experience, innovation, and available additional resources).

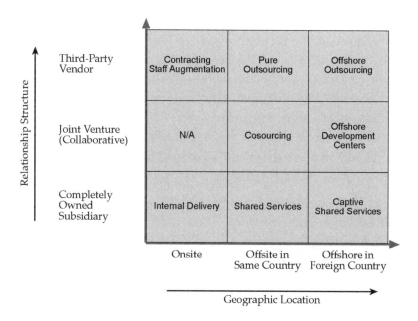

Figure 2.2: First-Generation Offshore Business Models

Offsite Onshore Shared Services

The shared services approach eliminates many of the common but duplicate processes, activities, and staff that individual business units have and brings them together to achieve critical mass. Paying for each business unit to manage its own finance and accounting, human resources, or information technology support is costly. These "cost center" functions while necessary are not strategic. It makes more sense to consolidate these nonstrategic processes and generate economies of scale.

Companies execute the shared services model by bundling selected supporting processes and activities into a separate division or organization. This entity treats these processes as its core business and is measured by its own unique profit and loss (P&L). Bundling services into an independent organization means that some or all of the employees who support them also have to move to the new entity.

Offshore Captive Shared Services

Taking the shared services and housing them offshore leads us to the captive shared services delivery model. The product of this "do-it-yourself" offshore model is a center set in a foreign country that is dedicated to serving the different business units or sales, general and administrative (SG&A) functions of a large company. This model is very common in multinational firms that wish to control their BPO operations, quality, and intellectual property. Some companies that have chosen this model include Standard Chartered Bank, GE Capital International Services (GECIS), British Airways, and American Express.

American Express was the first to establish a back-office, captive shared services center in India in 1993. Other companies that have followed suit include British Airways in 1996 and GECIS in 1998. Since 2000, a growing number of Global Fortune 500 firms including AOL, Citigroup, Dell, Hewlett-Packard, HSBC, and J.P. Morgan Chase have established captive operations.

Cosourcing

Cosourcing is the term that describes companies that execute a shared services center with an external vendor. Cosourcing, a fancier term for joint venture, is a collaborative relationship based on shared objectives that reflect the appropriate balance between control and flexibility. Cosourcing is a viable model for organizations uncomfortable with outsourcing a complete business process; outsourcing some parts to a joint venture with a vendor may offer a temporary or final solution.

The cosourcing model aims to combine the strength of the vendor and the client. Consider the case of AT&T and Accenture, who announced a five-year, $500-million, cosourcing arrangement designed to transform AT&T's residential credit and accounts receivable management functions and provide new capabilities and efficiencies. In particular, the agreement is designed to help AT&T expand its service portfolio, increase marketing flexibility, improve uncollected receivables, enhance operational efficiency, and reduce costs.

On its side, Accenture will manage the integration of planning, initiative execution, and collections processes across multiple organizations within AT&T Consumer. Approximately 45 AT&T employees whose work is within the scope of the agreement will transition to Accenture. In addition, approximately 250 other AT&T employees will be part of the cosourced operation and remain on the AT&T payroll.

The cosourcing agreement has been structured so that AT&T will retain control of business planning, credit policy, and customer interaction. Accenture will lead the transformation program and be responsible for operating the credit risk management and collections functions. In addition, Accenture will build and deploy capabilities to enable AT&T to support its growth objectives while mitigating risk and reducing uncollectibles.

Cosourcing is an option when firms don't have the skills or the money to set up a shared services center on their own or simply don't have the management bandwidth given the magnitude of the other tasks on their plates. The advantage for companies that cosource is that they don't have to pay for everything upfront. The advantage for vendors is that they gain a guaranteed revenue stream.

Offshore Development Centers

In the software industry, joint ventures with offshore vendors are common, so common that the industry developed a term for them: offshore development centers (ODCs). An ODC is a dedicated, customized, and secure development center established by a vendor for a customer who needs to outsource substantial software development, maintenance, or engineering work. The customer and the external contractor jointly own the ODC. This model gives the customer more control but requires much greater management attention.

In the mid-1990s, GE began a businesswide initiative to establish dedicated software and engineering development centers with several Indian vendors such as Tata Consultancy Services, Satyam, and Patni. Each vendor established facilities dedicated to GE with separate entrances, security, and firewalls in cities such as Mumbai, Bangalore, Hyderabad, Delhi, and Chennai.

These software and engineering development centers are extensions of GE's individual business IT or engineering teams and ultimately report to the global business chief information officer (CIO) or engineering leader. The CIO reviews current suppliers, selects new ones, and negotiates contracts. These centers have proved highly successful, growing from just over 600 software designers in 1995 to 6,500 in 2002. In 2001, GE's savings from the project exceeded $250 million and are projected to grow to $600 million in 2003.[5]

In 2002, GE established two wholly owned software development centers (as opposed to the jointly owned centers we just described) to develop key in-house expertise for more highly valued and proprietary software. Increasingly, many U.S. technology companies are considering starting 100%-owned subsidiaries in countries like India instead of working with an offshore IT services vendor. The main reasons being: 1) the cost savings associated with an offshore subsidiary can be as high as 40% when compared to a vendor partnership; 2) direct control on hiring and retention of offshore resources; and 3) the ability to retain intellectual property within the company.

A typical ODC provides the services outlined in table 2.2.[6]

Facilities Management	Operations Support	Staffing, HR, and Training
■ Office infrastructure ■ Physical security ■ Communications infrastructure ■ Technology equipment ■ Standard office software	■ Data security and backup ■ Computer maintenance ■ Systems administration ■ Accounting services ■ Office administrative support ■ Visa and travel support ■ Government liaison	■ Recruiting and hiring ■ Orientation and training ■ Retention program ■ Taxation and HR compliance ■ Employee benefits ■ Outplacement

Table 2.2: Services Provided by Offshore Development Centers

How Does the ODC Model Work?

To understand the role of an offshore development center, it is useful to look at the lifecycle of a typical third-party vendor software development or maintenance project. At the beginning of the project, the ODC assigns a small team of two to five with varying skill sets — business analysts, project managers, and IT professionals — to visit a customer site and determine the scope and requirements of the project.

Once the initial specifications of the engagement are documented, the project managers return to the offshore location to supervise a much larger team of ten to 50 IT professionals dedicated to the development of the applications. A small team remains at the client's site to track changes in scope and address new requirements as the project progresses.

Once the development stage of the assignment is completed and tested, a team returns to the client's site to install the newly developed system and ensure its functionality. At this phase of the engagement, the vendor will often enter into an ongoing agreement with the client to provide comprehensive maintenance services from one of its offshore software development facilities.

In contrast to development projects, a typical maintenance assignment requires a larger team of ten to 20 IT professionals to travel to the client's site to gain a thorough understanding of all aspects of the client's system. The majority of the maintenance team subsequently returns to the offshore software development facility where it assumes full responsibility for day-to-day maintenance of the client's system, while coordinating with a few maintenance professionals who remain stationed at the client's site. By pursuing this model, the company completes a significant portion of its project work at its offshore software development facilities.

Sophisticated project management techniques, risk management processes, and quality control measures such as ISO 9001 and the Capability Maturity Model are necessary to complete projects seamlessly across multiple locations. These processes govern all aspects of the software product lifecycle, from requirements to testing and maintenance.

The software product engineering and IT industry has grown rapidly over the last decade through the provision of outsourced programming and IT services. In an era where the innovation is around software, we expect the ODC model to be widely adopted.

Staff Augmentation, Contracting, or Temporary Services

The oldest onsite outsourcing model is staff augmentation, contracting, or temporary services. In this model, corporations leverage supplemental staff to contain costs and handle overflow work. Staff augmentation reduces the costs associated with hiring, benefits, and termination, as well as the expense of recruiting, training, and retaining personnel. In-house resources can be redeployed on revenue-generating and strategic activities.

The staff augmentation model can also utilize offshore resources. Actually, many offshore vendors first started as "body shops" that provided staff augmentation. These vendors thrived in the late 1990s when it was extremely difficult to find qualified employees.

Pure IT or Business Process Outsourcing

Pure outsourcing is the most classic of the first-generation offshore outsourcing business models. In this model, companies delegate one or more business processes to an external provider that owns, administers, and manages the processes based on predefined and measurable service level metrics.

Pure outsourcing is based on a multiyear (five- to ten-year) contract with a single vendor for all the in-scope services. It comes in two forms: information technology outsourcing (ITO) and business process outsourcing (BPO). In this model, vendors usually handle a large part of the customer's IT or process needs. The two reasons most commonly given by companies that select this model are 1) lack of staff with appropriate skills and 2) not enough time to do the job right.

The advantages of this model are a lower cost of procurement, reduced management overhead, and service provider familiarity with client needs. The disadvantages are the captive or even exclusive relationship and the tendency of service provider investments to set the pace for innovation.

First-Generation Offshore Outsourcing

In this model, foreign companies come to the United States or Europe to sell projects. These projects are then executed completely offshore with local, low-cost labor. This model was first seen in contract manufacturing and then spread to IT. In the IT sector the tasks included Y2K remediation, euro conversion, software development, and application maintenance.

The first generation of offshore outsourcing was attractive for CIOs in the financial services, high-tech, and retail industries that did not want to hire in-house staff or expensive consultants to do simple tasks. In addition, the U.S. unemployment rate during the 1990s was very low, which made it hard to recruit employees. As a result, many organizations turned to offshore outsourcing vendors to take care of their staffing problems. This facilitated better utilization of in-house personnel. It also helped them to rapidly turn projects "on" or "off" based on business demand.

The first generation of offshore outsourcing did have some limitations. Its modus operandi was to throw low-cost talent at a variety of problems, which works well enough for defined commodity tasks that do not require much communication; however, in a business process environment (customer care or transaction processing) that requires more interaction, the classic hand-off model is not a good match. Much more integration between the firm and the offshore vendor is necessary.

The Second Generation of Offshore Business Models

As customer needs evolve, second-generation business models are emerging. They tend to be more sophisticated and to span multiple models of the first generation (see figure 2.3). These combination models include:

- Global delivery or blended outsourcing models (practiced by large global vendors),

- Hybrid delivery model (practiced by midsize and large offshore vendors),

- Global shared services center (practiced by large multinationals),

- Build-operate-transfer (BOT) model (practiced by risk averse corporations), and

- Offshore multisourcing model (practiced by experienced multinationals).

Global Delivery Model

A global delivery model (also called blended outsourcing) is one in which a company outsources to a multinational service provider such as Accenture, EDS, or IBM that offers a mix of onsite, offsite onshore, and offshore resources.

Take the case of Accenture, which is transitioning its service offering mix to a global delivery model in an effort to improve its cost structure and margins. In response to the rate pressure from offshore firms, Accenture has been establishing its own offshore and nearshore presence, with more than 40 low-cost delivery centers worldwide. Accenture has more than 8,000 employees in offshore and nearshore locations such as India, China, the Philippines, and Spain, up from 4,000 in 2002 and expected to increase to 12,000 by year-end 2004.[7]

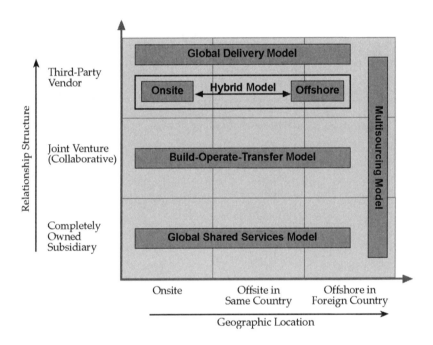

Figure 2.3: Second-Generation Offshore Outsourcing Business Models

The global delivery model allows vendors to innovatively distribute and manage engagements across multiple global locations. The advantage of this model is that the company initiating the outsourcing receives a lower rate without the risk. If faster time to market is a primary delivery objective, the global delivery model can accommodate this requirement by divvying up work efforts across onshore, nearshore, and offshore development facilities. Large corporations that hire major global outsourcers such as Sykes, SITEL, Convergys, Wipro, or Infosys often prefer this distributed approach. The distribution of outsourcing activities may vary according to the demands of the project.

Vendors have a variety of marketing names for the global delivery model: best shore, any shore, right shore, and multishore. Whatever it is called, its objective is the same: to distribute and manage engagements and resources across multiple global locations, thereby allowing the service provider to better respond to client requirements from around the globe. If disaster strikes any of the vendors's locations, it can immediately shift work to other locations so that there is no interruption in business processes.

The biggest advantage of the global delivery model is that it saves the client from investing in a huge team of employees. It adapts to the client's changing requirements and, if there is a sudden need for more resources, the service provider can supply them at once to the client and later relocate them to other, more convenient locations.

The global delivery model is the preferred model of choice for large consulting companies. Their close customer relationships and enormous domain knowledge have made them formidable competitors. They can quickly enter markets such as India or the Philippines and take advantage of the low-cost labor. Their capabilities and customer bases permit them to scale up their offshore operations rapidly.

Hybrid Delivery Model (Onsite and Offshore)

Hybrid outsourcing combines onsite and offshore services to deliver results at reduced costs. The hybrid outsourcing model, also known as the dual-shore model, is quickly becoming the most common model for the midsized service providers headquartered offshore in countries such as India.

How does this work? Consider the case of a software development project: The local onsite team manages the project's program management office (PMO) and handles the client-facing components of the project, such as requirements gathering and user-interface development. The onsite operation may control a defined portion of the project that requires interaction with the business subject matter experts and software architects onsite. The offshore facilities take care of the coding, testing, and bug fixing so work can be performed around the clock.

In a dual-shore model, requirements gathering and the development of detailed specifications is done onsite, while programming or process work is done offshore. This model maximizes efficiency in resources and costs. Ideally, 20%–30% of work is done onsite whereas 70%–80% is outsourced offshore depending upon the criticality of the project.

This model is one of the most popular to have emerged so far. Its proven benefits include continuous, near 24-hour work cycles; the ability to structure and assemble teams with diverse, multiple skill sets; lower-cost resources; and the ability to quickly scale (up or down) depending on the requirements. Part of its success can be attributed to the fact that this model enables clients to directly interact with the service provider through the onsite team and simultaneously enjoy the benefits of offshore outsourcing.

This model has its own set of challenges including project management and administration costs, optimization of cross-cultural communication, and the supervision of onsite teams.

Global Shared Services Model

Global shared services centers, also known as captive centers or offshore insourcing, are a combination of onshore shared services and offshore captive centers. The objective is to consolidate the scattered, autonomously run internal services operations of a multinational organization into mega-service centers. Another objective is to create a customer-focused mind-set and dedication, which enables high-quality, cost-effective, and timely service. The global center is run as an independent business, with its own budget and bottom-line accountability. GE, HSBC, and American Express are considered by many to be the most sophisticated in deploying this model.

How does this work? To understand this model better, let's study the best-practice example of GE Capital International Services (GECIS). GECIS provides back-room services to GE Capital businesses and GE industrial businesses at significantly lower costs and higher quality levels. GECIS began with simple data processing and has moved up the value chain to support more complex processes from diverse businesses across GE. GECIS has nine Centers of Excellence (CoEs) in the following areas: finance and accounting, insurance, collections, customer fulfillment, industrial and equipment, analytics, learning and remote marketing, IT services, and software. Table 2.3 lists some of the situations and processes that three of these CoEs handle.

GE Contact CoE	GE Finance CoE	GE Transaction CoE
<ul><li>A store representative calling for approval of a credit card purchase</li><li>A credit card holder with a question or reporting a lost card</li><li>A automobile owner calling to report an accident</li><li>A medical systems field engineer ordering a spare part</li><li>Collection calls to a credit card holder requesting past due payment</li></ul>	<ul><li>Over 60% of GE's accounts payables — 6 million invoices annually</li><li>Daily cash settlement to private label credit card services</li><li>Account reconciliation for 28 GE businesses</li><li>Financial planning and analysis</li><li>Financial closing for six businesses</li><li>Balance sheet reporting for 11 businesses</li></ul>	<ul><li>Application claims</li><li>Claims processing</li><li>Billing</li><li>Collections</li><li>Underwriting</li><li>Loan approvals</li><li>Order processing</li></ul>

Table 2.3: Services and Processes That GE's Centers of Excellence Handle

GECIS also supports other back-office functions. GECIS's IT-enabled services provide help desk and network management. The analytics center conducts data mining and analysis for GE and its customers. GECIS e-learning assists with employee training and assessment. GECIS even employs doctors to evaluate and classify medical claims. Currently, GECIS is the largest captive shared services employer in India with more than 11,000 employees. This number is expected to increase to 20,000 by mid-2004.[8]

Captive shared services centers have significant advantages. First, they have guaranteed markets for their services and an established management hierarchy. They also alleviate some of the organizational issues such as control and politics that crop up when firms relocate back-office activities offshore to external vendors. Multinational captive centers are leading the way in the establishment of the global shared services business operations.

Build-Operate-Transfer Model

For many of the companies that have started their own foreign subsidiaries, the process has not been as smooth as they expected. They faced obstacles — legal, taxes, hiring, and management — from start to finish. While some companies have taken a long time to attain a steady state, some are still struggling, and a few even closed down their operations.

The increasing number of captive subsidiary failures led to the evolution of a new business model in the offshore services industry called build-operate-transfer (BOT). In this model, a firm contracts with an offshore partner to build a shared services or offshore development center and operate it for a fixed interim period. The logic behind the BOT model: The offshore partner can initiate operations and reach operating stability much faster than it can with an in-house effort.

A typical BOT is built and managed in three phases:

1. **Build.** The offshore partner provides a complete solution for building a presence in a particular country. The clients receive their own office space and establish their own brand identity at a lower price than comparable outsourcing arrangements. The vendor's staff takes care of all administrative and legal issues, from real estate, utilities, and permits, to computers, communications, and office supplies. The vendor also provides the professional support staff and operating licenses to run functions such as call centers.

2. **Operate.** The offshore partner provides a comprehensive set of operational management services, from HR and staffing, to accent training, accounting, payroll, legal, facilities, and security. The clients are able to focus their management time on their core business rather than on operational issues.

3. **Option to Transfer.** The offshore partner cannot lock in clients. The clients have the option to bring the operation in-house at any time. The outsourcing contract should detail a well-defined process to ensure a smooth transition. Typically, the contract includes a clause that says the client has the option to buy the entire operation after a

fixed period. A BOT gives the client the ability to realize the benefits of offshoring quickly with limited execution risk while minimizing upfront costs and long-term financial risks.

Building your own subsidiary in a foreign country requires much knowledge and information about the country and culture, as well as the right personnel. If you aren't up to the task of gathering this information, then the BOT solution may be the right answer for your company. The BOT model is usually found in the civil and construction engineering business, especially in the maintenance of highways and airports. Now the BOT model is becoming popular in the offshore outsourcing world.

BOT models tend to build on first-generation ODC models. With the ODC model, the basic framework is in place for the "build" and "operate" parts. With BOT there is an additional option to "transfer" the operations after a certain period. This arrangement provides customers with bottom-line enhancements and fully offloaded costs, risks, and ownership of the new venture. The risk of execution is minimized and the money can be spent on core functions.

Offshore Multisourcing: Hub-and-Spoke Model

Similar to the Chinese proverb that states a clever rabbit will have three openings to its den, many companies will hire multiple offshore vendors to mitigate risk.

Multisourcing is the practice of using multiple offshore suppliers to reduce the power that a single monopoly vendor might have. This also helps companies achieve the advantages of a best-of-breed strategy. Citibank and American Express have both taken a multisourcing approach that resembles a classic hub-and-spoke model. They will have offshore operations of their own, as well as three or four partners with whom they collaborate. This is an interesting model as the businesses get some of their partners to actually work with them in their own hub centers, train them, and then let them go back to the spoke center.

New York–based Guardian Life Insurance Company embraces a multisourcing approach. The insurer contracts with Patni Computer Systems (Mumbai), NIIT Technologies (New Delhi), and Covansys (Michigan). Instead of awarding one major, long-term contract to a single supplier, Guardian is mitigating risk by working with a consortium of vendors to create a multilocation, distributed delivery model.

The rise of multisource deals could be a sign that companies are taking a more cautious, risk-averse approach to outsourcing. In the case of Guardian and others, multisourcing works because the organization has the internal ability to manage and integrate multiple providers (products, projects, and services) to derive a single solution.

When should organizations choose full-service outsourcing (using one provider) over multisourcing? It depends on the maturity of the organization. Companies that are new to outsourcing tend to multisource until they get comfortable with the whole process. When they renegotiate contracts later, they tend to give more thought to using one provider. Often, to reduce complexity, very large businesses will look for one dominant provider and that provider will then work with a big network of companies.

Understanding the Offshore Revenue Models

No discussion of offshore business models is complete without some mention of the underlying revenue models. In order to help you understand the revenue models, we should note that offshore outsourcing comes in two flavors:

1. Task-oriented (piecemeal) — outsource my mess for less, or take my tasks and complete them for less money.

2. Process-oriented (comprehensive) — take over my business processes and provide them back to me as a service.

The task-oriented and process-oriented revenue models are quite varied in offshore outsourcing. The task-oriented BPO contracts tend to gravitate towards time and material and fixed-price. The process-oriented BPO contracts range from cost-plus to fuzzier risk-reward models. Let's look at each revenue model in more detail.

Time and Material Revenue Model

The simplest pricing model is time and materials (T&M) billing. The T&M model is an attractive option when scope, specification, and implementation plans of a project are not easy to define at the outset.

The challenge in the T&M model is adhering to very strict project management and reporting practices whereby task sheets are generated on a daily or weekly basis for each of the employees on the project. If there is lax oversight of the work, then T&M can become very expensive.

Fixed-Price Revenue Model

Outsourcing vendors use the fixed-price or fixed-time model to effectively sell their services to clients. Customers are attracted to this model because of the upfront commitment on timing and the concept of risk sharing on potential cost or time overruns.

Under this option, the customer pays a prenegotiated fixed price for the complete project, which is linked to well-defined deliverables. This is suitable for customers with clear requirements and project schedules. Changes in scope are subject to a predefined fixed hourly rate and must follow a standard, already established change request procedure.

Cost Plus Revenue Model

This model is typically used in tandem with the build-operate-transfer model or for complex multiyear, multi-element arrangements. It is also the model behind the dedicated development center (an extension of a company's software engineering facility). It is popular among large companies that seek long-term gains from offshore outsourcing. These contracts are principally structured on a fee-for-service basis and stipulate that the vendor receives a fee that is no greater than the client's historical cost of operating the functions assumed by the vendor. For some components of the outsourcing fees, vendors provide negotiated discounts from the client's historical costs. After vendors have recovered their costs or achieved a negotiated minimum cost reduction, they may be required to share further savings with the clients in a negotiated gain sharing arrangement.

Risk-Reward Revenue Model

Vendors that enter multiyear partnerships with clients favor risk-reward or gain sharing models for outsourcing contracts. Since the goal of outsourcing is to help clients become more effective in their business operations, vendors are open to linking their revenues with the actual benefits their clients realize.

This type of contract is also known as value pricing, or "pay as you save," whereby the outsourcer builds first and is paid as savings materialize. These are performance-based contracts, tying payments to business performance.

The drawbacks of this model are that revenue recognition on the vendor side becomes an important accounting issue. Vendors typically can recognize revenues and profits as work progresses based upon the proportion of costs incurred to the total expected costs. Vendors maintain for each of their contracts estimates of total revenues and costs over the respective contract term. For purposes of periodic financial reporting, vendors accumulate total actual costs incurred to date under the contract.

Summary

A crucial issue in ensuring offshoring success is selecting the appropriate business model. Offshore business processes have a variety of organizational forms ranging from captive centers to third-party outsourcing vendors. The distribution of activities across the various delivery models may vary from one project to another depending on the effort involved, speed of execution, level of interaction, and the cultural and time zone differences.

Another issue that managers need to pay attention to is the underlying revenue model. Current revenue models for outsourcing and offshore vendors are similar to those of traditional service firms or professional service organizations, such as accounting or law firms. In general, revenues are determined by the number of billable consultants, their utilization, and average hourly bill rates. We envision more progressive revenue models developing over time.

In summary, the more time you invest upfront in choosing the right business model, the higher your probability of success.

Chapter Three

The Business Process Offshoring Landscape

"For a successful technology, reality must take precedence over public relations."

— Richard Phillips Feynman

Introduction

You might expect a $180 billion oil and gas behemoth like British Petroleum (BP) to do its own accounting. And it might, if it wasn't cheaper to pay an external vendor to do it. That external vendor is IBM Global Services, which agreed to handle BP's accounting for ten years. In the initiative's first two years, BP has saved about $52 million. Over the next eight years, it anticipates saving $200 million more.[1] As part of its contract, BP expects IBM to continuously drive down costs using a global delivery model.

Sustained sales and earnings growth are vital to the survival of every firm and are critical for evaluating and compensating management. Outsourcing of processes is increasingly becoming the cost management tool of choice to foster earnings growth alongside alternative strategies such as mergers or acquisitions.

Increasingly, corporate strategists are encouraging a close examination of offshore outsourcing. As we pointed out in Chapter 2, the options for executing offshore outsourcing range from transition of one or more business processes to a captive center, external service provider, or joint venture, which, in turn, owns and manages the selected processes based upon defined and measurable performance metrics.

This chapter builds on the foundation of the previous chapter and breaks down the term "business process" into its constituent parts. Our rationale for the breakdown? In order to create strategic value you must have a clear understanding of underlying business processes so you can address the question of what to offshore.

In this chapter, we provide an integrative framework to help you understand the range of business processes that are migrating offshore. To illustrate how the different processes are being offshored, we study two best-practice companies, Dell and American Express. We identify the different process groups — information technology, customer care, finance and accounting, human resources, and transaction processing — and set the stage for the rest of the book.

Business Process Focused Offshore Outsourcing

Which processes are heading offshore? According to Richard Swanson, director of BPO Services at Patni Computer Systems, a global consulting and IT services provider, "The services that are working best offshore are those that are labor intensive, well structured, repeatable, nonproprietary, and low risk to the business. These are the kind of processes that can be moved offshore the easiest."[2]

In order to define the opportunities for you, we will first break down offshore outsourcing into value-added categories (see figure 3.1). The targeted business processes generally fall into seven broad categories:

1. Finance and Accounting (F&A) — accounts payable, accounts receivable, risk management, and general accounting.

2. Customer Care — customer selection (marketing campaigns), acquisition (telemarketing and telesales), retention (service and support), and extension (cross-sell and up-sell).

3. Human Resources (HR) — employee support, payroll, recruiting, performance management, benefits administration, and training.

4. Transaction Processing — billing and payment services, indirect procurement, and administration services such as tax processing, claims, and policy processing.

5. Information Technology (IT) — software and application development, systems maintenance, packaged software implementation and integration, and architecture design services.

6. Supply Chain Management — transportation and logistics, direct procurement, and warehouse and inventory management.

7. Manufacturing — contract manufacturing (which currently accounts for more than 50% of the outsourcing market) and research and development.

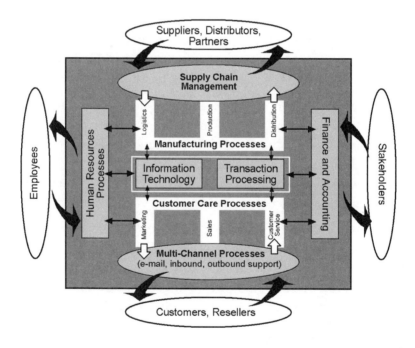

Figure 3.1: Business Process Categories

Initially, offshore outsourcing companies concentrated their efforts on manufacturing and IT application development and maintenance. In the last three years, their focus has broadened to include other processes such as customer care and back-office transaction processing. We believe the opportunity for offshore outsourcing is feasible for processes that are standardized, easily measured (in terms of service levels), relatively centralized, and, in many cases, high-volume.

The broad spectrum of processes means that offshore service providers can specialize in one category or even a subcategory, based on the complexity of the process. This specialization has been critical to the growth of the offshore outsourcing market.

To understand the nuances of the different process segments, it is useful to look at how Dell is approaching offshore outsourcing. Dell's uniqueness lies in its sophisticated use of offshoring to drive down cost.

Best-Practice Case Study: Dell's Low-Cost Locations

Outsourcing has been the cornerstone of Dell's direct business model. In fact, outsourcing is considered one of the primary reasons Dell has been able to grow from a company that reported $18.2 billion in revenues in 1999 to a company that reported $35.4 billion in revenues in 2003.

Dell is concentrating on big-picture issues, such as how to continue reporting year-over-year increases in sales and how to penetrate new markets. The soft economy and the decline in corporate technology spending forced Dell in 2002 to get creative in finding news sources of revenue. Along with cutting costs through offshoring, the company is entering new markets, such as printers, storage, and handhelds.

The business requirement to support these new customers at a low cost is further fueling the offshore outsourcing trend at Dell. To maintain its lead as a low-cost leader, Dell is migrating its business model to a global delivery model. In this case study, we outline the different Dell offshoring initiatives under way in Ireland, India, Russia, and Taiwan.

Offshore Call Centers in Ireland

Established in December 1992, Dell Bray was one of the first call centers to land on Ireland's shores and was followed by Dell Cherrywood in August 2000. The two centers are charged with providing sales and support to Ireland, as well as to individuals and small and midsize customers in the United Kingdom.

Dell chose Ireland for several reasons: 1) Europe is a key market; 2) the country has a low-cost business environment; 3) the labor pool is educated, IT savvy, and English-speaking; 4) several government subsidies exist; and 5) the supplier and telecom infrastructures are robust.

Some of the other reasons companies cite when asked why they picked Ireland for offshoring are the overlap in the U.K. and U.S. business day, the compatible cultures, Ireland's proximity, and the lower attrition rates.

Offshore Help Desk and Technical Support in India

In June 2001, Dell announced the formation of Dell International Services, a division of Dell Computer India Pvt Ltd. The division was established to provide technical support to U.S. home and small business customers mainly through call centers located in Bangalore and Hyderabad, India.

According to Dell, the Indian support center objectives were threefold:

1. To push Dell closer to its goal of providing service worldwide and enabling its philosophy of "call anywhere, resolution anywhere."

2. To expand service for customers in the consumer segment, beginning with the United States and extending to other countries in the future.

3. To support the growing Indian customer base.

Dell listed many of the same reasons its competitors have cited for setting up in India — the ability to provide a 24x7 or "follow-the-sun" model of service, a favorable cost structure, and access to a vast, skilled, English-speaking workforce.[3]

In 2001, the technical support center had 200 seats; as of March 2003, the number of employees had jumped to 2,000. The center has also added Australia, New Zealand, and Ireland to the countries it services from India. In addition to providing users e-mail- and telephone-based technical support, Dell International Services has added software development and hardware product design to its responsibilities.[4]

Dell's Offshore Failure

After successful trials with the consumer segment, Dell expanded its round-the-clock technical support center in India to handle calls from its U.S. corporate customers. This plan, however, ran into problems. There was an onslaught of complaints from the very same customers the center sought to support. Customers were not satisfied with the level of support they were receiving and complained that the Indian technical support representatives were difficult to communicate with because of thick accents and scripted responses.

Since corporate customers account for about 85% of business, Dell had to bow to customer pressure.[5] It moved tech support for some corporate customers back to call centers in Texas, Idaho, and Tennessee. However, calls from home PC owners will continue to be handled by the technical support center in Bangalore, India.

Dell clearly has to adjust its strategy by providing more accent neutralization, employee training, and service quality management at the Indian technical support center.

Offshore Software Development in Russia

Dell, like Boeing, Motorola, Citibank, and Intel, has traveled to Russia to outsource software development. Although India is regarded as the big fish in the offshore software development pond, Russia is climbing the charts with its huge pool of low-cost engineering talent. One of the leading offshore providers in Russia is LUXOFT with whom Dell decided to collaborate in mid-2002. The outcome of the partnership was a dedicated software engineering center located in Moscow.

The best-of-breed engineers were hired according to criteria that Dell set to ensure that the team had the experience, domain knowledge, and education that it sought. The Moscow-based center follows Dell's practices, methodologies, and culture and complements Dell's European IT centers located in Great Britain, France, and Ireland.

The center supports Dell's internal IT requirements for its constantly changing Web site and e-commerce portal and develops enterprise and system software for the global market. The Russian center allows Dell's IT departments to concentrate on more critical, value-added technology tasks, while keeping the scale of IT deliverables at the current pace or an even faster pace, which gives Dell the ability to accelerate the sales machine to support a market capture strategy.[6]

Offshore Production in Taiwan

In manufacturing, Dell executives were faced with the interesting challenge of devising new solutions in an industry that refuses to stand still. The dynamics of the PC industry change virtually every month: Product lifecycles shorten, and demands for reliability, flexibility, speed, and quality escalate. To keep pace, Dell undertook a wholesale revamping of its business processes, from design and forecasting, to raw materials acquisition, production, distribution, and customer follow-up.

One of the results of its revamping was a decision to offshore more production to partners in Taiwan and China. Taiwan is not new to offshore manufacturing. In fact, many high-tech companies have been outsourcing some manufacturing process steps there for almost two decades. However, most of their outsourcing has been at interim Stages 1 or 2 (see table 3.1). These companies have not yet taken full advantage of the outsourcing model, which can further reduce cost of goods sold, decrease overhead expenses, and more quickly introduce new products to the global market.

Offshore Manufacturing Stage	Characteristics
Stage 1: Noncore components	Convenience, flexibility, and alternative source of supply
Stage 2: Commodity but core components and assemblies	Offshore most of printed-circuit-board assemblies
Stage 3: Offshore manufacturing of entire product lines	Reconsider entire manufacturing strategy, examine whether current contractors are the best fit, and minimize management costs. Dell does the design and the partners do the rest.

Table 3.1: Stages of Offshore High-Tech Manufacturing

Dell has migrated from Stage 2 to Stage 3. For instance, in November 2002, Dell disclosed that it offshored production of its handhelds to Wistron, a provider of both original design and manufacturing (ODM) and contract electronic manufacturing (CEM) services. Competing for the contract were Compal, MiTAC Technology, and High Tech

Computers, but Wistron proved it was the only company that could meet Dell's extremely low contract price of $170 per unit. With such low margins per unit, the only way Wistron could afford to take the contract was if it was guaranteed a large order. By selecting Wistron to produce its handheld, Dell has been able to pass its savings on to the customer.[7]

As Dell has learned over the years, offshore outsourcing also raises unique challenges that cannot often be anticipated. For instance, Taiwan is in an earthquake zone. In September 1999, the country was hit by a violent earthquake that tragically killed thousands and affected nearly every aspect of daily life. One of its effects was to halt manufacturing at an industrial park for PC components nearby to Dell. Due to its lean inventory, Dell had to slow production and could not take advantage of the PC price hike because it had a limited buffer inventory.

The Bottom Line

Dell is evolving into a true multinational. By 2007, the company hopes to double sales to $60 billion, with 50% derived from non-PC business, in contrast to the 19% of total sales non-PC business contributes today.[8] Dell won't achieve those numbers through U.S. sales alone, which brings us to back to India, and, to a much lesser extent, Russia and the other countries to which it offshores work. Not only do these countries represent a chance to cut costs through offshoring and a way for Dell to diversify its offshoring portfolio, they, India and China in particular, represent an untapped market for Dell's products.

What is intriguing about Dell's offshore outsourcing strategy is its evolution. It began with an initial focus on reducing transaction costs and progressed to the next step of maximizing cost savings. To achieve those savings, the company needed to make process improvements that fueled productivity gains, so they turned to automation. Then, to realize more savings, Dell moved to process reconfiguration. Dell is systematically moving up the value chain and sending more complex business functions offshore.

Segmenting the Offshore Business Process Landscape

As the case study of Dell illustrates, the offshore business process landscape is quite complex and varied. Dell is unique because it is not taking a piecemeal approach to offshoring by outsourcing one task at a time. Instead, it has chosen the more risky approach of offshore outsourcing entire processes.

Based on the analysis of various best-practice companies such as GE and Dell, it is clear that there are five main categories of business processes that companies are sending offshore. They include information technology, customer care, finance and accounting, human resources, and transaction processing (see figure 3.2). In this book, we have chosen to focus on the five most widely outsourced categories. We will not cover manufacturing and supply chain management.

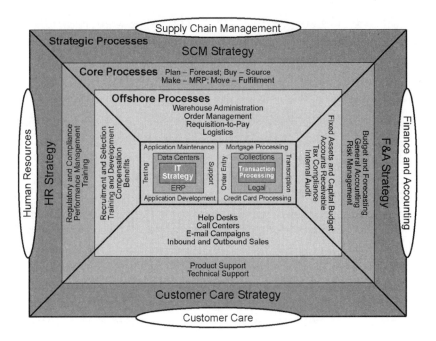

Figure 3.2: Offshore Process Landscape

When evaluating whether or not to offshore any of these business processes, three questions need to be answered:

1. Can you offshore the process without losing your competitive advantage?

2. If you offshore the process, will it generate incremental value to justify the effort?

3. Can you offshore the identified process without losing control of it?

Information Technology Processes

Information technology (IT) hardware and software companies were the first to move into the offshore sector. Back in the mid-1980s, the model was to use offshore labor for low-end, low-cost work such as language localization, device and printer drivers, and motherboard production.

However, as the offshore outsourcing phenomenon took off, Fortune 1000 companies started contracting with offshore companies to do other types of work like Y2K remediation. The focus gradually shifted to application maintenance, support of existing products, and, eventually, new application development.

Today, the range of possible IT processes that can be offshored includes:

- **Application development**, which spans designing, developing, and installing software for a variety of IT systems. Applications range from single-platform, single-site systems to multiplatform, multisite systems. A project may involve the development of new applications or new functions for existing software applications. Each development project typically involves all aspects of the software development process, including definition, prototyping, design, pilots, programming, testing, installation, and maintenance.

- **Application maintenance**, which is usually for large software systems that need modifications, enhancements, and product support. It includes migrating to new technologies while extending the useful life of existing systems. Projects may involve re-engineering software to migrate applications from mainframe to client/server architectures or to migrate from existing operating systems to Unix or Windows NT. For companies with extensive proprietary software applications, implementing such technologies may require rewriting and testing millions of lines of software code.

- **Application testing**, which focuses on critical aspects such as quality assurance, building automated test suites, performance metrics, capacity planning for peak business demands, validation testing, test automation, execution, defect tracking, and reporting.

- **Support services** for constantly changing applications and technology that span help desk, scheduled maintenance, security issues, remote diagnostics, and documentation development.

- **Implementation services**, which are end-to-end application hosting services that allow customers to transfer the responsibility of maintaining, enhancing, and managing custom and packaged applications to the vendor. They also include product lifecycle management, prototype development, technology evaluation, proof of concept, application hosting, and training.

- **New product engineering services**, which encompass Web Services design, product and process analysis, and simulations and range from basic changes to complex designs. In addition, they may involve customizing the latest object-oriented design, modeling, and engineering software to specific user requirements.

Figure 3.3 shows the different offshore IT categories.

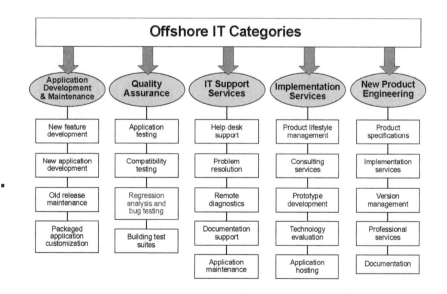

Figure 3.3: Offshore IT Processes

Customer Care Processes

The customer of today is very different from the customer of yesterday. With each passing day, customers gain more knowledge and, consequently, more demands for companies.

The Internet created a new customer who is armed with more intelligence about prices and greater service expectations and is driving companies to focus efforts and money on customer care. Within the process category of customer care, there are many subcategories ripe for offshoring.

- **Support** entails everything from responding to the customer's initial inquiry, product question, and status update, to the invoice query and the order confirmation. Most of these issues are handled through contact centers via voice-based phone support, e-mail, or live chat.

- **Marketing** provides comprehensive marketing functionality such as direct mail marketing campaigns, telemarketing, telesales, lead qualification, lead tracking, and customer surveys.

- **Sales** support cross-selling and up-selling opportunities, inbound and outbound sales, acquisition programs, campaign management, and retention programs.

- **Technical support** processes assist customers with resolving a product or service problem.

- **Customer analytics** provides content and applications to measure, predict, plan, and optimize customer relationships.

Figure 3.4 shows the different offshore customer care process categories.

Technical support and help desk are often the first customer care processes to go offshore. However, this is not as easy as it appears. The case of Dell's help desk problems was highlighted earlier. Lehman Brothers also faced similar problems. In December 2003, Lehman Brothers stopped using Wipro Spectramind, an Indian outsourcing firm, for its internal IT help desk. Lehman wasn't satisfied with the level of service it received and brought the help-desk function back in-house. Offshoring technical support while attractive can be fraught with pitfalls if not planned carefully.

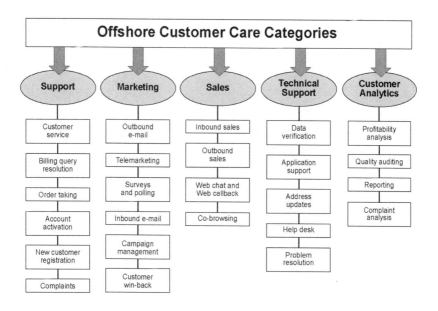

Figure 3.4: Offshore Customer Care Processes

Finance and Accounting Processes

From accounting to travel management, firms need to analyze voluminous data sets to understand, report, and generate value. Within this process category, many subcategories can potentially be offshored.

- **Transaction processing** enables enterprises and their business networks to handle customer- and supply chain–related financial processes. Accounts payable, accounts receivable, credit management, bill presentment and payment, in-house account management, cash and liquidity management, and dispute management are typical transaction processing subprocesses.

- **General accounting** records quantities and values from financially relevant transactions in value-creation processes and maintains a consistent, reconciled, and auditable set of books for statutory reporting, management support, and use as a source for analytic applications. Subprocesses include general ledgers and subledgers, bookkeeping, and project accounting.

- **Financial management** encompasses financial statements, revenue and cost accounting, and product and service cost calculations.

- **Financial reporting** supports greater transparency in financial reporting, performance monitoring, integrated strategic planning, business consolidation, and effective stakeholder communication. Typical subprocesses include financial reporting, sales tax filing, shareholder services, and budgeting and forecasting.

- **Tax processing** is dependent on the general ledger, which is a collection of all balance sheets, income, and expense accounts used to keep a business's accounting records. General ledger posting reports, quarterly local tax returns, federal tax returns, W-2 forms for all employees, and unemployment tax returns are the subprocesses housed under tax processing.

Figure 3.5 shows the different offshore F&A process categories.

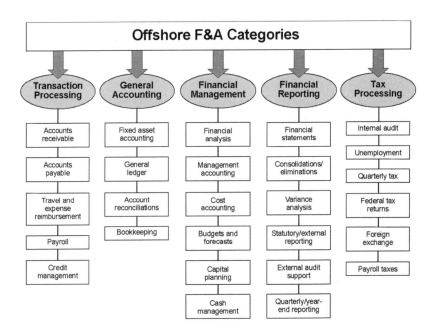

Figure 3.5: Offshore Finance and Accounting Processes

Human Resources Processes

Human resources (HR) is a complex business function that covers a range of processes, from recruitment and retirement, to basic transactions and workforce development.

The initial targets for HR offshore outsourcing are the HR departments of the Global 500 companies. According to *FORTUNE* magazine's Global 500 list for 2002, large corporations employed more than 47 million people, and the median number of employees for these corporations was approximately 63,000, in multiple locations and countries. An employee base of this magnitude presents enormous complexities: Multiple HR groups for different business units exist, and corporations lack central information repositories or integrated HR technology infrastructures. Simplifying this complex organizational structure and lowering the cost of providing employee services is the primary driver of HR outsourcing.

The HR process category contains many subcategories that can be offshored.

- **Compensation services** involve managing deferred compensation, stock options, and long-term performance; analyzing payroll data; keeping track of attendance; recording and paying payroll taxes; and issuing payments to employees.

- **Benefits management** spans a broad range of services that include managing health, medical, 401(k), pension, and life insurance plans; overseeing eligibility and vacation schedules; tracking leave; maintaining retirement earning histories; and supervising the enrollment and termination of benefits.

- **Employee relations** is based on companies' efforts to promote and maintain effective relationships with all employees. This includes capabilities that enable employees through a variety of channels (help desk, Web portal, and voice) to conduct day-to-day transactions. Specific tasks include employee development, employee record management, employee communication, labor management, local compliance issues, training needs identification, training administration, and specialized training requirements.

- **Workforce management** covers the creation of workforce strategies that help to effectively deploy and measure human capital. It also includes developing candidate pools, assessing and selecting candidates, and managing recruiting. For large multinationals, recruiting and workforce planning involves establishing and administering expatriate and domestic relocation policies and programs, addressing and managing the special needs of the expatriate employees, and handling the repatriation of employees.

Figure 3.6 shows the different offshore HR process categories.

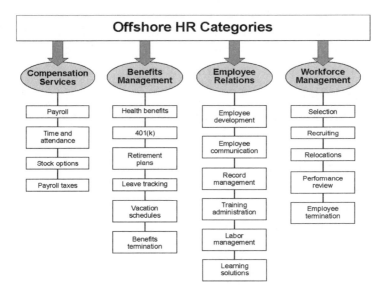

Figure 3.6: Offshore HR Processes

Transaction Processing

While back-office transaction processing may be boring, the accuracy and timeliness of the information it delivers are the legs upon which today's companies stand.

As the offshore market matures, back-office services are becoming more specialized and vertical-specific. For instance, in the mortgage industry, companies are outsourcing loan processing. In healthcare, companies are outsourcing medical transcription and medical record administration.

In insurance, companies are outsourcing claims processing and policy administration. Figure 3.7 shows the different offshore transaction processing categories.

To better understand offshore transaction processing it is useful to look at a real-world case study. In the world of offshore transaction processing, American Express is considered by many to be a best practice. By moving its transaction processing offshore, the company has created tremendous efficiencies in its internal back-office services. American Express's offshore presence also gives it the ability to manage membership growth and still keep operating costs in check.

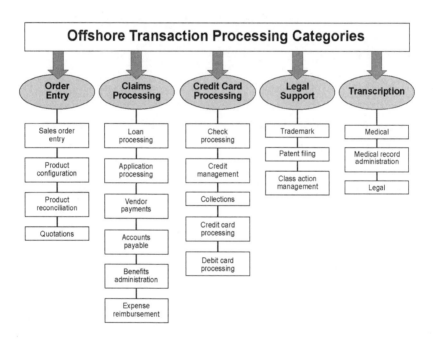

Figure 3.7: Offshore Transaction Processing Categories

Best-Practice Case Study: American Express

American Express (Amex) started offshore operations in the early 1990s and is regarded as a pioneer who helped to prove the viability of the global captive center business model. The company continues to build on its lead and expand its offshoring scope to support more transaction processing and customer support processes.

American Express is a mature organization that employs a hybrid of the onshore, offshore outsourcing, and insourcing delivery models. It has entered into several strategic relationships with BPO providers in Gurgaon, New Delhi, Mumbai, and Bangalore in India. In addition, it has set up a proprietary American Express Global Service Center in New Delhi to offer voice- and data-based customer services, fraud and risk modeling, and financial processing to customers worldwide.

Company Overview

Founded in 1850, Amex is engaged in the business of providing travel-related, financial advisory, and international banking services to customers throughout the world.

- Through Travel Related Services (TRS), Amex offers travel-related products and services including its flagship Gold, Platinum, Optima, and corporate charge cards; card member lending products; travelers checks; and corporate and consumer travel services.

- With the aid of its financial advisory services and products division, the company markets its real-estate brokerage, financial planning, and investment advisory services, as well as products such as insurance, annuities, investment certificates, and mutual funds.

- The American Express Bank concentrates on private financial institution and corporate banking, as well as personal financial services and global trading.

Amex's growth strategy has three major components: 1) expanding its international presence, 2) strengthening its charge card network, and 3) broadening its financial services offerings. Amex reported revenues and net income of $23.81 billion and $2.67 billion, respectively, in 2002. The company's long-term internal targets include 8% annual revenue growth, 12%–15% earnings growth, and an 18%–20% return on equity. To achieve these goals, a strategy to improve overall business performance was put in place.

Amex's Offshore Strategy

Amex incorporated its offshore strategy into its overall plan to improve business performance. Following 2001, one of the most difficult years in its recent history, Amex was even more determined to build a sustainable platform for long-term growth. The company is strengthening its business model and the underlying economics by improving its risk profile and investing in business-building activities.

All these activities are clustered around three corporate initiatives: Six Sigma quality, e-business, and global shared services. Let's look at each in more detail.

Amex has turned to Six Sigma to enhance quality and productivity in key business processes and to eliminate costly errors. Six Sigma is a performance improvement technique for fine-tuning products and processes that companies use to strive for a near-perfect goal of operating with only 3.4 defects per million activities or opportunities. Amex is also applying Six Sigma principles to product design and development in order to build in quality from the customer perspective.

Amex's e-business initiative centers on leveraging the Internet to lower costs. Amex has made a number of its services available to customers online. For example, according to Amex's 2002 annual report, within the United States, 80% of its card servicing transactions are now online. In fact, it conducts more online interactions with customers than it does by telephone or in person. The Internet also serves as an important product development and customer acquisition channel for both the card and financial services businesses. The company is also moving more internal processes, such as the procurement of goods and services, to its intranet.

Amex is transforming traditional processes with insourcing, outsourcing, and offshore captive shared services centers. Amex expanded its global servicing network (insourced) by leveraging educated workforces around the world, outsourced its data operations to IBM, and signed outsourcing agreements with providers such as Wipro Spectramind to deliver customer service from India and the Philippines. It also opened a captive customer service center in India to complement its existing network.

Of all the outsourcing strategies Amex has adopted, the shared services center approach focused on transaction processing captivates us the most. The history of shared services in Amex dates all the way back to 1993 when the company used a global shared services strategy to implement organizational and cultural change initiatives.

Operational Efficiency Through Offshore Captive Centers

In the early 1990s, Amex Travel Related Services (TRS) had more than 46 transaction processing sites, each employing 20 to 40 employees. These sites performed various tasks related to the processing of credit card records, account activity, or transactions. They sprawled across North America, Latin America, EMEA (Europe, Middle East, and Africa), and APA (Asia Pacific and Australia). They were internally focused, geographically fragmented, inflexible, and legacy bound. Duplications and inconsistencies made these sites inefficient and costly.

To cut costs, Amex devised a shared services strategy to consolidate, standardize, and re-engineer scattered support activities. The corporation consolidated the 46 sites into three financial resource centers (see table 3.2). These three shared services centers consolidate credit card authorization, accounts payable, general ledger, and other administrative services at one location serving a geographical area. They were designed to reduce costs, standardize business processes, leverage enabling technology, and produce economies of scale in transaction processing. They operate as cost centers with costs charged across the different business units. By treating it as a cost center rather than a profit center, there are significant tax advantages.

To distribute the workload, Amex selected Phoenix, Arizona, as the location to serve the Americas and Brighton, United Kingdom, as the location to serve Europe. After some review, Amex picked India as the location for the third center dedicated to handling Japan and APA (J/APA). This center, called the Financial Center East (FCE), was established in Gurgaon, India, in 1994.

Before Amex Implemented Shared Services Centers	After Amex Implemented Shared Services Centers
■ 46 transaction processing sites each employing 20-40 employees ■ Geographically fragmented ■ Process duplications and inconsistencies ■ Lack of customer focus ■ Operating on inflexible, legacy applications	■ Transaction processing in three sites (Phoenix, Brighton, and Gurgaon) ■ Consolidated operations ■ Standardized processes ■ Customer-focused ■ Leveraging technology and skills expertise

Table 3.2: American Express's Migration to Shared Services Centers

Why India? Amex had considerable operating experience in India before opening the shared services center. The seed for the decision to locate in India was planted in 1993 when Amex launched its Indian rupee–denominated card. The Indian operations began to resemble other units in terms of servicing, number, and complexity of transactions. However, its cost per transaction was lower by 40%–50%. In addition, the quality of the output — throughput, errors, and rework — was superior.

The FCE's labor pool is also high quality: It comprises a mix of MBAs, engineers, chartered accountants (certified public accountants), and other graduates. With more qualified and better-educated staff, the number of first-call resolutions of customer problems was higher, and issues were resolved more easily. The lower cost per transaction and superior quality caught the attention of management, which picked India as the location for the third shared services center.

In the early days, the FCE processed transactions that supported the Amex card business and serviced local geographies of J/APA. Since then, the FCE has grown by leaps and bounds to service all of Amex's businesses and become a global service provider. It has evolved to provide accounts payable, cash applications, general ledger, and forecasting services to divisions in Asia, Europe, North America, and Latin America. Today, 58% of the work completed at the FCE is for the J/APA operations, 20% for European operations, 24% for U.S. and Canadian operations, and 8% for Latin American operations.[9]

The evolution of the FCE's capabilities has been steady. In 1995, Amex sent the first process to the center. In 1997, it became a business unit servicing all geographies. In 1998, the FCE streamlined its processes through a major process improvement and re-engineering exercise. In 1999, it began performing high-end activities such as financial analysis and forecasting. By 2001, the FCE had turned into a global back-office processor with end-to-end capture-to-reporting capabilities and employed more than 3,000 employees working three shifts. Encouraged by its success with the FCE, Amex began a pilot in 2003 to look at the viability of servicing customers in the United Kingdom, Australia, and Canada by English-speaking telephone representatives based in India.[10]

Back-Office Transaction Processing BPO

To better understand how the FCE adds value, let's go behind the scenes of an Amex card purchase. Amex credit and charge cards allow card members to charge purchases of goods and services around the world and online at establishments that have agreed to accept them and to access cash through ATMs at more than 500,000 locations worldwide.

The FCE's Role in Processing Card Transactions

Approximately 35.4 million Americans carry an American Express card, and the total cards in circulation reached 57.3 million by year-end 2002. The company's charge volume reached $311 billion in 2002, with approximately 25% coming from card members outside the United States.

A significant amount of accounting reconciliation and processing has to happen daily to guarantee that the correct people are charged and the appropriate vendors are paid on time. Processing, checking, and posting the customer payments to their credit card balances also has to be carried out promptly. Behind the completion of all of these tasks is the FCE.

The FCE's Role in Dispute Resolution

Where did this charge on my credit card come from? Frequently customers dispute charges made to their cards. Processing these disputes requires human intervention, which means it is expensive and time-consuming. This is another scenario in which the FCE has a starring role and adds value with its low cost, high-quality staff.

Dispute resolution begins when customers call Amex customer service to assert that a merchant charged them for a purchase that they did not make. The customer service representative sets up a "dispute case" in the system that is routed to the FCE, which initiates a chargeback process to reverse the transaction presented by the merchant. The FCE withdraws the amount from the merchant account and temporarily deposits it back into the customer's account. An investigation is conducted.

If the merchant refutes the dispute, then the FCE works with the cardholder to provide documentation to support the chargeback claim. This must be done within a certain period or customer rights are lost. A "second" chargeback occurs. The merchant has a certain length of time to respond. At this point, the merchant can accept the second chargeback and reimburse the disputed amount or ask to arbitrate the case.

Clearly, there are many steps involved in the dispute process, which can take several months. But the FCE has reduced the turnaround time in the dispute resolution process.

The Return on Investment

As Amex moves into new markets, lower costs and better quality become enormous competitive advantages. Processing transactions out of India costs about a quarter of what it does in the United States mainly due to the differences in labor costs. Labor costs in India are very attractive for Amex. For instance, chartered accountants typically receive a salary of $7,000 per year, while CPAs in the United States require an annual salary of $40,000.[11] Beyond lower labor costs and higher quality, perhaps the most significant benefit the FCE offers Amex is the flexibility to delegate common tasks to the FCE.

Amex's ROI also came in unexpected ways, such as incremental discounts from vendors for prompt settlement. By reducing the turnaround time of invoice payment, the discounts were quite substantial. In an interview Raman Roy, CEO of Wipro Spectramind and considered by many to be the primary force behind Amex in India, said that the incremental discounts that Amex received were more than the salary bill in India.[12]

Summary

Offshore outsourcing has come a long way in a short time. Corporations largely understand traditional IT outsourcing and are beginning to get comfortable with more complex process outsourcing.

When we began looking at offshore outsourcing, we were surprised to find so many different players in the market, each with its own unique niche. We have attempted to simplify this complicated space by dividing the many processes into a number of broad process categories.

In general, firms are organizing their offshore activities around some or all of the following five core areas: Information technology, customer care, finance and accounting, human resources, and transaction processing.

Our objective in Chapters 4 through 8 is to conquer some of the complexity with more detail and precision.

Chapter Four

Information Technology Offshore Outsourcing

"If everyone is thinking alike, then somebody isn't thinking."

— General George Patton

Introduction

Senior managers have a few demands for their information technology (IT) organizations. Topping the list are reduced infrastructure complexity, a better return on investment (ROI) from their technology investments, more system integration and interoperability, faster time to delivery, more predictable availability and response time, and better security. Oh, and all at a lower cost.

Overworked IT organizations have to drive operational efficiencies while simultaneously supporting customer relationship strategies. Shrinking IT budgets without a corresponding decline in IT needs also help to explain why offshore outsourcing is quickly becoming mainstream.

The range of IT offshore contracts spans the technology-related spectrum, going well beyond software maintenance to include state-of-the-art product development, packaged application customization, deployment and maintenance, database administration, help desk support, data center management, and data analysis.

In this chapter, we explore IT offshore outsourcing in detail. We begin by looking at why companies are offshoring IT. Then, to provide a better context, we look at the evolution of IT offshoring — past, present, and future. We discuss the different types of IT offshoring and illustrate through case studies — BellSouth and Guardian Life Insurance — how some market leaders are approaching it. At the end of the chapter, you will be able to apply this understanding to your organization and to explore systematically the steps in offshoring an IT project.

Why Are Companies Offshoring IT?

With the promise of better quality, cheaper resources, and faster development, more and more IT organizations are going offshore. Among the Fortune 500 companies, more than 200 currently send some of their IT work offshore to India. IBM expanded its offices in Bangalore, India, to handle engineering work. Oracle has more than 3,000 employees in India doing research, developing software, and staffing help desk centers. AT&T Wireless hired Tata Consultancy Services (TCS) to set up a global development center in India to supplement its customer support.

Of all the industries, the information-intensive financial services industry leads the business world in IT offshoring. A case in point is the global investment bank Lehman Brothers. In 2001, Lehman saw that its revenues were diminishing and its IT costs were ballooning, so it initiated an offshore strategy to reduce its IT costs by 2003. A sizable part of the $700 million in IT costs was tied up in salaries for Lehman's total IT staff of 2,000.[1]

After a detailed analysis that included attending conferences, analyzing public documents, interviewing competitors, and talking with several outsourcing vendors, Lehman determined that it could optimize IT expenses. To gain experience and executive buy-in to the offshore model, the investment bank kick-started the process by initiating 80 pilot projects in the application development and maintenance area.

Lehman reviewed as many as 15 vendors and picked three — Wipro Technologies, TCS, and Infosys. The investment bank conducted fixed duration, limited scope projects with these vendors. One of the goals of the pilots was to let project managers become familiar with managing offshore vendors and fixed-price contracts, as well as providing vendors with business requirements. Lehman is estimated to have spent $8 million on 80 pilot projects over a six-month period.[2]

Based on its experience and ROI data from the pilots, Lehman set up two dedicated offshore development centers (ODCs) with Wipro and TCS. It expects to obtain a 40% costs savings on development and cut costs by $50–$70 million in a three-year period.[3] The company is considering expanding the scope of its IT offshoring by creating its own captive center staffed by Lehman employees to do mission-critical software development, infrastructure maintenance, and research analysis.

Lehman is not alone in shifting work to lower-cost software development locations. Its competitors — Goldman Sachs, Merrill Lynch, Bank of America, Deutsche Bank, and others — have also adopted offshore strategies in an attempt to gain a cost advantage.

The financial services industry is an early adopter of the IT offshore model. Currently, about 20%–25% of U.S. companies outsource IT. We expect the offshore component to increase considerably from current levels over the next three years. The reason for the growth: Cost savings from offshore outsourcing are too compelling to ignore.

Let's look at the evolution of IT outsourcing and offshoring to understand the current state better.

Evolution of IT Outsourcing and Offshoring

IT outsourcing (ITO) has evolved considerably in the last decade. It has cycled through different business models: IT contractors or staff augmentation, legacy software project outsourcing, packaged software outsourcing, offshore development centers, and captive development centers (see figure 4.1).

Contractors and Staff Augmentation

ITO had its origins in the hiring of contractors to fill short-term capacity voids or one-time project ramp-ups. Not surprisingly, IT service firms broadened their scope to accommodate projects that required more than staff augmentation. Over time, some IT service firms began to recognize the importance of wrapping processes, methodologies, and project management disciplines around the technical skill sets of their employees.

In the early days of ITO, overseas development and contracting services were primarily used by multinational independent software vendors

(ISVs) like Microsoft, enterprise software companies like SAP, and global IT consulting firms like Cap Gemini. These firms had the resources and business experience to manage offshore projects. During this period, a number of offshore service suppliers such as Wipro and Infosys steadily gained the experience and knowledge of how to successfully implement large-scale projects by working side by side with various companies.

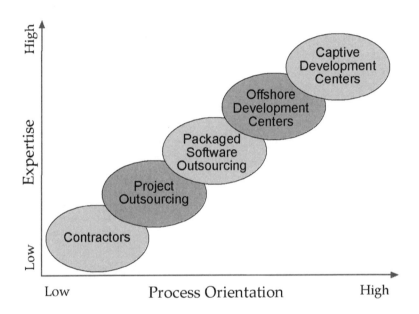

Figure 4.1: The Evolution of IT Outsourcing and Offshoring

During the fast-growth 1990s, there was an enormous gap between the amount of work to be done and the people available to do it. This resulted in a boom in staff augmentation, or body shop, services. Many service providers simply acted as a staffing agency. In some cases, they sent people with temporary visas to work under contract for clients. The type of tasks performed in these settings tended to consist of application maintenance, application development, and mainframe-to-client/server migration projects.

Legacy Software Project Outsourcing

The second wave was legacy IT outsourcing, which entailed an outsourcer handling old company information systems. The year 2000 and euro conversion projects allowed many offshore firms to gain a foothold in the U.S. and European market places. In those two particular cases, the sheer volume and time pressure involved in performing date remediation forced large companies to consider offshore alternatives.

Having proven themselves capable of finding and correcting Y2K problems, the offshore firms began seeking business opportunities in areas such as system design, application development, and maintenance. Companies began wondering: if vendors could complete the Y2K conversion, why can't they also maintain and enhance legacy applications? Offshore vendors were happy to meet this customer request.

Due to the market demand, offshore firms began to establish a local presence to provide customer interaction–intensive IT services such as business process consulting, functional requirements definition, requirements specification, and high-level design. Once ambiguity about how a system or business process should work was resolved, the software development project could be sent overseas for actual programming and testing. At the same time, with the bulk of development and related activities occurring offshore, there was an increased need for project coordination between client sites and offshore facilities.

As suppliers became more involved in complex projects and business-critical client initiatives, there was an increase in onsite activity as supplier project managers, analysts, and architects became involved in requirements gathering and analysis, strategy planning, solutions architecture, prototyping, and design work.

Packaged Software Outsourcing

The third wave of ITO was emerging technology outsourcing, which involved bringing in an external vendor to help implement new technology. In the late 1990s, offshore vendors began to expand their service offerings, moving from subcontract coding and body shop work to custom software development, application maintenance, quality testing, systems integration, legacy system migration, and technical training. The next phase of this evolution was providing support for enterprise application projects.

This model gained traction with the increased adoption of packaged applications from vendors such as SAP, Oracle, and PeopleSoft. In the late 1990s, the explosive growth of enterprise applications resulted in a worldwide demand for skilled IT workers, while the combination of low wages and large populations of technology workers created new opportunities for offshore suppliers.

Enterprise e-business initiatives, coupled with an explosion in the global demand for IT skills, also opened up opportunities for offshore contractors in Web applications and emerging technologies such as enterprise application integration (EAI) and mobile computing.

Offshore Development Centers

ITO's fourth wave was partial or complete offshoring. For large companies it makes sense to have a dedicated offshore development center (ODC). This is equivalent to having a remote software team that is providing development or maintenance support. This team complements but does not replace the company's internal staff. ODCs are established only after the software vendor and the IT organization have already worked together on offshore projects and both sides are confident that the relationship will work. In every ODC relationship, mutual trust and professional project management are critical.

Consider the case of Target Corporation, a $26 billion retailer. To reduce costs, Target set up a dedicated ODC in Chennai, India, with Tata Consultancy Services (TCS). Using the hybrid onsite-offshore model of delivery, TCS provides application development, maintenance, and production support to all of Target's divisions in e-commerce, customer management, stock control, warehouse, supply chain, credit, and corporate services.

Another company that set up an ODC was MasterCard International, one of the most recognized brands in the world for global payments. MasterCard recognized that offshore outsourcing could not only save money but also generate it. In June 2001, MasterCard launched an ODC with Mascon Global. Mascon-MasterCard Global Technology Services develops and maintains software for MasterCard's core processing functions — authorization, clearing, and settlement. The business model behind this is a joint venture with Mascon owning 51%.[4]

Although the offshore development model has been largely associated with multinational enterprises, a growing number of midtier firms and

IT service suppliers have also become involved in or are exploring development projects either directly or with offshore partners.

Captive IT Development Centers

Next in the evolution of ITO are captive IT development centers, which are basically efforts by large companies to maximize the value of offshore outsourcing. As companies gain experience with offshoring, some are looking to set up their own captive centers to increase efficiency and innovation. Software companies such as Microsoft, SAP, IBM, Oracle, and Intel have chosen the captive development center route.

Consider the case of Oracle. In a bid to retain a cost advantage over its competitors, Oracle is developing its own captive centers in India. At the end of August 2003, Oracle India employed 3,200 people in its three units: India Development Center, India Support Center, and Oracle Solution Services India. Oracle is shifting a large portion of its developmental work from its three other centers — California, Sydney, and Dublin — to India.

Oracle's competitor SAP AG has adopted a similar strategy. In 1998, SAP created a strategic development center called SAP Labs India. Since then, it has become one of the fastest-growing SAP subsidiaries, employing approximately 1,000 people. It is an integral part of SAP's global development network and is engaged in collaborative software engineering that facilitates the delivery and maintenance of solutions.

Captive IT development centers, however, are not for every company. Some firms that have started on this path have sold their Indian operations to vendors. For instance, Wipro bought Ericsson's research and development units in India, and HCL Technologies, one of India's largest IT services firms, bought a 51% stake in the holding company of Deutsche Software (Deutsche Bank's IT services subsidiary).

Offshoring IT Processes

IT offshoring allows companies to operate their core businesses while utilizing offshore vendors or resources to manage their technology needs. Interestingly, most of the work going offshore used to be done in-house and is estimated to be a $600 billion market.[5]

Which in-house IT solutions are candidates for offshore outsourcing? It depends, given that IT covers a wide range of services — traditional legacy application management, packaged application development, desktop support, data centers, network management, infrastructure management, and application testing. Let's look at each in more detail.

Application Development and Maintenance

Application development and maintenance (ADM) organizations are struggling to meet the new and more complex demands of businesses. Continuing shifts in underlying application infrastructure and a lack of skills necessary for developing and deploying more modern applications remain serious stumbling blocks for many companies.

Offshore resources help alleviate some of these issues by leveraging expertise and low-cost alternatives for needs such as new feature development, driver development, new application development, packaged application customization, and old release maintenance.

To understand how this works, consider the case of Toshiba, one of the largest suppliers of semiconductors, electronic components, and storage devices. Toshiba wanted to revamp its business processes to reduce order-to-delivery lead time, minimize inventory, increase customer service levels, and enhance supply chain visibility. Toshiba recruited Infosys, based in Bangalore, India, to help with business process definition, project management, package evaluation, implementation, user training, and post-production support.

Infosys developed for Toshiba a stock allocation system; a distribution system for managing the sales channel through distributors; a sales commission system; and an early shipping advance (ESA) system to increase inbound supply chain visibility.

Alternatively, companies that are uncomfortable with the distance and potential political uncertainties of Asian countries are looking nearshore for application development as a risk mitigation strategy. Tufts Health Plan, a health maintenance organization (HMO), outsourced development of administrative applications for its managed-care business to Keane Inc., a U.S. outsourcing firm that operates a service center in Halifax, Nova Scotia, Canada. Keane offers a global delivery model of onsite, offsite, nearshore, and offshore.

To address the needs of wary customers looking for a lower risk profile, many Indian and Russian firms are opening ADM centers in Canada. For instance, Wipro Technologies opened an ADM center in Windsor, Ontario. These firms are creating a broader range of geographic options for their customers.

Quality Assurance

In the current competitive technology era, the increased complexity of software applications magnifies the risk of failure. Application developers need to cope with such issues as compressed "go live" dates, frequent application changes, a lack of well-defined requirements, increased security concerns, and unpredictable user loads. Consequently, testing assumes a critical role in application development and maintenance.

Application testing is usually subsumed under the quality assurance (QA) function. QA is the pattern of all actions necessary to provide confidence that the application fulfills customer expectations (that it is problem-free and able to perform the task for which it was designed). The QA of a commercial product usually involves alpha testing, in which an early version of the product is tested at the developer's site, and is then improved accordingly. A complete version of the product is then made available for beta testing by a larger set of users. Faults identified during beta testing are fixed before the product is released.

Testing focuses on critical aspects such as building automated test suites, performance metrics, capacity planning for peak business demands, validation testing, test automation, execution, defect tracking, and reporting. Consider the case of World Book Online (WBOL), the Web site division of the encyclopedia and publishing company. It is a subscription-based service for schools and libraries in the United States, Ireland, the United Kingdom, and Australia with more than 2 million hits per day.[6] In 2001, WBOL offshored enhancement and maintenance of its Web site to Tata Infotech in India.

Tata Infotech conducted functional testing of WBOL's application in nine different operating systems and 15 different browsers. The project covered three types of application testing:

- Functional testing, which captures, verifies, and replays user interactions automatically, so software developers and QA engineers can identify defects and ensure the user experience is smooth.

- Scalability and availability testing, which involves increasing the load at the same time as augmenting the infrastructure and verifying that the system response is kept within the set targets.

- Security testing, which ensures that the application is not vulnerable to buffer overflows, replay attacks, session hijacking, and denial of service attacks.

Tata Infotech supported WBOL from its software development center in Bangalore, India, and executed this project by connecting to the WBOL server via the Internet.[7] With Web applications serving millions of users, application testing takes on greater importance.

Infrastructure and Support Services

Managing technology and applications can be challenging. It's not surprising that CIOs are focused on reducing the hidden costs of applications such as testing, integration, and ongoing network support. Companies can incur costs in the following ways:

- Scheduled maintenance, which includes routine maintenance tasks or preventive maintenance tasks resulting from break-fix problems.

- IT operational issues such as 24x7 monitoring of application performance, both inside and outside the firewall, immediately alerting IT personnel to problems before they can affect the customer.

- Help desk end-user support and new service provisioning requests, as well as remote diagnostics (password reset and desktop control).

- System problem resolutions related to desktop, notebooks, operating systems, shrink-wrapped products, office productivity applications, and network connectivity.

- Documentation development, which details all of the application requirements, code, and support procedures.

Many companies that want to focus on their core competencies decide to outsource IT support. Coors Brewing Company, the third-largest brewer in the United States, is one example. Over the course of ten years, the brewer has doubled in size. For the company's business units, such as the internal IT department, managing that growth became problematic. Coors wanted to retain the technologies related to producing and selling beer but was open to outsourcing other IT work.

In 1991, Coors decided to outsource strategic infrastructure, desktop support, application development, SAP application support, and network management services to Electronic Data Systems (EDS) in a five-year agreement. By utilizing EDS's Best Shore services methodology, Coors was able to reduce the cost of application management by as much as 40%.[8] EDS's Best Shore methodology and others like it determine the optimal mix of sourcing options for the customer — onshore, nearshore, and offshore — based on risk tolerance, degree of cost savings desired, language requirements, and other factors. For EDS, the Best Shore service creates shared economies of scale. For instance, EDS New Zealand is undertaking applications work for Coors Breweries and the Royal Bank of Scotland Group, as well as contact center work for U.S.-based ChevronTexaco.

Implementation Services

Some offshore vendors offer a complete, managed hosting solution that takes the responsibility of their customer's servers in its facility, customizes the infrastructure, and manages the servers. Vendors also provide end-to-end, managed application hosting service solutions that allow companies to transfer the responsibility of maintaining, enhancing, and managing custom and packaged software applications like SAP or Oracle.

Typical implementation services include: product lifecycle management, business consulting, requirements gathering and analysis, prototype development, professional services augmentation, technology evaluation, proof of concept, application hosting, and training.

Consider the example of First Data Corporation (FDC), which processes financial transactions and fund transfers for many financial institutions, as well as 2 million merchants. The company estimates that it processes more than 5 billion payment transactions yearly worth $250 billion. As a large company with two separate IBM mainframes to support, FDC decided to spend its energies elsewhere and outsource some of the support, maintenance, and enhancement of its mainframes to Cognizant.

Each time FDC launches a new service, the two mainframes have to be updated accordingly. The timing of mainframe updates is critical. FDC wanted as little disruption to its business operations as possible. Cognizant assists FDC with this task working remotely from India, as well as from the onshore FDC site. Thanks to the Internet, Cognizant can access FDC's application code and test production data seamlessly from offshore. The two companies use e-mail to communicate major implementation changes to application software or critical event dates.

The difference in time zones (FDC is headquartered in Denver while Cognizant's three development centers are based in India) allows FDC to have a quicker turnaround on fixes, a faster time to market, and extended working hours. The labor cost savings, a major driver of most offshoring initiatives, are significant as well.[9]

New Product Engineering and Enterprise Software

New versions, new features, and new products are the lifeblood of the enterprise software industry. To survive, start-up and established companies have to bring products to market faster and faster. Doing everything in-house is no longer an option. As a result, more product companies are outsourcing to specialists skilled in enterprise software product engineering.

Consider the case of San Francisco–based Embarcadero Technologies, a leading provider of database and application lifecycle management solutions. Embarcadero relied on an Aztec Software team to help it take a new integration product, Embarcadero DT/Studio, through the entire product lifecycle — from development to maintenance. Aztec's contribution to the DT/Studio tool helped Embarcadero more quickly establish a competitive market position for the product.

Even Google, the innovative search technology company that connects millions of people around the world with information every day, is heading offshore. Google, based in California, announced plans to open its first offshore engineering R&D center in Bangalore, India. Google wants to expand the resource pool of computer science and engineering candidates from which it hires. According to Wayne Rosing, Google's vice president of engineering, "We just want more really great engineers. It's clear there are a significant number of really talented computer scientists in India."[10]

Product engineering involves performing the tasks to build and maintain enterprise software using appropriate methods and tools. The purpose of product engineering is to perform a well-defined process that integrates all the activities to produce correct and consistent products.

Product engineering tasks include analyzing system requirements, developing requirements, creating the architecture, designing the software, implementing the code, integrating the components, and testing the software to verify that it satisfies the specified requirements. When changes are required, affected work products, plans, commitments, processes, and activities are revised to reflect the approved changes.

Now that you have seen the different types of IT processes capable of being offshored, let's look at two case studies — BellSouth Corporation and Guardian Life Insurance — to understand the decisions management is tasked with making.

Offshore IT Case Study: BellSouth Corporation

BellSouth is a Fortune 100 telecom company headquartered in Atlanta, Georgia, that serves more than 46 million customers in the United States and 15 other countries. Incorporated in 1983, the company provides an array of local and long-distance voice, broadband data, and e-commerce solutions to customers.

The Business Need: Rapid Operating Cost Reduction

BellSouth, like others in the telecom services industry, is riding the roller coaster of a boom-bust economic cycle. The boom period arrived with the passage of the U.S. Telecommunications Act of 1996. Market leaders such as AT&T, WorldCom, BellSouth, Verizon, and Qwest spent vast sums of money to keep up with advances in broadband data delivery, wireless, and fiber optics in order to protect their lead against competitors, such as WilTel, XO, and McLeodUSA. During the boom period the telecom industry received over $1.3 trillion from the equity markets, according to *Forbes* magazine.

In 2000, the tides turned on the telecom players. The number and variety of threats facing them exploded. A slowdown in economic growth and a meltdown in Internet stocks created a profound change in market psychology. The public markets slammed the capital windows shut, and cash-strapped carriers found it difficult to raise money. The glut in network capacity exacerbated the situation. As a result, the telecom industry fell into a downward spiral, with the industry losing more than $1 trillion in market value.

The telecom industry was (and continues to be) under severe pressure to reduce capital and operating costs. Carriers began to cut back on capital spending. They also began to look at ways to decrease operating expenses. IT spending was one area that caught their eye. It is estimated that IT spending is about 20% or more of the total budget of a telecom company. Offshore outsourcing of costly IT and back-office services is particularly appealing, especially in an environment where companies are fixated on controlling operating costs.

A Brief History of IT Outsourcing at BellSouth

Outsourcing is not a new phenomenon at BellSouth. It was in the 1990s that business leaders first began asking, "Is IT application development and maintenance something we're good at and something we should be doing, or should we outsource this?" At BellSouth, senior management was asking that same question and came up with an answer.

In 1998, BellSouth selected Accenture as its IT outsourcing strategic partner to help it achieve improved service levels, on-budget performance, and on-time delivery. As part of that agreement, Accenture supports the entire solutions stack, including customer care, network, billing, marketing, finance, Web Services, human resources, and payroll, across all of BellSouth's U.S. operations.

The company also partnered with EDS in 1997 for operational support, signing a $3 billion, ten-year outsourcing contract. This contract covered BellSouth's mainframe computer operations, midrange operations, help desk, and desktop support for more than 50,000 computers. EDS operates data centers for BellSouth in Atlanta, Georgia; Charlotte, North Carolina; and Mobile, Alabama. EDS dedicates more than 1,800 employees to the BellSouth account.

In 2001, BellSouth faced a problem typical of many companies after the Internet bubble popped: a shrinking IT budget without a corresponding decline in IT needs. To combat the rising cost of ongoing maintenance and enhancement of IT applications, BellSouth began strategically evaluating its offshoring capabilities to further reduce IT expenses, and Project Horizon was born.

Project Horizon: Offshoring IT

Project Horizon's business objective is to use offshore resources to further reduce maintenance and development costs of IT applications, while maintaining the same workload and service levels and taking advantage of the differential cost savings that offshoring can provide.

The first step of Project Horizon was to review the options for reducing IT costs. One of the options was to move some of its development and support work to a non-U.S. Accenture delivery center.

The Project Horizon team looked at several locations: India, Spain, Canada, the Philippines, Brazil, and Australia. In order to mitigate risks associated with moving work offshore, the team reviewed the security, safety, government stability, disaster recovery capabilities, and infrastructure of these countries.

After a long evaluation, BellSouth chose India as the pilot site. The reasons were: more than 60% of vendors with best-in-class process maturity (CMM Level 5) are located in India; more than 40% of Fortune 500 companies utilize India for their application support; and BellSouth will have access to highly skilled, low-cost resources.

Project Horizon Pilot Offshoring Site: India

Project Horizon was the product of BellSouth and Accenture's joint planning. BellSouth is using Accenture's global delivery capability to execute Project Horizon in phases. The initial phase was a four-and-a-half-month pilot (April 2003 through September 2003). The scope of the pilot included transitioning 17 development and support roles that

Accenture provides for three BellSouth applications to the Bangalore, India, delivery center.

The applications selected reflect a variety of business units and technologies. The Project Horizon team chose the pilot applications using a formal process that ranked applications based on 11 categories (including head count, complexity, stability, and impact on the business customer). After the team evaluated the results, it was able to choose three applications suitable for the pilot: network (applications and infrastructure), BellSouth Works (customer markets), and management accounting (shared services).

The pilot aimed to: 1) prove that development and support in a non-U.S. location would be transparent to the business units, 2) measure the resources required for smoothly transitioning the work to India, and 3) gauge the potential savings in store for BellSouth. BellSouth plans to transition 634 full-time employees offshore over a five-year period.

Managing Offshore Risk

Some of the important issues that BellSouth's IT management considered during the pilot planning phase included:

- Security of BellSouth information in a non-U.S. location. BellSouth conducted a site visit to India to make sure that the Bangalore delivery center's physical security met its requirements. BellSouth also requires regular employee background checks.

- Control of confidential customer data. All BellSouth data stays in the United States. A "no download" data policy is enforced via security components built into the infrastructure.

- Disaster recovery plan for work sent to India. The Bangalore delivery center has a full disaster recovery plan. The plan was structured to comply with BellSouth's security policies and standards.

Risk management is a big deal when evaluating offshore opportunities. Although offshoring services may yield companies substantial cost savings, it benefits them to do their homework before rushing offshore to India, the Philippines, or elsewhere. The risk of not conducting the necessary due diligence is too great.

Expected ROI and Results

The current business case suggests moving one-third to one-half of BellSouth's IT application work offshore, which equates to 600–900 positions over the next four years. This cost savings initiative will enable BellSouth to reduce IT expenses and save 45%–70% in outsourcing costs, which translates into an estimated savings of $275 million over five years (2003–2007).

If the project proves successful and results in a $275 million windfall for BellSouth, the company could have a lower cost structure than its troubled telecom counterparts. The BellSouth case study illustrates how the constant need to reduce total IT operating costs and pass gains along to customers in terms of lower prices is rippling through the whole economy, affecting not only how business is done but also where it is done.

Offshore IT Case Study: Guardian Life Insurance

IT offshore outsourcing has become an integral part of some insurers' operations. The insurers moving offshore include Aetna, MetLife, Prudential (United Kingdom), Swiss Re, and Royal & SunAlliance. In order to understand what is prompting insurers to move offshore, let's look at Guardian Life Insurance Company of America.

Guardian is one of the biggest players in the U.S. mutual life insurance industry. It offers 3 million people life and disability insurance, as well as retirement and investment products such as mutual funds and annuities. The company also provides employee benefit packages, which include life insurance, health insurance, and pension plans, to 5 million participants.

Eager to reduce costs, bring new products to market faster, and redistribute resources, Guardian was one of the first among its insurance industry peers to adopt outsourcing, both onshore and offshore. Like many companies new to outsourcing, Guardian proceeded cautiously and began outsourcing functions that did not affect customers but did touch employees. They included travel services, event planning, and management of 401(k) plans. Future targets include claims, billing, accounts payable and receivable, payroll, and cash management.[11]

Moving Towards Offshoring

Guardian took its time and did its due diligence. The insurer first began offshoring with a pilot in March 2001. It earmarked several small development projects for participation in the pilot. After the company began seeing positive results and had become more comfortable with the idea, its IT offshoring initiative grew to include all types of development for all of the company's divisions.

Guardian followed up its initial foray into offshoring by announcing two contracts to send IT work to India in September 2002 and March 2003 with Covansys and Patni Computer Systems, respectively. It later decided to add a third Indian vendor, NIIT Technologies, to its offshoring mix.

Guardian signed up Covansys, a global provider of technology and consulting services based in Michigan, with three development centers in India and three in the United States. Covansys was given the multimillion-dollar task of supporting and developing Guardian's group insurance applications along with other select technology and business projects, such as client data, claims reporting, and proposal processing systems. Covansys's primary objective was to integrate and enhance Guardian's legacy systems.

The two companies agreed to an 80-20 model in which 80% of the work is completed offshore at Covansys's Indian development centers and 20% is conducted on location with Guardian. This model generally yields companies the most savings while allowing them to maintain input into and control over the offshoring relationship.

When exploring what model to use in an offshoring project, Venu G. Vaishya, vice president for application maintenance and development and offshore solutions for Covansys Corporation, explains that the company will consider several factors including how complex and stable the application is, how many systems the application in question has to interface with, or if it's a vendor-supplied package. Answers to these types of questions drive what model is adopted. Vaishya says, "There are cases when we start the engagement with a 60-40 model and, over a period of one to two years, graduate it to an 80-20 model."[12]

The next IT vendor that Guardian picked was Patni Computer Systems based in Mumbai, India. With a contract worth $35 million over seven years, Patni agreed to help Guardian launch new life and annuity products, perform gap analysis, and implement IT systems that aid Guardian in adopting to the changing insurance industry. The goal is for the two companies to hit a 20% onsite/80% offshore model. Currently, Patni completes 70% of the work from its development centers in India.

The last IT services provider to be awarded a contract by Guardian was NIIT Technologies, also for application maintenance and development. NIIT's multiple locations were particularly attractive to Guardian especially with the long-running tensions between India and Pakistan. Using different geographic locations for offshoring is a common approach to mitigate company risk.

Expected ROI and Results

All of Guardian's application development and maintenance projects are characterized by a mix of onshore and offshore consultants and internal employees. Guardian also makes it a point to remain actively involved in its overseas IT projects, thereby avoiding a recurring coordination problem in IT offshoring.

As Venu Vaishya of Covansys Corporation sees it, the only thing limiting the IT offshore outsourcing model is the customer's willingness and ability to participate in managing the project. "It has to be a collaborative effort. The customer has to be engaged on all levels."[13]

Guardian took pains to make sure it fully participated in its offshoring projects. It set up a formal development process, created company-wide technology standards, and implemented project management software through its project management office. This last initiative, the project management office, helps the company to supervise every step of an outsourced IT project. The office also handles the monthly meetings aimed at reviewing specific metrics — customer satisfaction, offshore leverage, productivity, knowledge retention, and quality metrics — as well as any issues that develop. Guardian also instituted a policy of housing all source code and data in-house and encrypting all data that moves from offshore to onshore.

If these ventures into offshoring prove beneficial, and so far they have — the company has already recouped its initial investment costs in the

three IT offshoring projects and saved an additional $12.5 million —
Guardian will likely continue on its offshoring path, with a project in
dental claims entry soon to follow.[14]

How to Create a Business Case for Offshoring IT

Is IT offshoring right for you? Can you reach a consensus as to which
processes are core and which are noncore? With which offshore vendor
should you partner? Whatever you decide, you must take a structured
approach, beginning with articulating your strategy and developing a
robust business case.

Before IT offshoring can become part of your overall business strategy,
you will have to go through the following six steps:

1. Evaluate whether an offshore IT strategy is suitable for your
   organization,

2. Identify core and noncore IT processes,

3. Justify your decision to offshore IT by estimating the potential ROI,

4. Design an offshore engagement model,

5. Select vendor(s) and negotiate the contract(s), and

6. Develop an implementation plan.

We tackle the first three steps below and devote the third section of this
book to describing the last three steps in detail.

Strategic Vision: Why Are You Considering Offshoring IT?

What strategic scenario is your company facing? Are cost pressures,
increased competition, and a challenging revenue growth environment
leading you to re-evaluate your cost structure in an effort to enhance
performance? If so, then your organization is probably devoting attention
and resources to internal core competencies and considering outsourcing
noncore competencies.

The first task of IT offshoring is understanding the expectations and
assumptions behind the decision to outsource. At this point, you don't
have to identify which applications are targets or make a detailed business

case. The goal is simply to reach a consensus among stakeholders on whether or not to offshore IT and why it may be appropriate or necessary for your organization.

If stakeholders are not in favor of offshoring IT, then the project moves no further. If, however, they are in favor, then the outcome of this first step is a succinct statement of your company's offshore business objectives and of the priorities and measurable goals of the IT operation. A strong statement helps stakeholders identify the areas of benefit that are most important to achieving the organization's primary business objectives. You might want to specify targets, such as reducing application development costs by 20% by 2005.

According to Dennis Callahan, CIO for Guardian Life, "It's very important that people driving the outsourcing create a comfort level with their senior management, staff and business areas dependent upon it. Companies can't just go off in a vacuum and successfully outsource."[15]

Choosing to offshore IT is a serious decision that can be complicated by various internal political battles; therefore, it is vital that a stakeholder consensus is reached before moving ahead with IT offshoring and that all key stakeholders agree with the statement of business objectives and measurable goals.

Scope: Core versus Noncore IT Processes and Applications

The next step is figuring out the scope of the project. Which areas of your business could be offshored to the benefit of your company? What are you not doing well? In other words, which IT processes should you retain and which processes should you send offshore?

Figure 4.2 illustrates the pyramid of IT processes. The processes (or commodity services) at the bottom of the pyramid that tend to be low in strategic value are good candidates for offshoring. They include software development, application testing, legacy application maintenance, help desk support, application customization, and remote diagnostics. Certain areas like project office or IT strategy tend to be too strategic to be offshored or even outsourced.

The types of IT projects being offshored is changing. Innovation is beginning to overtake application maintenance in the category of projects that are going offshore. According to Shirish Netke, vice president of marketing at Aztec Software, "The number one priority in companies right now is repurposing their existing assets. CIOs are not willing to spend any more money than necessary on packaged application software like CRM or ERP. They are looking at investing in services-oriented architecture composed of elements like enterprise portals, integration engineering, and network identity management. These projects are increasingly being executed with a hybrid onshore-offshore business model."[16]

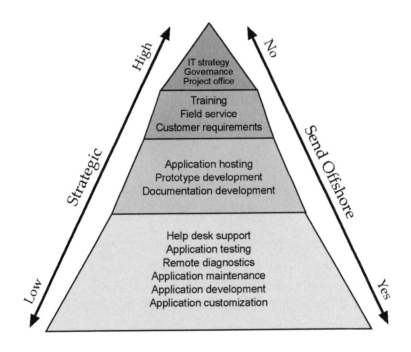

Figure 4.2: Core versus Noncore IT Processes

The scope of your project should be based on the degree of risk your company is willing to shoulder in order to achieve its desired balance of cost and quality. To assess the risk and difficulty of IT offshoring, many companies start with one pilot project with an offshore company and then steadily expand the relationship based on positive results.

A good example of a gradual scope escalation model is Best Buy, a $15-billion specialty retailer headquartered in Minnesota. Best Buy's offshore experience began in November 1999 when it outsourced some application system management to Tata Consultancy Services (TCS), based in India. Since 1999, the relationship has grown, with TCS providing Best Buy services in the areas of application development, maintenance, performance engineering, process definition, and deployment.

After you determine what the broad scope of your offshore project is, the next step is to examine the chosen applications in some detail. The typical method of assessing IT applications is to develop a template that allows you to capture consistent information for each application. The template should cover the following:

- Which business areas and processes does the application support?

- Which technology platform does it run on?

- Which development languages and tools does the application rely on?

- How does it integrate with other applications?

- What are the required resources such as support, enhancement, and development workload (historic, current, and planned)?

- What service levels — target and actual — does it currently achieve?

- What are the real costs associated with each application — metrics such as salaries, contractor rates, and office space costs?

Populate the template for each application under consideration for offshoring. Much of this information may be readily available, or it may be necessary to conduct a series of interviews with key staff. It is important to talk to those employees who have experience with the day-to-day management of the applications to ensure that your information is accurate and up-to-date.

After collecting the application-specific information, your next step is to map the resources to the applications portfolio. You should wind up with a multidimensional map of the applications, processes, resources, costs, and workload.

Developing the Financial Justification

After a core versus noncore capability and application assessment, the next step is to develop a business case that quantifies the financial side of the offshore equation. This includes return on investment (ROI) estimations by collecting detailed data: What are the specific benefits of offshore outsourcing? What are the costs of offshore outsourcing? What are the associated risks? Let's look at them in detail.

Tangible Benefits of Offshore IT

In offshore outsourcing, the most common expectation companies have is a clear tangible benefit of labor cost savings and faster time to market. In a recent survey of several senior and corporate IT managers, 44% ranked reducing and controlling costs as their number-one reason for outsourcing to non-U.S. locations.[17]

Low-Cost Labor Arbitrage. Before your company can realize labor cost savings from offshoring IT, you have to know what your current IT labor costs are. You should determine what your labor costs are by analyzing a solid baseline of current spending including employees and contractors.

Faster Time to Market. With offshore outsourcing, companies can utilize a "follow the sun" development model. They can turn the time differences between onshore and offshore locations into an advantage by building projects in a 24-hour development cycle. While offshore resources concentrate on development, in-house teams can "test the build" the next morning and create new information and documentation to be sent to the offshore team later that day.

Bob Evans, CEO of Symphony Services Corporation, a company that specializes in outsourced offshore software development solutions for commercial software companies, said, "A simple example is company A releases its new generation twice a year, and company B releases three times a year. In the course of two years, company A makes four releases and company B makes six releases, and is, in effect, one year ahead of company A."[18]

Should you tap a larger pool of trained and available IT skills at very low wages through offshore outsourcing? Can you leverage offshoring to provide a faster solution to meet business needs? If you answered yes, then you are ready to move ahead. Best-practice firms are finding that offshoring reduces IT labor costs by about 40%, a compelling number in any economic environment.

Intangible Benefits of Offshore IT

Your business case for offshoring IT will be stronger if you substantiate your numbers with nonfinancial benefits. These so-called soft benefits are difficult to translate into dollars, yet they must be closely evaluated, as they will contribute to a potentially larger ROI.

Less Recruiting, More Refocusing. By outsourcing projects to offshore development teams for design and development, companies can concentrate on other areas of business, rather than spending hours recruiting local professionals for noncore activities. Companies gain access to best-of-breed talent without the huge recruiting investments associated with them.

Business Flexibility and Agility. With offshore outsourcing, companies can increase IT staffing flexibility and gain access to an expanding base of world-class IT skills. Thus, companies can quickly respond to business opportunities with flexible capacity resource deployment. Using offshore development programmers and technical professionals for short- and long-term projects is a cost-effective necessity as technology rapidly changes and expertise becomes harder to find or more expensive.

Quality and User Satisfaction. Many offshore IT vendors, such as Patni, have ISO 9001 certification and institutionalized Six Sigma processes. Many have been successfully assessed at the highest level, Level 5, of the SEI-CMM — the Capability Maturity Model of the Software Engineering Institute. The vendor quality focus translates into minimized error rates and tangible time and cost savings. Third-party quality certifications are rapidly becoming a must-have.

Costs of Offshore IT

In addition to considering the benefits of offshoring IT, there also are costs — visible and hidden — to take into account. You should expect to incur one-time vendor selection, transition, and layoff costs, as well as ongoing contract management costs.

Vendor Selection Costs. When choosing your offshore vendor, selection costs will include documenting requirements, sending out RFPs, evaluating the responses, and negotiating the contract. A project leader or team may work full-time on vendor selection. All of this preliminary work represents an opportunity cost. There are also legal fees and travel expenses. The entire selection process can take from six months to a year, depending on the nature of the engagement.

Transition Costs. It takes from three months to a year to completely hand the work over to an offshore partner. Expect no savings but rather significant expenses such as management time and travel during this initial period. For example, you may have to pay for knowledge transfer, that is, when the offshore vendor's employees visit your site to learn your applications.

Severance and Retention Bonuses. Laying off your employees as a result of offshoring leads to severance costs and retention bonuses. Additional costs result from the need to retain employees as consultants to share their knowledge with their offshore replacements. R. Venkatesh Iyer, president and chief operating officer of NIIT SmartServe, the BPO unit of the eighth-largest IT services company from India, agrees. In addition to companies not committing enough resources to offshore projects, NIIT SmartServe believes that one of the top three mistakes customers make when they offshore processes is "...not making an effort to manage the change for the employee whose job is being outsourced, not realizing that his cooperation is essential for process mapping and tacit knowledge transfer."[19]

Contract Management Costs. Managing the offshore relationship is expensive. There is a significant amount of work in invoicing, auditing, and ensuring cost centers are charged correctly. You will also need to make sure projects are meeting milestones specified in the contract.

Costs are closely related to expected service levels such as time to market, quality, or throughput. If you want a very high service level, then you have to pay a lot more. It is important to articulate the service levels your business requires, as well as a framework for performance measurement to ensure that the costs of the outsourcing engagement are objectively measured.

Finally, estimate the total cost, which includes labor, management, coordination, travel, and other expenses. Frequently, managers think that they are saving 50% offshore, but they forget to factor in the resources they expend every time they have to sort out some problem. The rule of thumb is that IT productivity has to be high enough to make it worth the extra management time and attention that is invariably required.

What Are the Risks of Offshoring IT?

In every business case it is important to assess the execution risk that is involved. There are several risks that one must consider when sending IT work offshore.

Loss of Knowledge and Innovation. As the bulk of IT work moves offshore, the knowledge and experience that come from coding applications and solving business problems, the source of many business process innovations, could move offshore.

Potential Breach of Security. Security is a major concern. You must take precautions to ensure the confidence, security, and integrity of the company-sensitive information you send offshore. All the data that vendors and customers exchange should be encrypted, and all communications should be relayed through a secure VPN connection.

The Potential for Poorer Quality. Quality of the offshore work is a concern. You must make sure that the offshore vendor clearly conveys the technical guidelines for the code or product to everyone on the project team. The vendor should have quality assurance procedures and dedicated personnel, giving you confidence that it will deliver a quality product.

Language and Cultural Barriers. Language and culture differences are a concern in some areas of IT. A project that makes sense to a U.S. worker, such as creating a Web interface for teens, may be foreign to offshore workers. To mitigate this risk, many offshore vendors situate experienced project managers locally to guide the offshore team.

Summary

CEOs and boards are demanding that their companies use IT to execute faster, better, and cheaper despite flat or shrinking IT budgets. According to the Gartner Group, by 2004, eight out of 10 CIOs will have direct marching orders to move offshore at least part of their technology services. Four out of 10 will already have done so.[20] The economics are hard to resist.

For many CIOs and business executives, the decision to base IT activities offshore is a well-trodden road — the cost, quality, value, and process advantages are proven. Moreover, at a time when IT organizations are struggling with poor credibility and budgets are being scrutinized, offshore outsourcing has become a valuable tool. The risk of the IT offshoring decision is mitigated by the fact that many offshore vendors are very competent and are using quality methodologies such as the Capability Maturity Model (CMM), Six Sigma, and ISO 9001.

The early success of pioneers such as Microsoft, Oracle, and GE legitimized the global sourcing of IT, and adoption expanded as companies relied on offshore providers to supplement projects and overcome IT resource shortages. Recent improvements in telecommunications and advances in collaborative tools and processes make offshoring even more attractive to companies. Despite the well-publicized benefits of IT offshoring, considerable risks and logistical challenges lurk in the shadows. Obstacles range from the challenges of managing widely dispersed projects, to cultural nuances and geopolitical uncertainties. Overcoming them necessitates considerable knowledge and experience.

Is IT offshoring a fad or a mega-trend? We believe that the rush to incorporate offshore vendors into an overall IT strategy is an irreversible mega-trend as enterprises move forward with strategic rebalancing of their priorities and ongoing cost reduction initiatives. But one thing is clear: The more aggressive a company's offshore strategy, the more money it can save. To get more and more savings, companies will have to embrace more risk and overcome new management challenges.

Chapter Five

Customer Care Offshore Outsourcing

"The customer is always right."

— Gordon H. Selfridge

Introduction

Want to buy a product? Pick up the phone and order it. Have a question about a product? Log on to the Internet and send an e-mail to a customer contact center. Have a complaint about a bill? Go to the Web and chat with an agent. Multifunctional contact centers that handle all of these scenarios are a $650 billion industry employing 4 million people in the United States alone.

While a contact center's function is critical, its location is not. If a customer has a question or a problem with a product, does the call center agent answering the phone have to work for the company that sold the product, or even be in the same country? In today's global economy, the answer is no. Consider the following examples:

- A U.K. travel company specializing in making airline, hotel, and car reservations had multiple customer service centers located in the United Kingdom and Ireland. The company decided to develop a South Africa-based offshore strategy to provide low-cost inbound customer service and cross-selling capabilities.

- A satellite television company serving millions of households had multiple customer contact centers. The company decided to develop an India-based offshore plan to reduce its customer care costs.

- A telecom company providing residential voice and data services had multiple processing centers for dealing with new connections and billing queries. The company decided to develop a Philippine-based offshore strategy to reduce processing costs while increasing quality levels.

These examples illustrate a mega-trend — the offshoring of customer care. Companies in multiple industries including financial services, travel, retail, telecom, and media are racing to develop and implement an offshore strategy. For instance, General Electric Information Services, which offers consumer credit cards for retailers such as J.C. Penney, has 3,000 call center employees in the United States and 11,000 in India.[1] The rationale for offshoring customer care is simple: Customers are not interested in the mechanics (how, where, and what) of customer care. They are interested, however, in quick, high-quality service.

The number of companies outsourcing and offshoring their contact centers is rising steadily. Consider the case of Procter & Gamble, or P&G, which is outsourcing its customer relations to Sykes Enterprises. Using a blended onshore/offshore model, Sykes and P&G will work together to handle the more than 6 million customer service inquiries P&G receives annually through multiple channels including telephone, e-mail, postal mail, and fax on its 300 brands worldwide. Sykes is also managing P&G's global fulfillment services, which include product information mailings, coupons, and other items.[2] P&G intends to utilize Sykes's global network of support centers throughout the United States, Latin America, Europe, Africa, and Asia.

P&G's actions are representative of the offshore trend. High-touch customer care is the focal point of many firms. The reason? The competitive advantage gained from product or service innovations is fleeting. Companies have to constantly look for new, low-cost ways to maintain contact with customers in order to survive in the dynamic market. So it should come as no surprise that businesses are trying to create value and reduce costs. To execute this strategy, companies have no choice but to consider offshoring customer service as a key part of their overall strategy.

In this chapter, we define offshore customer care and how it has evolved. We discuss which customer care processes are being offshored. Using two case studies — Delta Air Lines and BT Retail — we illustrate two different approaches to offshoring customer care. Finally, we discuss how you can create a business case for offshoring.

Why Are Companies Offshoring Their Contact Centers?

There are four primary reasons for creating an offshore customer care strategy: cost, flexibility, quality, and better employee retention.

First, of course, is cost. The greatest expense of customer care centers is labor. Companies look to offshore to India, the Philippines, or Ireland because talent is available at a fraction of the price it is available in the United States. For instance, we estimate that a call center in India can hire a new graduate with a four-year degree, English skills, and technical skills for about $12 per hour. The average bundled cost for a U.S. call center agent is estimated to be around $34 per hour. Obviously the cost difference is substantial, especially if you have several thousand agents.

Flexibility is the second reason for creating an offshore strategy. Offshore vendors can handle large volumes of incoming customer requests — voice and data — at peak times. The vendors can serve as a release valve for companies whose in-house centers may experience an overflow, such as when a company rolls out a new campaign or product. Staffing for peak times translates directly to costs. With offshore resources more flexible and available, handling these types of situations becomes easier.

The third reason for developing an offshore strategy is quality. In countries such as the United States, filling call center positions with university graduates is a difficult and costly feat. However, in many offshore destinations, a highly educated labor force is readily available. If properly trained, this high-caliber workforce can be a powerful advantage in improving overall service quality.

Derek Holley, president of eTelecare, the largest outsourced contact center company in the Philippines, says, "In India and the Philippines, hiring a university graduate over a high school graduate offers a tremendous increase in worker quality for only a minor increase in cost. In the United States, where the wage differential is much greater, it doesn't make as much sense."[3]

Better employee retention is the final reason for offshoring. One of the major headaches of contact centers is turnover. Since people are the largest component in a contact center, retaining the best people is key. Bringing a new agent up to speed can take four to 12 weeks of costly training.

Ashish Kumar of 24/7 Customer, a provider of voice- and e-mail-based customer support services in India, says "The challenge in the U.S. is to retain people because most of them perceive the call center jobs to be a parking space for a while, and then they will go and do more and better things. In India, it's a big career opportunity for most of the people who are coming out of college. It is something they can really build their future on because it is a growing industry."[4]

Why are contact centers and customer care at the forefront of offshoring? Let's look at the evolution of the customer care industry in order to understand how it's migrating towards offshoring.

A Brief Overview of the Customer Care Industry

All customers at some point or another deal with a contact center. The sheer size of the contact center industry underscores the broad role it plays in modern business. It has a variety of names including call centers, service centers, customer care centers, support centers, or multi-channel support centers. All are used interchangeably to describe the support aspect of the customer care industry.

There are an estimated 75,000–100,000 contact centers in the United States alone employing 4 million people. A typical U.S. support center is approximately 42,000 square feet, has 432 workstations, and can handle in excess of 12,000 user transactions per day.[5] Organizations spend an estimated $160–$180 billion annually in direct expenditures to run contact centers. Included in this figure are ongoing staff and telecom costs, as well as capital expenditures on technology and facilities.[6]

Clearly, finding, targeting, supporting, and retaining customers, the core themes of customer care, is big business. However, the way that companies carry out these activities has changed considerably over the last four decades.

The Evolution of Customer Care

During the last decade, the call center, an integral part of customer service, has expanded from a simple phone operation to a full-service interaction center capable of handling all customer queries via any channel — telephone, e-mail, fax, postal mail, and the Web.

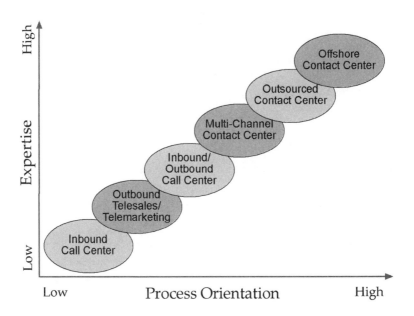

Figure 5.1: The Evolution of Customer Care

Outbound Sales

In the late 1970s, the state of the art was outbound telesales. The technology was primitive — an outbound agent would have three basic tools: a rotary-dial phone, a stack of 3"x5" index cards, and a pencil. Prospective leads were picked from phone books and each agent cold called people. Agent burnout and turnover were high, and the process was time-consuming and inefficient.

The invention of the automatic call distributor (ACD) in 1973 led to a more sophisticated customer care industry. With predictive and preview dialers, reps no longer had to manually dial and could make more calls per hour. In fact, predictive and preview dialing is estimated to have increased outbound productivity by 300%, an event that created the call center industry.[7]

In traditional call centers, the agents were split up based on whether they handled inbound or outbound calls. Companies soon realized that this division didn't make sense for two reasons: Agents dedicated to one mode were underutilized, and time and resource management was difficult. Following a TV commercial or direct mail campaign, inbound calls might spike by several hundred percent. Days later, when inbound calls dropped off, the previously swamped agents would have nothing to do, while the outbound agents were busy dialing out offering new discounts to customers. The next step in the evolution was the migration from pure inbound and pure outbound to a blended model of inbound and outbound calling.

The Inbound/Outbound Call Center

By the early 1990s, inbound duties had evolved to span sales, order taking, basic technical support, and help desk support, while outbound duties had grown to include collections, surveys, and data verification. Given the range of tasks being performed, call centers, staffed by generalists (who could handle both inbound and outbound calls) and powered by ACDs, mushroomed. Duties were shifted based on need, which helped to spread the work among all agents and minimize downtime. This increased productivity and further fueled the demand for more call center automation.

In the mid-1990s, computer telephony integration (CTI) gave companies new ways to combine the power of the computer with the telephone. CTI, initially based on client/server architectures, allowed better integration between the data and voice environments — putting more information on the desktop. Businesses began concentrating on the relationship between the agent and the customer. The objective was once and done, that is, complete the process during a single call. The goal: empower agents to serve customers better.

The Multi-Channel Contact Center

Until 1995, most call center activity was voice. The Internet and e-commerce changed that. Companies began to add e-mail, Web chat, and co-browsing capabilities to their existing call centers to support their online customers. This is when people first started referring to call centers as contact centers.

The online channel evolved quickly. Its first use was as a marketing vehicle with brochureware Web sites that were a combination of corporate annual reports and product information. Brochureware soon gave way to e-commerce transactions, which evolved into self-service portals that provided presale, sale, and post-sale support. With enhanced broadband access, online self-service is becoming the primary channel in certain industries.

Despite the proliferation of online channels, customers instinctively reach for the phone when they need help. As a result, the trend in the late 1990s was towards multi-channel contact centers. These centers allow firms to integrate service, sales, and marketing efforts across multiple channels. They are driven by the premise that each customer interaction is an opportunity to cross-sell and up-sell.

Outsourced Contact and Service Centers

For companies that did not want to build their own call centers, outsourcing them became a viable option for businesses in the late 1990s. Also called service bureaus, outsourcers are used by companies that need help handling a sudden surge in call volume.

Corporations also turn to outsourcers when they are interested in testing out a marketing campaign that will generate demand but are not willing to invest in building additional call centers to handle the workload. Microsoft took this approach for its U.K., Irish, French, and German customers. The company outsourced its preferred support center to SITEL, which serves Microsoft customers from its centers in Dublin, Ireland; Paris, France; and Krefeld, Germany.

Customer care vendors work hard to balance three requirements in customer service: new cross-channel experiences, lower service cost, and increased sales from each customer contact.

The Offshore Contact and Service Center

Increasing customer satisfaction while lower servicing costs has been the goal of businesses for the last three decades. However, this goal is getting harder to achieve due to constant changes in customer care.

The customer care industry has changed along three different dimensions:

1. More business process support (marketing, sales, fulfillment, customer inquiry, and support);

2. More customer contact points (sales departments, retail branches, call centers, and Web sites); and

3. More contact channels (mail, telephone, e-mail, and Web chat).

Given these different dimensions, the cost and complexity of customer care is escalating. We estimate that live voice costs between $4 and $8 per contact, interactive voice response (IVR) costs about $1–$2 per contact, Web self-service between $0.05 and $0.30 per contact, and e-mail averages $3–$10 per contact. Given these figures, it easy to see why offering customers a multi-channel integrated experience at a low cost is becoming very difficult.

For a while, companies thought that using technology to digitize customer care would solve their problems. There was a period when people thought that the Internet would decrease the need for contact centers. Despite all the technology, customers still want to talk to an agent.

To further reduce the cost of agent support, companies are beginning to complement their onshore call centers with offshore call centers. The objective is cost control, service improvement, and seamless support. (Seamless support is the vendor's ability to provide customer support without the customer knowing that he has been directed to a third-party representative, possibly in another country.)

Top on the list of objectives for many companies is cutting costs of customer care. HSBC, the world's second-largest bank, announced in October 2003 that it would move 4,000 jobs in five U.K service centers mainly in data processing and call center roles to India, Malaysia, and China starting in January 2004. HSBC's chief executive said that going offshore was "essential" to remaining efficient and competitive.

HSBC has good company. Many large British companies such as Lloyds TSB, Barclays, British Telecom (BT Group), Abbey National, and Prudential are choosing the same path. These firms are expanding their offshore call center operations into service centers capable of processing new customer registration, account opening, application processing, address updates, and billing query resolution.

Now that you understand the evolution of the customer care industry, let's examine the processes that make up offshore contact centers.

Offshoring Customer Care Processes

To minimize the total cost of customer care, companies are trying a variety of models — in-house, shared services centers, outsourced, and offshored. Of these, offshore is gaining momentum as a new model.

The offshore customer care processes are divided into three categories — customer support, marketing and sales, and technical support.

Customer Support Processes

Customer support helps organizations better manage relationships by facilitating all customer-facing processes — presales information, order taking, order management, and post-sale support. The processes also have to be aligned with the channels. Customers have the freedom to choose their preferred mode of communicating with companies, whether it is via live agent, e-mail, or the Web.

Regardless of the selected channel, faster, more meaningful responses result in more satisfied customers. How to satisfy the customer better and yet keep costs low is the challenge facing companies. To solve this dilemma, companies are offshoring these channels: voice-based phone support, e-mail support, and live chat.

Voice-Based Phone Support

This is the cornerstone of the call center. Technology advances allow for a much more sophisticated experience for the confused or troubled customer. Utilizing integrated customer and product data, reps can resolve issues and answer questions more quickly and accurately than ever before.

Ambergris Solutions is a leading Philippine-based provider of customer care, inbound sales, and technical support solutions. One of its clients, a Fortune 100 computer manufacturer, is using 300 Ambergris agents to answer customer billing inquiries, communicate order status and shipping information, accept additional orders for spare parts and peripherals as well as order changes, set up returns transactions, and handle complaints. It took the two companies seven weeks and three days from when their partnership began to integrate the first call. After the 90-day initial ramp period, Ambergris had a service level of 86%, bypassing the target of 80%, and an average handle time of 6.54 minutes in comparison to the target of 7.5 minutes.[8]

Yahoo! also decided to seek some outside help in providing voice-based phone support to its many customers. In July 2003, the company signed a customer care agreement with Convergys Corporation. Convergys has as many as 15,000 workers in the Philippines and India. Under the agreement, Convergys will provide voice-based phone support to Yahoo! customers calling with general inquiries and billing-related questions on its premium products and services.

How does this work? Convergys deploys many international private leased circuits (IPLCs) with diverse telecom carriers to establish a highly reliable and lower latency connection between the U.S. hub and an international gateway in India. The calls are received and answered by Convergys India Services (CIS). CIS opened its first call center in India in December 2001. Since then, it has created 6,000 jobs at four Indian call centers and has plans to open a fifth.[9]

E-Mail Support

E-mail management is a critical issue for companies like Expedia.com, eBay, or Lands' End, which deal with millions of customers and are bombarded by service e-mails. Increasingly, the customer expects a reply to an e-mail query within a few hours, not a few days. Let's say that answering each e-mail takes ten minutes. When you multiply processing-time-per-e-mail by the number of e-mails per month, you are looking at a significant amount of time and money spent on responding to e-mails.

To keep these costs under control, some companies are moving them offshore. For example, Amazon.com has an e-mail contact center in India operated by Daksh, a New Delhi–based call center outsourcer. AltaVista, a provider of search services and technology, selected 24/7 Customer of India for its e-mail-based customer support.

How does this work? Software can help to route and track customer e-mail messages and online forms to the appropriate agents. When a customer complaint comes up on a representative's screen, routine responses are rapidly assembled from a library of prescripted remarks. These remarks are customized with the customer's name and other relevant information and then sent electronically, permitting the representative to move on to solving the next problem. Such real-time interaction is becoming an important component of all contact centers.

Live Chat and Video Interaction

New customer service applications help companies provide superior customer service by enabling real-time interaction via text chat through a Web browser. Live chat services cover Web site navigation, co-browsing, online search, information support, and online transaction and technical support. Having a service rep just a click away gives customers the reassurance that if problems occur, help is easily and readily available.

TransWorks, a provider of BPO services operating out of India, has recently added Web chat to its e-mail product line. One of its clients, a financial services company was using the Internet as a channel to acquire customers. This company was struggling to deal with the flood of e-mails sent by prospective customers in response to an online advertising campaign. TransWorks agreed to handle the client's presale inquiries and monitor the effectiveness of the campaign. The relationship was subsequently expanded with Web chat in order to facilitate real-time interaction with prospects.

Sales and Marketing Processes

Sales and marketing are the bread and butter processes of every company. Sales and marketing initiatives are not only people- and technology-intensive; they are expensive. Applications required for a sales and marketing initiative range from, data warehouses, data mining technologies, analytic software, and campaign management software, to e-commerce reporting tools and Web logs.

Some of the sales and marketing processes offshored include inbound and outbound sales, cross-selling and up-selling, marketing campaign management, and retention management using customer feedback surveys. Let's look at each in more detail.

Inbound and Outbound Sales

Offshoring sales is a growing trend. Take, for instance, SBC Communications, headquartered in San Antonio, Texas. SBC hired ChaseCom to manage its small business accounts. ChaseCom has call centers in Texas, Chile, and India and offers "win back" services, which involve calling customers who have left SBC to try to get them back.

Another important aspect of sales is targeting and acquiring new customers. A credit card company enlisted ICICI OneSource, a leading Indian vendor, to manage two outbound campaigns designed to increase its customer base. The first campaign centered on acquiring new, preapproved customers through telemarketing for four different products. The second campaign involved trying to persuade existing cardholders to sign up for add-on programs, such as balance transfers. ICICI OneSource dedicated 220 agents to handle the calls. To be more effective, ICICI OneSource set up balance transfer coaching, as well as incentives for agents who were successful at getting customers to transfer their balances.

Cross-Selling and Up-Selling

More and more companies view cross-selling and event-driven marketing as tools that provide a strategic advantage for their marketing departments. By implementing a cross-sell strategy and including the applications necessary to track customer contacts, event triggers can be established to identify prospects for additional sales. For example, in banking, an event such as a large deposit triggers a salesperson to call a customer and ask if he or she is interested in investment options.

Retention and Customer Surveys

Listening to the customer is one area that has evolved in recent years. Companies have realized the importance of understanding customer requirements and needs. Almost all best-practice companies have a customer feedback mechanism in place to listen to the customer.

Offshoring provides a low-cost alternative for collecting customer data, either through telephone or e-mail based surveys.

Technical Support Processes

Technical support processes assist customers with resolving a product or service problem. Help desk applications automate the management and resolution of product support calls and improve the efficiency and effectiveness of the help desk process.

How well companies provide highly available, reliable technical support affects how long they retain customers. Technical support teams not only assist customers experiencing technical difficulties; they help customers become comfortable with a company's products and services. Some of the major technical support services offered by offshore outsourcing firms follow.

24x7 Technical Support and Problem Resolution

Help desk staff verify a customer's service-level status (the level of support the customer is entitled to receive), open trouble tickets, track specific tasks needed to resolve problems, maintain permanent incident histories, and capture support costs for chargebacks.

America Online (AOL) takes customer technical support seriously. AOL Member Services, the customer support arm, is a global organization available 24x7x365 and can be reached by telephone, TTY (for the hearing-impaired), e-mail, and online in a specially designed chat environment. The group helps members who request assistance with registration, billing, and account reactivation and cancellation. It also supplies technical support and forgotten password help and takes orders for AOL software.

AOL Member Services has several call centers located in New Mexico (1,200 employees); Florida (1,600 employees); Utah (850 employees); Arizona (700 employees); Oklahoma (1,200 employees); India (1,900 employees); and the Philippines (850 employees). The Indian center handled 10 million customer calls between July 2002 and July 2003.[10]

Installation and Product Support

As consumers continue to buy more products online and the concept of self-service increases in popularity, consumers will need help with installation or maintenance support. Although some people may prefer to walk into a full-service store and buy a computer from a knowledgeable salesperson, many elect to log on to a Web site, configure their PC, and await its arrival on their doorstep three days later. Although the second scenario makes the purchase process easy, it creates a lot of not-as-easy installation work for computer novices. This is precisely the reason that companies such as Dell are utilizing offshore resources to help manage the numerous questions that always arise.

When Mitsubishi introduced the first high-definition VCR, it asked Source One Communications to support customer inquiries. Based in New Jersey, Source One is made up of a global network of outsourced call centers located in New York, Manila, Toronto, London, Johannesburg, and the Philippines. Source One agents have handled tech support for Mitsubishi since 1998 and provide technical support for all of Mitsubishi's home theater equipment, including TVs, VCRs, DVDs, and satellite receivers.

Innovation also figured into Source One's product support services. Initially, productivity was low because agents had to physically leave their desks to search through hard copy product manuals. Digitizing the legacy manuals allowed agents to access them online, which improved service quality due to more accurate information at their fingertips. Mitsubishi experienced a savings of more than 10% of overall call costs.[11]

The migratory trend to offshore service centers marks an important new chapter in customer care. Let's see how Delta Air Lines and the British Telecom unit BT Retail are approaching this new era.

Offshore Call Center Case Study: Delta Air Lines

Delta Air Lines is the second-largest airline in the world in terms of passengers carried and the third-largest as measured by operating revenues. Since the terrorist attacks on September 11, 2001, Delta and the airline industry have faced unprecedented challenges. Due to a downturn in travel, Delta's net losses totaled $2.5 billion for 2001 and 2002. The airline industry has experienced substantial revenue declines and cost increases, creating industrywide liquidity issues that have resulted in two major airlines filing for bankruptcy.

In order to survive, cost reductions became the primary objective of Delta's management. In 2002, Delta announced that its cost management initiatives (such as cutting 16,000 jobs and 72 aircraft from its fleet) achieved a cost savings of $1.5 billion in 2002. Hungry for more innovative ways to increase profits and slash costs, Delta decided to offshore operations related to customer reservations.

Offshoring Select Customer Reservation Processes

Delta has more than 6,000 employees in 20 reservation call centers. The company chose to outsource customer reservations in order to free up its own reservation agents to handle customers' more immediate needs. To pick the right activity for the offshoring proof of concept, Delta used several screening criteria.

- The process had to have a large cost base due to the number of employees involved.

- The offshore process had to be labor-intensive.

- An ample number of skilled, full-time vendor employees had to be able to support the process overseas.

- A significant wage level differential between the United States and the chosen offshoring country had to exist.

Delta conducted careful location due diligence and found that the United States had a fully loaded wage rate of $46,000, while the Philippines had a cost of $7,300 and India stood at $6,000.[12]

Based on the location shortlist, Delta initiated a search for vendors, utilizing a four-round vendor selection process. At the end of the process, Delta reached agreements with two vendors to handle select worldwide customer reservations functions — Wipro Spectramind at a facility in India, and Sykes Enterprises at one of its Philippine centers.

The two vendors were charged with handling the following reservation processes: general sales calls; frequent flyer service support; reject and queue handling; and incoming baggage service calls.

Handling general sales calls is aimed at providing coverage 24x7x365 for phone calls from customers regarding potential bookings, as well as ticketing. Supporting Delta's frequent flyer program consists of ensuring that customer account information is correct and that any mileage issues are taken care of. Resolving reject messages and handling queues means clearing up any problems that the automated booking system earmarks for agent intervention, such as an expired ticket. Lastly, managing inbound baggage customer service calls translates into handling questions about lost or missing luggage.

To maintain quality, Delta has service level agreements (SLAs) in place. The airline and the vendor monitor customer care agents and evaluate their performance based on specific metrics, with both parties submitting their scores for review and quality control. In order to monitor an operation that is thousands of miles away, Delta uses contact center management software from Witness Systems that captures voice and screen data from agent workstations, which can be viewed in real time or archived.

While the Wipro Spectramind operation went according to plan, the call center in the Philippines was later cancelled. Delta cited security reasons in the uncertain Philippine political environment as the reason for putting the Sykes call center on hold.[13]

Quantifying the Value and ROI for Delta Air Lines

Delta's primary goals for offshoring are to obtain significant cost savings and productivity improvements. The company expects to realize initial distribution cost savings from its offshoring project of as much as $26 million in 2003.[14]

The $26 million is derived from the cheaper labor rates of workers in India. The lower wage rates in India mean that Delta can hire at least seven people for every one customer care agent the company employs in the United States, or, put another way, the Indian call center will be seven times as productive. Within the first eight weeks of offshoring reservation processes, Delta watched its average call handling time for baggage services drop from 639 seconds to 454 seconds and the quality of call handling exceed expectations.[15]

The ROI of offshoring is sometimes magnified due to tax savings. Companies willing to do business offshore often benefit from tax breaks. For example, when Sykes established its first call center in the Philippines, the government gave Sykes "pioneer status," which is an incentive for first-time businesses with seven years of income tax exemptions. Sykes's clients indirectly benefit from the tax break if the company is able to pass on the cost savings.[16]

The ROI is further improved if you factor in the long-term costs of employee acquisition, retention, and training. There is no shortage of well-educated call center candidates in India and the Philippines. Unlike their American counterparts, call center employees from these countries tend not to view customer service as tedious, so they are less likely to leave, which results in lower attrition rates and employee training costs.

When calculating ROI, you also have to factor in the cost of training. Wipro Spectramind does incur some training costs through voice and accent labs where employees practice their American accents or through employee tutorials covering the regulations of the U.S. Department of Transportation (depending on the client) and even U.S. pop culture. The cost of this training, however, is more than offset by the wage differential between the two countries.

Offshore Contact Center Case Study: BT Retail

When people in the United Kingdom call a friend or surf the Internet, there is a good chance that British Telecommunications, or BT Group, is working quietly behind the scenes. The company competes in the markets of local, national, and international services; broadband and Internet products and services; and IT solutions. BT's services and products touch over 20 million business and residential customers.

The company is split according to the audience it serves: BT Retail works with businesses and residential customers; BT Wholesale specializes in network services and solutions; and BT Global Services sells to multisite organizations all over the world.

Facing increasing competitive threats to its core business, BT Retail has set the challenging target of £1.5 billion in new revenue growth over the next three years. One of the ways BT hopes to achieve this target was unveiled in February 2002. That was the month that the company announced a transformation strategy aimed at enhancing its call center capabilities and reducing its costs.

BT Retail's management felt that its network of contact centers did not allow it to achieve its strategic goals: reduce customer dissatisfaction by 25% per year, deliver consistent customer service in a cost-effective manner, and remain competitive. To streamline the call center environment, BT Retail decided to develop a network of Next Generation Contact Centers (NGCCs).

Next Generation Contact Center Initiative

The BT Retail call center network is massive and complex. It handles 2.3 million calls per day that deal with directory inquiries, residential services, business services, operator assistance, and emergency services. Before the NGCC initiative began, the calls were handled by 16,000 agents at 150 call centers spread over 104 sites. BT estimated that it spent £560 million a year on its call center operations (one-third of BT's entire cost base).[17] Its goal was to reduce costs by £150 million by 2004, while at the same time enhancing customer satisfaction.

The mission of the project is to deliver outstanding customer interactions primarily by upgrading existing centers, eliminating some of the existing centers, and opening new ones with the aid of a £100 million investment. Before upgrading or shutting down centers, managers looked at:

- The size of the center.

- Suitability as a "next generation" contact center.

- Geopolitical factors.

- Costs incurred as a result of remaining open or shutting down.

- The impact the center had on BT Retail's individual business units.

- The impact the center had on customers and employees.

BT's NGCC initiative to consolidate its large call center network is in line with the larger trend of companies converting their call centers into multifunctional contact centers that handle customer queries regardless of what channel they go through. Carol Borghesi, director of BT's NGCC initiative, summed up the motivation for the project this way: "Creating a smaller network of leading-edge, multifunction contact centers is key to making dramatic improvements to the quality of customer service."[18]

So far, the contact center restructuring program is estimated to have yielded £86 million in cost savings, on track to hit the company target of £150 million in savings by year-end 2004.[19] To further support the cost reduction goal and improve customer satisfaction, BT is embracing an offshore customer care strategy.

Offshoring Next Generation Contact Centers

The next phase of the NGCC strategy includes the offshore outsourcing of customer care to two new contact centers in Bangalore and New Delhi in India. BT anticipates that the sites will employ 2,200 people by March 2004. The centers in India will initially handle parts of the company's directories and conferencing work.[20]

The NGCC offshore contract is estimated to be worth $160 million. At the time, the contract was the largest BPO engagement an Indian company had ever been awarded.[21] In order to select its vendor, BT put a number of services out to bid. There were 12 bidders in the initial round. BT shortlisted several and then chose two partners — Progeon, the BPO unit of Infosys, and HCL Technologies.[22] For the New Delhi NGCC, BT picked HCL Technologies, a company that offers BPO and IT services from eight global delivery centers — five in India (3,100 seats), one in Ireland (580 seats), one in Malaysia (200 seats), and one in the United States (580 seats). In response to questions as to why BT selected HCL as its partner, the CEO of BT Retail, Pierre Danon, highlighted HCL's presence in 14 different countries as a strength, in addition to the working relationship the two companies had formed in 2001 when HCL acquired a 90% stake in BT's Belfast, Northern Ireland, contact center.

HCL's training methods were another point in its favor. For any project it undertakes, HCL trains its employees rigorously. Sujit Baksi, CEO of both the India and Northern Ireland BPO units of HCL Technologies, pointed out that the average length of training in the industry is four weeks, but HCL devotes almost 23 weeks to training its employees. If you factor in the month or so it takes for an agent to be brought up to speed, that's about 29 weeks of training.[23] The training differs depending on the BPO project undertaken and the client's preferences.

The structure of the offshore organization also affects the training. Sanjay Kumar, founder and CEO of offshore call center firm vCustomer, states, "For every ten people, we have a team lead. For every 15 people, we have a quality lead. For every four team leads, we have a product manager. For every six quality leads, we have a quality manager. At the end we provide both leadership and quality mentoring at better ratios with correspondingly improved results in individual performance."[24] Training all these people on the various nuances of processes is an intense activity. Figure 5.2 outlines some of the types of training that an employee for an offshore outsourcing firm might undergo.

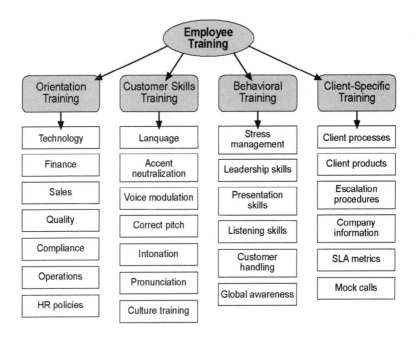

Figure 5.2: Types of Training Offshore Vendors Offer Employees

To handle the telemarketing, directory, and conferencing work that BT is offshoring, HCL plans to recruit 1,000 employees including executives, data analytic experts, and software engineers by year-end 2003.

To manage its offshore presence, BT has sent its managers directly to India to oversee the two new Next Generation Contact Centers. Since the India centers are part of BT's overall strategy, the company has no intention of "lifting and dropping" the project into HCL's lap, so BT site managers oversee the facilities.

While BT has been hesitant to release numbers regarding offshore outsourcing, it did say that it has realized value in the form of quality improvement and productivity gains from its offshore NGCC initiative.

Creating an Offshore Customer Care Business Case

Procter & Gamble, Delta Air Lines, AOL, and HSBC are all early adopters of the offshore customer care model. Why did they adopt this strategy? The rapid changes in customer care technology, global competition, and pricing pressures have made it difficult for companies to cost-effectively maintain in-house the necessary personnel to handle all of their customer care needs. This has resulted in more and more companies trying to measure how effective their customer service is and really try to understand what they can do to improve their customer service process. To improve and fix problems, companies are increasingly turning to outsourcers to perform specialized tasks, functions, and entire processes.

Should Offshore Customer Care Be Part of Your Strategy?

An offshore evaluation should follow a disciplined approach from planning through negotiation and implementation, to ongoing management of the relationship. The typical planning, analysis, and design steps in an offshore customer care evaluation include:

1. Conducting a feasibility study.

2. Analyzing the requirements of the offshore project in detail.

3. Identifying core and noncore processes and creating a business case.

4. Designing the service level agreements together with the vendor.

5. Building, implementing, and maintaining the offshore relationship.

6. Deciding whether to renew or terminate an offshore contract.

This section focuses on the all-important first steps of the planning phase. A major part of the planning phase is the feasibility study. The feasibility of offshore customer care is determined by a series of screens that every offshore strategy should pass before further, detailed evaluation. The first is the core competency screen. If the function to be outsourced contributes centrally to the organization's success (core competency), then that process probably is not a strong candidate for offshoring. But do not confuse a critical function with a core competence, as the former probably should be outsourced to a best-in-class provider.

Which Processes to Retain and Which to Offshore

Although saving millions of dollars has an immediate appeal, take time to assess if it really makes sense to move a particular process offshore. In figure 5.3, we look at which processes are ideal candidates for offshoring and which processes are best left alone. Many customer care initiatives require a low level of service knowledge and are low touch. These two factors make them ideal candidates for offshore outsourcing.

When the offshore discussion starts, many people immediately say that anything that is noncore can be outsourced. But the reaction Eric Paljug, vice president of marketing at vCustomer, gets from some of his prospects is "What is noncore about my customer service?"

Many companies feel that they have to own everything the customer does. Paljug elaborates, "For example, an automaker owns the customer experience — the design and the specification of what a car is — but they do not own the manufacture of each component of the car." In the same way, the entire customer experience is core, but the actual delivery of customer service is much more process driven as opposed to being an inherent competency or differentiator. "Once prospects understand the idea of what is core and noncore, that is when they start to outsource."[25]

In contrast, companies could take the stance that customer care is the very front line of customer relationship management. Contact center reps can make or break a longstanding relationship with just one interaction. Knowing as much as possible about the customer and how to meet individual needs is critical to building loyalty. With the right training and infrastructure, an outsourced contact center ought to be just as helpful as an in-house center. But will the outsourced reps be interested in building customer loyalty? After all, they work for a third-party vendor. Without the proper preparation, training, compensation, and company loyalty, why should they bother cross-selling, up-selling, or spending extra time with your most valuable asset — the customer? These are some of the issues that need to be considered before sending your customer service functions to another company.

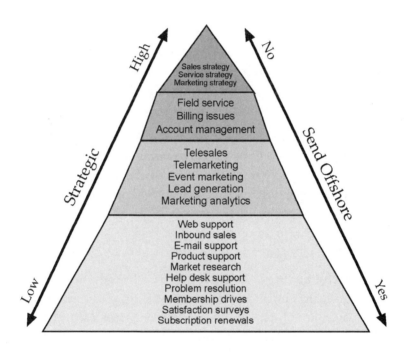

Figure 5.3: Core versus Noncore Customer Care Processes

Developing the Financial Justification

Do you understand the current cost structure of your customer care operations? You need to familiarize yourself with it before you can estimate how much you can save by offshoring. Once you have a good idea of your current cost structure, you are ready to move to the next phase of the feasibility study: quantifying the benefits and costs of the offshoring decision. Companies must conduct a rigorous ROI analysis to decide whether the cost savings and overall advantages of running an offshore operation will outweigh the disadvantages.

The benefits of offshoring can be divided into three categories: tangible, intangible, and strategic. Traditionally, CFOs have used only tangible benefits to estimate ROI numbers, such as lowering head count, and have underestimated potential value. Intangible benefits such as customer satisfaction or costs like customer dissatisfaction are not easily measured. Each of these categories must be considered in the decision to offshore.

Tangible Benefits of Offshore Customer Care

The most tangible advantage of offshoring call centers are the cost savings. Apart from that, local governments in offshore locations sometimes pick up the tab for incentives such as training and tax concessions. Their motivation is to make it more attractive for companies to offshore operations.

Savings in Direct Costs. Our analysis shows that savings from operating customer care centers offshore versus operating them in the United States or the United Kingdom are estimated to be between 25% and 50%. Canada provides operational savings of 10%–20%. In Jamaica and the rest of the Caribbean, companies save 25%–30%. In India and the Philippines, savings are around 40%. The savings predominantly come from differences in wage rates for customer service agents.

Computing the Savings. In table 5.1, we illustrate how to calculate your possible savings in labor costs from offshoring contact centers. For simplicity, we assumed that: 1) U.S. call center agents earn $12 per hour; 2) offshore agents earn $3 per hour; and 3) an agent, whether in the United States or offshore, works 2,080 hours per year (40 hours per week and 52 weeks a year).

Number of Call Center Jobs	Total Annual Salary in U.S.	Total Annual Salary Offshore	Total Annual Savings
50	$1,248,000	$312,000	$936,000
100	$2,496,000	$624,000	$1,872,000
500	$12,480,000	$3,120,000	$9,360,000
1,000	$24,960,000	$6,240,000	$18,720,000
5,000	$124,800,000	$31,200,000	$93,600,000

Table 5.1: The Labor Savings from Offshore Customer Care Centers

Intangible Benefits of Offshore Customer Care

Several intangible benefits associated with offshore centers also deserve attention. They include effective recruiting and retention, improved quality and productivity, better customer satisfaction, operational excellence, and speedy problem resolution.

Retention. Say "call center" to most Americans, and they think of tedious, low-paid, dead-end jobs fielding complaints about phone bills or bank statements. In contrast, employees in many offshore markets regard the position of contact center rep as a career. The higher the retention rate, the lower the level of spending on recruiting and training. Considering the time and costs associated with training new agents, it becomes easier to maintain quality service at a low cost.

Computing the Savings. While not obvious, the savings here can be substantiated. Suppose that 1) a firm spends $2,000 on average to advertise, recruit, screen, interview, select, and train a customer service rep at an acceptable level of proficiency and productivity, and 2) in the offshore region, the attrition rate is 20%, while in the United States, the attrition rate is 60%. Table 5.2 presents an estimate of these savings.

Number of Call Center Jobs	Annual Attrition Costs in U.S.	Annual Attrition Costs Offshore	Total Annual Savings
50	$60,000	$20,000	$40,000
100	$120,000	$40,000	$80,000
500	$600,000	$200,000	$400,000
1,000	$1,200,000	$400,000	$800,000
5,000	$6,000,000	$2,000,000	$4,000,000

Table 5.2 The Attrition Costs of U.S. and Offshore Customer Care Centers

Improved Customer Satisfaction. Better agent retention leads to more experienced agents, which can lead to higher customer satisfaction. Customer satisfaction is tied to how well an agent delivers. An experienced, knowledgeable, and efficient agent who enjoys his job stands a stronger chance of meeting his customer's expectations and hence satisfying them.

Better Labor Quality and Productivity. Quality and productivity often improve when operations are moved offshore. The calls handled per staff per shift and the productive hours worked per call center staff per year tend to increase. One reason for the improvements is low employee turnover. People in offshore countries strive to obtain contact center jobs, and once they land them do not want to lose them. Another reason for better quality and productivity is that offshore centers are able to hire better educated and more skilled employees. The average call center agent in India has two to four years more of education than a U.S. agent has. If trained well, these agents can provide better service and quickly adjust to changing customer needs.

Process Excellence. With a laser-like focus on process improvement, offshore customer care centers also deliver a substantial reduction in call handling costs. Most offshore vendors are using initiatives including COPC-2000, ISO 9002 certifications, and Six Sigma to offer superior quality and process improvements.

Strategic Benefits of Offshore Customer Care

The long-term benefits of offshore contact centers are better customer loyalty, improved revenue potential, and an ability to support growth.

Improved Customer Stickiness. The long-term impact of increased customer satisfaction, process improvements, and speedy problem resolution is a definite jump in customer loyalty. If customers always receive superb service, then reduced churn follows.

Revenue Enhancements. The workforce skill enhancements from offshore operations will translate to, in the end, better customer acquisition and cross-sell and up-sell execution. Experienced, skilled agents are able to free up their time by quickly resolving customer issues. This free time could be set aside for revenue-generating activities.

Support Growth. With access to customer service capabilities and educated workforces around the world, offshore customer contact centers can support growth. Companies can establish a global servicing network through offshoring that enables them to improve both the cost and quality of the overall service infrastructure, expand capacity, and increase flexibility to meet the needs of their growing businesses.

Costs of Offshore Customer Care

Balancing out the benefits of the offshoring equation are the costs. The first significant cost is a one-time transition expense that covers lease terminations, severance, and disposal of current assets. Ongoing costs for telecommunications, operations, and program management also contribute to the offshoring price tag.

Telecom Costs. Telecom costs will rise as the majority of voice and data traffic traverses thousands of miles to its end offshore destination.

Overhead Costs. Maintaining and supporting ongoing operations offshore is typically more expensive than it is onshore for various reasons. Business trips are usually longer and more expensive than trips to domestic contact centers. For example, a flight from New York to California is about $300, while a flight from New York to Mumbai, India, is around $3,500. In addition, visiting different countries can add to operational costs, such as provisions for transportation, lodging, and meals.

Program Management Costs. Many companies also forget to account for program and project management costs. In order to ensure that the offshore engagement is running smoothly and per contract, project managers, along with possible technology or call center subject matter experts, need to be dedicated resources. This adds to the overhead.

Training Overhead. Offshore contact centers will only be successful if agents can establish empathy with customers and overcome the cultural divide. As a result, significant accent and cultural training is required. If servicing a U.S. client, training might include American history, government, and language including popular phrases and slang.

Training also includes accent neutralization. Agents in countries such as India, the Philippines, or Jamaica may have too heavy of an accent to be understood by their American or English customers. Accent neutralization is necessary before the agents can interact with customers. Somshankar Das, president and CEO at e4e, a business process and technology solutions outsourcing company, says, "Now you can actually have agents switching from a British accent, to a U.S. accent, back to an Indian accent."[26] The emergence of multi-accent agents is a new trend.

Performance Measurement Costs. Metrics such as total cost-per-call and total cost-per-resolution are a key aspect of any call center. Total cost-per-resolution looks at when the customer problem was resolved as opposed to each individual call. Total cost-per-resolution is if the customer calls and the problem is not resolved and they call a second time, then the total cost-per-resolution considers both calls. If you measure cost-per-call instead, the numbers are deceiving. You also need metrics such as first-time resolution statistics and dispatch rate. So when you evaluate vendors, conduct due diligence on the metrics they use.

Summary

In this chapter, we examined the emerging dynamics in offshore contact centers. Contact centers are strategic to the health of industries such as financial services, telecommunications, insurance, consumer goods, airlines, technology, and governmental agencies. Because of the growing role they play in maintaining customer satisfaction and, more recently, in generating revenues, the challenges of planning, building, and managing offshore contact centers must be effectively addressed.

Creating a high-value offshore contact center is a strategic imperative in today's economy. Growth for offshore customer care solutions and services will be driven by the trend of global Fortune 1000 companies turning to offshore outsourcers to provide cost-effective, high-quality customer support solutions. We also anticipate an acceleration from in-house onshore call centers to an offshore model, which provides customer care solutions at significantly lower costs.

Finally, is offshore customer care a trend or a fad? We expect offshore customer care is here to stay, as long as firms are looking for a high-touch/low-cost strategy. However, like the re-engineering movement of the early 1990s and e-commerce wave of the late 1990s, only some companies will be able to get it right. The process requires commitment, planning, and collaboration across the organization. The returns in improved efficiency, heightened customer loyalty, and contributions to profitability are reasons enough to begin the journey.

Chapter Six

Finance and Accounting Offshore Outsourcing

"An investment in knowledge pays the best interest."

— Benjamin Franklin

Introduction

Finance and accounting departments today face unprecedented pressure. Companies find themselves under the more watchful eyes of federal and local governments thanks to the wave of corporate scandals that led to tighter regulations such as Sarbanes-Oxley in the United States. At the same time, business processes are speeding up due to automation. Tracking every company financial transaction is no longer optional. It's mandatory.

Recording and reviewing every financial transaction is an enormous, time-consuming task. To make the task more manageable, CFOs and managers have begun to separate their core financial activities from their noncore financial activities and outsource the processes labeled noncore.

Contracts to handle standard, discrete processes in finance and accounting (F&A), such as accounts receivable, general ledger, billing, customer invoicing, and collections, have begun to pile up in the inboxes of best-practice providers.

F&A processes are migrating offshore rapidly. For multinational companies, offshoring F&A functions seems inevitable. Pioneers in F&A

offshoring utilized a captive shared services center business model to send many F&A functions to countries such as India.

- Ford Motor Company has more than 400 people in its business services center in Chennai, India, conducting accounting operations for Ford worldwide.

- Through e-Serve International, an offshore business processing outfit based in India formed by Citigroup in 1999, Citigroup employs approximately 3,000 people in Mumbai and Chennai, India, where they handle finance and loan processing. e-Serve supports Citigroup's operations in 25 countries from one global contact center, four call centers, and two global processing sites.

- GE Capital Services opened India's first service center in Delhi in 1993. Its 12,000 employees now handle accounting, claims processing, and credit evaluation services for more than 30 GE divisions.

- Deutsche Bank has set up a wholly owned subsidiary in Bangalore, India, for global cash operations and electronic payment processing. The Indian subsidiary processes payment transactions for Deutsche's entities including those located in New York, Frankfurt, London, and several Asian countries. Initially, the subsidiary has processed electronic payments in dollars, euros, and other currencies.

The number of F&A tasks that companies can offshore has grown exponentially as have the number of business model and country options. In this chapter, we look at the evolution of finance and accounting, the processes that constitute F&A, and three companies that have adopted F&A offshoring —British Airways, Alpha Industries, and Risk Management Alternatives — in order to give you insight into how this segment of offshoring works.

Why Are Companies Offshoring Their F&A Operations?

In his autobiography, Jack Welch credited Peter Drucker with the concept of taking one's back-room operations and making them someone else's front room. Welch wrote, "Back rooms by definition will never be able to attract your best. We converted ours into someone else's front room and insisted on getting their best."

The strategy espoused by Welch has become widely practiced. Rhodia, the $7.2 billion French maker of specialty chemicals, didn't hesitate to give Welch's strategy a try. In 2001, the company entered into a six-year contract with Accenture to transfer the bulk of its F&A functions to a shared services center in Prague. Rhodia's goal was to achieve improved performance and cost reductions across multiple countries.

Why Prague? Rhodia decided that moving to a Central European location where salaries and operational expenses are about three-fourths less than what they are in Western Europe was a sound business decision. The company laid off about 200 local employees and replaced them with Accenture's staff in Prague. The transition to the Prague shared services center was completed in phases (about 30–50 employees at a time), beginning in the United Kingdom and following with the French locations. By Rhodia's December 2002 target date, almost 90% of the transition, or knowledge transfer, had occurred. The lower cost of living and salaries in Prague should cut spending by 30% in two years and yield several millions in annual savings.[1]

Rhodia's F&A offshoring move is representative of many large firms. Fortune 1000 companies tend to regard F&A as part of the back room. Outsourcing it to a provider whose core competency is this very function means that better execution for both the client and provider is possible.

Firms are offshoring F&A for four reasons: cost, talent, availability, and technology. Cost is the primary reason why companies with high transaction volumes are sending their accounting work offshore. Companies with performance metrics in place to measure their gains report significant savings from offshoring F&A. They attribute their savings to salary differentials. For instance, the cost ratio of an Indian accounting professional and a U.S accounting professional is 1:10.

Another motive of countries electing to offshore F&A functions is advanced skill sets and talent that can handle the ever-changing regulatory requirements. Countries such as India, which have an abundant supply of accountants, are becoming a destination for F&A outsourcing. The average Indian accountant obtains significant hands-on experience before he becomes a CPA or CFA. He understands the basics of financial management and Generally Accepted Accounting Principles (GAAP) accounting thoroughly. In contrast, accounting talent is often in short supply in developed countries. Fewer college graduates are choosing an accounting career. In the United States, accounting departments struggle to retain lower-level staff. The availability of high-quality labor definitely helps offshore firms provide consistent, cost-effective service and achieve economies of scale.

A secondary driver of offshoring F&A is a desire to improve current service levels. Offshoring is often part of an overall restructuring program to improve the quality of accounting operations. The offshore F&A operating model appeals to executives not just because it provides the opportunity to cut costs, but also because it can reposition the F&A support organization. With offshoring, companies can finally move controllers from purely transaction-centric processes such as accounts payable (AP) and accounts receivable (AR) to more active work with line managers to improve cash flow and profitability.

Another factor that is making offshore F&A viable is the investment in single company-wide enterprise software platforms. Products such as SAP R/3, Oracle, and PeopleSoft have aided in the re-engineering of F&A processes, which has led to more consolidated, streamlined workflows. These applications are now enabling the next phase of cost reduction. With sophisticated Web applications and better security measures, new functions such as corporate finance, financial accounting, and management accounting can be moved offshore, especially if the firm is under significant cost reduction pressure.

A Brief Overview of Finance and Accounting

Accounting is almost as old as civilization. Accountants participated in the birth of cities, invented writing, and supervised the development of money and banking. During the Italian Renaissance, double-entry accounting was invented. Double-entry bookkeeping consists of a simple rule: Every debit must have a corresponding credit, and every credit a corresponding debit.

In 1494, Fra Luca Pacioli, the father of modern accounting, wrote *Summa*, a book devoted to record keeping and double-entry accounting. It laid out most of today's accounting routines, such as the use of memorandums, journals, and ledgers. His ledger included assets (receivables and inventories), liabilities, capital, income, and expense accounts. He described the year-end closing entries and proposed that a trial balance be used to prove a balanced ledger. There would be little modification to Pacioli's system for the next 500 years.

Accounting became more formal and organized in nineteenth-century Britain and twentieth-century America. Accountants, such as William Deloitte in 1845, set up shops named after their founding partners. It was the birth of the Big Eight.

In 1954, the accounting profession had its first encounter with digitization. Arthur Andersen's administrative services division computerized the payroll applications of a General Electric appliance division in Louisville, Kentucky. History books describe the delivery of the Universal Automatic Computer (Univac) to GE as the first installation of a mainframe computer at a business. It is said to have taken several trucks to transport the machine because the Univac weighed 30 tons.

For much of the seventies and eighties, the Big Eight accounting firms — Arthur Andersen, Coopers and Lybrand, Deloitte Haskins and Sells, Ernst and Whinney, Peat Marwick Mitchell, Price Waterhouse, Touche Ross, and Arthur Young — dominated the accounting landscape. In the mid-1980s, corporate merger mania took hold, and the Big Eight consolidated. Arthur Young melded with Ernst and Whinney, while Deloitte Haskins and Sells hooked up with Touche Ross, and Price Waterhouse merged with Coopers and Lybrand.

After the mergers, the accounting firms would never be the same. In the scandal that rocked the accounting world, Arthur Andersen was convicted of obstruction of justice for its role in the Enron debacle. The felony conviction meant the accounting giant could not submit audited financial statements to the SEC. This marked the end for Andersen. So the Big Eight dwindled to six, to five, and, currently, to four — PricewaterhouseCoopers, Ernst and Young, Deloitte and Touche, and KPMG.

The consolidation in the market place was paralleled by the consolidation within companies. During the 1990s, many companies adopted an internal shared services approach for F&A work, aggregating all divisions' finance and accounting processes in a separate center. By standardizing and centralizing F&A operations, companies were able to reduce head count and create a single administrative focus with a single set of information systems. The shared services model allowed individual management divisions to concentrate on their core competencies.

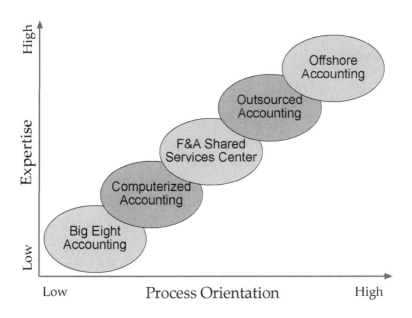

Figure 6.1: The Evolution of Finance and Accounting

In the late 1990s, the growth in internally managed shared services began to give way to direct outsourcing to external providers and to some interesting internal and external hybrids. For instance, travel company Thomas Cook AG, which has 14,500 employees and 1,000 locations worldwide, opened a new shared services center (SSC) in Peterborough, England, under a ten-year cosourcing agreement with Accenture. The agreement gives Thomas Cook's management full control over the center's strategy, policy, investment, and procurement, while responsibility for operational management rests with Accenture.

Many of the multinational firms that pioneered the SSC model are leading the way in F&A offshoring. These firms are moving core accounting and support operations to lower-cost offshore centers. For instance, American Express opened a shared services center in India to handle accounts receivable and payable, payroll, data capture, reconciliation, audit scheduling, and tax planning.

Many companies, as an offshoring first step, are utilizing "lift and drop" outsourcing or labor arbitrage that provides the first wave of savings by transferring processes "as is." The next step is to re-engineer processes and capture the value that offshoring is capable of delivering.

Offshoring F&A Processes

In this section, we delve into the specific accounting functions firms are sending offshore. In F&A, the A is offshored much more than the F. The difference exists largely because finance is more art than science, while accounting is more repetitive. Executives feel safer outsourcing generic accounting processes rather than operations that require analytical thinking. Modern accounting is characterized by standard procedures and an exacting attention to detail. While accounting requires expertise and systems, its constituent processes can be extremely repetitive, making it prone to human or system errors.

Commodity accounting tasks are often first in line for offshoring. They include accounts receivable, accounts payable, account management, reporting and analysis, compliance, and tax processing.

Accounts Receivable

Accounts receivable (AR) represents monies due by companies or individuals for products or services rendered. AR processes are responsible for billing services; suspense clearance (clearing any accounts that temporarily were used to record unclassified receipts and disbursements); encoding errors; and collections that are obtained through the invoicing of customers.

In October 2002, Time Warner Cable announced a multiyear service agreement with Convergys Corporation to operate and maintain its billing and customer care products. ICOMS (integrated communications operations management system) is Convergys's billing and customer care product that ensures cable companies accurate and flexible billing, a universal customer view, and the ability to cross-discount and cross-promote their products.

Accounts Payable

Accounts payable (AP) are the unpaid bills of the business; the money you owe to your suppliers and other creditors for goods and services received. AP transactions include: purchase orders (POs) and non-PO invoices, freight payments, consolidated statements, EDI transactions, phone bills, utility payments, prepayments, check requests, purchasing cards, employee and non-employee travel and entertainment expense reimbursements, debit/credit memos, check returns, check print and distribution, and ACH transactions.

The AP process involves settlement of vendor invoices across multiple locations, entities, and currencies. Typically invoices are scanned using imaging software in the country of origin. The images are retrieved using high-speed digital links in the offshore location. The invoice approvals are completed using a Web-based workflow system. Once approval is given, checks are printed in the local country and disbursed.

Consider a common AP scenario: A multinational firm wanted to reduce its overall operating costs. It sought a vendor that could provide quality back-office services for its AP management process at service levels similar to its in-house capability but at a cheaper cost. The firm's internal service center could not handle the process volumes and maintain the same level of service due to ongoing attrition of its workforce. The firm wanted the vendor to manage volumes at better service levels (even when they spiked by 10%), achieve a 30% reduction in overall costs, provide output with a negligible defect rate, give daily reports to the control group, and meet its information security requirements.

Account Management

Account management comprises the core functions that balance the books. The typical functions in account management include general accounting, bookkeeping, creditor management, financial reconciliation, fixed asset and liability accounting, and expense accounting.

In 2001, General Motors Corporation (GM) entered into a ten-year agreement with Affiliated Computer Services (ACS) to outsource a collection of F&A functions for North America and Europe. GM wanted to achieve considerable cost reductions and improve control. ACS services GM from centers in Arizona, Jamaica, and Spain. In order to ensure the quality of ACS's work, GM monitors the service level agreements, desk procedures, internal and external audits, onsite quality assurance teams, segregation of duties, delegation of authority, and process risk validations.

In April 2003, the North Carolina Department of Health and Human Services outsourced its electronic benefits transfer (EBT) services to eFunds Corporation. Under the contract, eFunds handles the electronic distribution of food stamp programs, including transaction processing, reporting, contract management, settlement, operations support, help desk services, and project management. In turn, eFunds, for cost reasons, sends the work to five offshore service centers it owns in India.

Regulatory Reporting and Analysis

Reporting and financial analysis has two components: internal reporting and external reporting. Internal reporting centers on financial information used by management as a basis for business decisions. External reporting revolves around disclosure and transparency to investors, regulators, and financial markets.

The typical tasks in reporting include: sales tax filing, statutory reporting, financial statement analysis, financial reporting, management report preparation, external reporting and shareholder services, and budgeting and forecasting.

The recent Sarbanes-Oxley Act shortens the period for preparing external reports, which could encourage accounting outsourcing. Large multinationals already need up to an extra month after they process transactions to collect and consolidate data for external reports. With the Sarbanes-Oxley ruling, companies legally have to issue reports more quickly, so they may look to outsourcers to help them meet the new federal regulations.

Compliance and Tax Processing

Corporations have to regularly file multiple tax documents. These documents include: general ledger posting reports, quarterly local tax returns, federal tax returns, W-2 forms for all employees, W-2 state withholding recaps, W-3 federal withholding recaps, year-end local tax reconciliations, and form 940 federal unemployment tax returns.

Procter & Gamble was one of the early adopters of offshore tax processing. The corporation has approximately 650 employees in Manila, the Philippines, who help prepare P&G's tax returns around the world. All the processing can be done in the Philippines, with just the final return submitted locally to the various tax authorities.

Accounting firms like Ernst & Young are exploring sending U.S. corporate tax returns to India. Even the smaller CPA firms are getting into the act. In March 2003, Boston-based CPA firm Rucci, Bardaro & Barrett (RBB) contracted Outsource Partners International (OPI), a provider of tax solutions, to take care of up to 70% of its tax returns processing. Under the arrangement, OPI will utilize its offshore processing center in India to provide RBB with completed tax returns, as well as Web-enabled digitized document management.

Offshore F&A Case Study: British Airways

Some companies choose to build offshore shared services centers (SSCs) internally, whereas others elect to partially or fully outsource their creation. British Airways PLC (BA) chose the former. The airline is widely regarded as a leading F&A player and one that pioneered the offshore model in the mid-1990s. BA has leveraged the offshore F&A model to drive down business costs and to generate incremental revenues.

British Airways Overview

British Airways is one of the world's largest airlines, ferrying 30 million passengers from one country to another annually. From hubs in London's Heathrow and Gatwick airports, the airline flies to 220 destinations in 94 countries. BA employs about 61,500 people worldwide.

The airline has a variety of F&A processes:

1. **Financial accounting** processes deal with the preparation of financial statements. Financial statements are standardized reports that airlines prepare for external parties such as shareholders.

2. **Management accounting** processes prepare information for internal use by airline managers in making decisions about the current and future activities of their organizations. They support a wide variety of managerial decisions.

3. **Financial supply chain management** processes enable collaboration within airlines and within their business networks by using defined business policies and shared services to handle all customer-related and supply chain–related financials.

4. **Revenue accounting** processes deal with the capturing, checking, and charging of flight coupons sold and flown worldwide. The coupon data represents actual revenues, which form the basis for accounting.

5. **Route profitability** processes cover all aspects of airline route profitability analysis, from single route aircraft economics to long-term network forecasting.

Moving from an In-House Model to an Offshore Model

The year was 1996, and BA was flying high. It reported record profits of £585 million for 1995–96, and stated in its annual report that its "financial results continue to set the standards for the industry." BA's stock value was rising. The company was celebrating its tenth anniversary of its journey from a state-run to a privately run business. There could not have been a more prosperous time in the history of BA. Yet in a gutsy move, the leadership, under CEO Robert Ayling, decided to transform the company — this time to position BA for the next millennium as the leader in an increasingly competitive market.

Unveiling the transformation plans for BA to employees, Ayling said, "To be a success in the next century, we have to bear in mind the transformation we achieved in the past and then do it all over again. Just as we created a new BA for privatization, we have to create a new BA for the new millennium."[2]

What spurred the bold decision to change? Ayling and his team sensed rapid shifts in the market in which they operated. They noted a few key trends: growing and more efficient competition, rising unit costs, more demanding customers, and decreasing yields. BA's management responded with a strategy that centered on cost reduction and labeled it the Business Efficiency Program.

The Business Efficiency Program

The Business Efficiency Program was the strategic plan for BA's second transformation for 2000 and covered virtually every aspect of business. As a "step change" efficiency drive — BA had cut its business costs by £900 million in the previous five years — it called for aggressive measures such as eliminating 5,000 jobs and selling or subcontracting some activities. The goals of the program were to meet new market and customer needs, restructure the workforce to ensure that it was equipped with the right skills, and achieve £1 billion in efficiencies.

Cutting £1 Billion in Costs. As part of the program, managers were asked to implement cost-cutting plans to improve efficiency. They were given performance and cost targets to bring operations in line with competitive prices. Ultimately, BA would consider selling or subcontracting activities if they could be done better or more cheaply externally. Some loss-making activities would be jettisoned. One of the first to go was the contract-handling unit at London Heathrow. It provided ticketing, check in, cargo, loading, and ramp handling services for 25 other airlines. The unit was facing stiff competition from eight other contract-handling firms and reported consistent losses. All 750 of its staff were offered voluntary retirement with severance pay or redeployment and retraining within the airline.

As part of the exercise, ticket processing, passenger revenue accounting (PRA), and other finance department processes were reviewed. This is how BA had the idea to offshore its PRA processes to India.

Offshoring Passenger Revenue Accounting

BA noted that its competitors had already transferred activities overseas, driven by the significant cost savings possible. Swiss Airlines, which hit on the idea in 1991, was one of the first to offshore account activities. Its operation in Mumbai, India, handles revenue accounting and frequent flier administration. The airlines that had dared to try offshoring talked about net annual savings being as high as 50%.[3]

BA realized it could not continue to compete effectively in the airline industry without changes. To bring costs in line with other airlines, it decided in November 1996 to eliminate 600 accounting jobs, more than half of the 1,100 U.K. workers in its PRA unit, over a period of three years. BA offered the affected employees the same options as it offered the employees in the contract-handling unit.

The PRA division handled accounting and ticket sales revenues for BA worldwide and for some partner and franchise activities. It also arranged all inter-airline billings. BA decided that half of the 600 jobs would become obsolete through process automation, while another third, or 200 jobs, would be transferred to India.

The World Network Services Offshore Captive Center

In November 1996, BA created 200 accounting jobs in its fully owned subsidiary in Mumbai, India, called World Network Services (WNS) Private Limited. (British Airways spun off WNS in February 2002.)

In its business case, BA expected to save £10 million, or $14 million, annually from eliminating 600 PRA jobs and transferring 200 to WNS.[4] The airline noted it could hire better employees in India for 20% of what they cost in the United Kingdom. The initial investment in WNS amounted to £1 million, and it was earmarked for total infrastructure and equipment.[5]

At the time, WNS had a high-quality office environment with 350 desks for nearly 1,000 staff working three shifts. The company employed only English-speaking graduates who had full access to the BA mainframe via a data pipe to London. It maintained a 100% uninterruptible power supply (UPS) and power generator backup that operated 24x7.[6]

WNS evolved in scope quickly. By 1999, it began to handle an array of back-office administrative processes for BA, including customer relations (handling complaint letters rather than phone calls), dealing with errors in the reservation systems, and keeping track of frequent flier miles.

The benefits of WNS were beginning to show in several areas. For example, the delays in answering complaint letters were reduced from more than two weeks to less than three days owing to multiple shifts. BA was even able to manage a peak in volumes during a cabin-crew strike in July 1997 by transferring the cancellation and rebooking of all reservations to WNS, meeting the short but significant demand by cross-training from other teams and volunteering staff for overtime.[7]

BA's offshore delivery model continued to evolve, changing from a cost center into a profit center. WNS became so efficient that it began undertaking this work for other airlines, which produced additional revenue streams for BA. By 1999, WNS obtained about 65% of its revenues from BA and 35% from other airlines, including Cathay Pacific, Canadian, and American Airlines.

Sensing growth opportunities, WNS expanded its operations, setting up a second site in Pune, India, in 1999 with an investment of £1.3 million. The site provides IT, administrative, and office support services to companies across the globe primarily in the transport and finance industries. The site served as a backup for the disaster recovery arm of Mumbai and vice versa.

The Economics of F&A Offshoring

BA enjoys a tremendous return on its investment in WNS. With the cost arbitrage between U.K. and Indian salaries, the airline saves about £2.6 million per year for the 200 accounting jobs it moved to WNS. Furthermore, there are improvements in revenue recovery.

To understand the revenue recovery savings better, let's look at the underlying process. Through coupon matching, WNS recovers money due from services provided to passengers traveling on BA. Coupon matching is the last link in the chain of money recovery process of passenger revenue accounting, or PRA. WNS also investigates and monitors any fraudulent activity and maintains the integrity of the revenue audit base.

First WNS receives a report of all unmatched used tickets. WNS holds these tickets in the system for three months to check if sale proceeds are delayed. Then it divides the actionable tickets into two types: prime and reject. Prime tickets require investigation to identify if revenue recovery is necessary through documentation. If so, WNS researches the prime tickets and prepares billing documents to recover revenues. The respective agent or passenger account is then debited.

A reject refers to a prime ticket that has already been billed but was disputed by the recipient of the bill (agents or credit card companies). In such cases, WNS acts on any rejection claims. The U.K. PRA unit prints and dispatches finalized accounting documents and letters. A workflow system allows efficient and speedy transfer of information between the United Kingdom and WNS, allowing the processing of passenger revenues in both countries.

WNS clears the unmatched tickets with a 98.5% level of accuracy. It clears prime tickets at an hourly rate that is 30% above the rate stipulated in the SLA.[8] Given these efficiency improvements and using some baseline assumptions (see figure 6.2), we estimate that BA recovers an additional £9 million per year in revenues for the 200 jobs moved. Together with the cost savings, we conclude the net savings to BA to be about £12 million per year, or $17 million per year.

BA also derives some intangible benefits from WNS. The training periods are shorter because the Indian staff has higher levels of education than its U.K. counterparts. Perhaps the most interesting of the additional benefits is that the size of the team providing the coupon matching service was reduced by half since inception due to agents' high productivity and process improvements. At present, WNS clears 100,000 prime tickets and 8,000 reject tickets annually. In 2002, the revenues recovered by WNS were £14.73 million, 20% more than the SLA stipulated.[9]

Variables	Before	After
Number of Accounts	200	200
Average annual salary	X_{salary}	$0.2\ X_{salary}$
Average time to clear per prime ticket	Y_{time}	$Y_{time}\ /1.3$
Level of accuracy in clearing prime tickets	90.0%	98.5%
Average revenue recovered per prime ticket	£150	£150
X_{salary} = £16,000 Y_{time} = 2.5 hours		

Savings from Cheaper Labor

Net savings per year   = 200*(0.8* £16,000)   = £2.6M

Improved Revenue Recovery from Higher Quality Work

(Before) Tickets cleared/year = 200*(0.9*(0.4*2000))   = 144,000
(After)   Tickets cleared/year = 200*(0.985*(1.3*0.4*2000))   = 204,880
(Before) Revenue recovered = 144,000* £150   = £21.6M
(After)   Revenue recovered = 204,880* £150   = £30.7M

Potential Savings per Year for 200 Jobs = 2.6 + (30.7- 21.6) = £11.7M ($16.6M)

Figure 6.2: Estimated Savings from Offshore Passenger Revenue Accounting

Commercializing World Network Services

WNS's future strategy required further investment to fully exploit the growing client base. To ensure that WNS capitalized on the rapid market growth, in 2002, BA sold a 70% stake in it to Warburg Pincus, a venture capital firm. The sale allowed BA to maintain a meaningful stake, while pursuing its strategy to focus on core its business.

By the time Warburg Pincus bought its stake, WNS was flourishing in its role of third-party BPO provider. It employed 1,400 people at its two centers in Mumbai and Pune. It reported 120% growth and $33.5 million in revenues in 2002–2003, its first year as an independent company. Currently, 60% of WNS's revenues come from 12 airline clients, and the BPO provider expects the airline sector to continue to contribute a significant portion of its future revenues. Other than BA, customers include Federal Express and Royal & SunAlliance.

The ability to see "the forest through the trees" separates industry leaders such as BA from the rest of the competition. By forcing itself to take a long-term view, evaluate its cost structure, and slash costs even in heady times, BA emerged a leader in leveraging offshore outsourcing to create growth opportunities for itself in an unconventional manner.

Offshore F&A Case Study: Alpha Industries

Now that we have discussed captive centers, let's look at an Ephinay Corporation case study that illustrates the inner workings of an onshore-offshore F&A model. Ephinay is an emerging venture capital–backed service provider exclusively focused on F&A solutions for Fortune 2000 companies. The corporation provides F&A outsourcing using a "multishore" combination with offshore and onshore delivery. Service centers are located in Phoenix, Arizona, and New Delhi, India, with headquarters in Charlotte, North Carolina.

Ephinay's first customer was a multinational Fortune 100 company that we will call Alpha Industries.[10] Alpha is a conglomerate that is involved in agricultural, food, financial, and industrial products and services. In the early 1990s, Alpha realized that it had to consolidate and integrate many discreet F&A subprocesses in ways that provided better control and were more cost-effective.

Creating a Shared Services Center

In the mid-1990s, Alpha decided to streamline its global accounting operations and procedures. It established a series of shared financial service centers in the United States, United Kingdom, Singapore, Australia, and France that would handle financial transactions for its respective geographies. The objective was to create an organizational model that enabled better service delivery complemented by the economies of scale offered by centralization.

To serve its U.S. businesses, Alpha invested around $5 million to set up a shared services center in a low-cost state. This center consolidated basic accounting functions for the region, in this case North America. However, instead of pulling existing accounting employees from the various scattered North American locations, Alpha created 115 new financial service jobs and directed its existing accounting employees in other locations to concentrate on performing special needs analysis and reporting while providing guidance on day-to-day accounting operations.

The center started off handling routine accounting procedures for ten lines of business in more than 100 locations. The routine procedures included accounts payable, accounts receivable, credits and collections, travel and expense reporting, and general accounting functions using electronic data interface (EDI) technology. By the end of 1997, the center had scaled up to assume responsibility for all of the North American product lines.

Offshore Outsourcing of Accounts Payable

Fast forward to 2002. Alpha wasn't ready to concede that it was finished looking for cost savings. When Ephinay approached Alpha with a proposal to not only cut costs further, but also improve quality of service and raise productivity, Alpha was intrigued.

Ephinay President Michael D. Gantt states, "Our value proposition is more than just labor arbitrage. We're offering a level of quality that leads to productivity for the customer. There's an element of dependability — particularly in finance and accounting — that is very important. Offshore players who think that they can just come in and offer to do something cheaply are going to find it hard to get business."[11]

Ephinay proposed that Alpha move some of its F&A processes, including accounts payable, to New Delhi, India. Alpha accepted the proposal, which is notable in itself because, as Andy Kankan, founder and executive vice president at Ephinay, observes, "An average finance controller or CFO, while he will always encourage other areas of operations to be outsourced, whether it's HR or some other area, is very, very conservative as far as his own operation goes."[12]

Ephinay began transitioning the processes over and applying its Six Sigma and process expertise to achieve the improvement objectives. As many BPO providers like to point out, where there is no quality, there is no cost advantage. Kankan led the transition team on its initial visit to the Alpha site. He explained that the team's mission was to "...identify the process steps, [examine] how the process would work if it was taken to a different location, [understand] whether it could be decoupled, what the linkages were, and whether technology would allow it to operate efficiently or not."[13]

The transition team's investigation yielded a positive case for moving some of Alpha's F&A processes offshore. Ephinay moved quickly. The Ephinay project managers and analysts visited the Alpha site in October. By February of the next year, they went live, and Ephinay began processing the first of what would turn out to be 450,000 invoices annually worth over $5 billion.

As a BPO provider to Alpha, Ephinay provides voucher processing, sales tax processing, and reporting services to Alpha's 21 business units. Ephinay's employees in New Delhi are responsible for ensuring that Alpha's many suppliers and vendors are paid correctly, in a timely manner, in accordance with various laws and procedures, and that they are easily able to identify the payment.

Sales tax processing is no less involved. When a business unit in a particular state purchases tangible goods, depending on the state, the supplier or vendor is required to pay a sales tax on the purchase. This simple requirement creates work for Alpha. When Alpha's AP unit receives the invoice, bill, or other payment request from the payee or vendor, it must review the vendor invoice and address two simple questions: Were tangible goods purchased? If yes, does the vendor collect the appropriate sales tax?

The sales tax issue becomes a legal responsibility and even a liability. How? When the vendor does not have a presence in the state, state governments shift the responsibility for reporting and paying sales tax from the vendor to the purchaser, Alpha in this case. The tax is referred to as use tax and includes both the basic state tax and district tax imposed by some counties. There are occasions when direct payments for tangible goods are processed and sales/use tax is not collected by the vendor. The purchaser, Alpha, is liable for the uncollected sales/use tax, and monthly payments are processed directly to the state by accounts payable.

As you can see, the services (verifications, calculations, checks, and procedures) that offshore outsourcing is delivering can be quite complicated.

Alpha's Return on Investment

The benefits to Alpha from the offshore services that Ephinay delivers include:

- Back-office costs that dropped by 60%;

- Six Sigma quality improvements in accuracy and cycle time;

- Enhanced control of financial processes; and

- New performance measures to monitor process results.

Last but not least, Ephinay is helping Alpha meet one of its primary objectives for offshore outsourcing: the creation of a blended delivery model and capacity for business expansion.

Offshore F&A Case Study: RMA

The British Airways case study illustrated a captive center model while Alpha illustrated an onshore-offshore blended model. To round off the discussion, let's look at a pure offshore outsourcing model in F&A. Risk Management Alternatives (RMA), a third-party debt collector based in the United States, has considerable experience leveraging F&A offshoring.

RMA presents an interesting F&A case study for two reasons:

1. In an interesting twist, RMA exemplifies the trend of outsourcing firms adopting offshoring to lower their cost structures; and

2. RMA proves that offshore outsourcing is not reserved strictly for the big companies. Small and midsize players are also offshoring.

RMA Overview

Operating out of Atlanta, Georgia, RMA is an outsourcing provider that helps companies with debt collection, accounts receivable management, and call center services. RMA was formed in 1996 and employs more than 4,000 professionals throughout the United States and international markets.

RMA's clients include major credit card issuers, telecom and utility companies, automobile finance companies, healthcare providers, and government agencies. The company's services help clients improve their operating performance by improving their cash flow, operating expenses, customer service, and retention.

Overview of the Debt Collection Industry

Have you ever received a call from your credit card company reminding you to pay your overdue account? If so, then you have encountered a not-so-commonly-known but huge service industry called debt collection.

At a basic level, the industry exists because people owe money. Credit grantors — credit card issuers, banks, car dealers, or retail stores — extend credit or offer payment installment plans to customers (consumers and commercial). Sometimes those customers fail to keep their end of the bargain and do not pay on time or at all.

Financial claims against customers for services, products, fines, loans, taxes, and other assessments for which payment has not been received are known as receivables. A receivable becomes a debt or delinquency when it is overdue or outstanding. Management of receivables, including debt collections, is an important function for a firm's internal liquidity.

Given its importance to companies' overall financial health and the fact that it's not easy to collect debts, executives often look to external expertise in the form of outsourcing providers to assume responsibility of receivables management. While some smaller firms outsource the entire receivables management process to a service provider, more firms choose to outsource only certain portions, such as debt collection.

To reduce debt collection costs, outsourcing firms are setting up operations in offshore locations such as India and the Philippines. Credit grantors and first-party and third-party collections agencies are looking closely at countries like India to handle a growing amount of U.S. consumer and commercial debt.

First-Party and Third-Party Collections

Figure 6.3 shows the transformation of a receivable into a debt and the phases thereafter. Debt more than 30 days past due is commonly called early-stage delinquency. Debt more than 90 days past due is termed late-stage delinquency. If even more time passes by and the debt remains uncollected, firms will write off the money owed as a tax-deductible expense. The debt is then called bad debt.

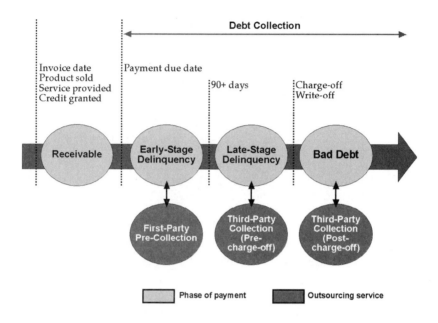

Figure 6.3: The Debt Collection Process

Figure 6.3 also charts different debt-focused outsourcing services available to credit grantors. In relation to outsourcing, the credit grantor is the first party; the debtor or the customer that owes money is the second; and the collection agency is the third.

In "early out," first-party, or precollection outsourcing, the collection agency helps with early-stage delinquencies. It contacts recently delinquent customers of credit grantors as the first party and solicits payments in a courteous manner. A relatively simple task, first-party contact is about reminding and resolving accounts, bringing in "easy money" without jeopardizing customer goodwill, and ultimately reducing the number of accounts that reach bad debt status.

In third-party collection service, an agency works with late-stage delinquencies in which accounts are unpaid for an average of eight months and the creditor has not received payment from the customer.

Figure 6.4 shows how this service works. Often creditors cannot locate customers who have moved or changed their phone numbers. The agency first obtains the customer's current address or phone number through a process called skip tracing. It then sends the customer a notice that allows her to dispute the debt or request verification of the debt.

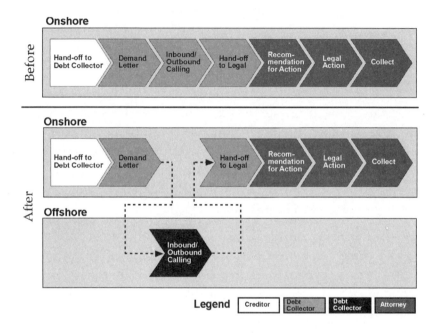

Figure 6.4: Offshore Outsourcing in Third-Party Collections

Once the customer is believed to have received the notice, the collector may call or write to the customer and demand full payment of the debt. If full payment is not possible, the collector helps the customer make arrangements to solve the problem. If the debtor does not cooperate, the collector will forward the debt to a collection agency and work with attorneys for legal action.

Collection agencies lend credibility and strength to the collections effort with a "third-party" authority. When debtors see that a creditor is using a third-party collector, they know the creditor is serious about recovering its money. In many cases, the debtor will respond with payment as soon as the debt collector contacts them because they know the debt collector will follow through until the debt is satisfied. However, the Fair Debt Collection Practices Act (FDCPA) directly regulates third-party collectors, setting forth strict guidelines designed to protect consumers from abusive, misleading, and unfair debt collection practices.

Offshoring the Collection of Early-Stage Delinquencies

Using technology, process improvements, and skill specialization, RMA reduces costs for credit grantors by up to 10%. But cost savings achieved through domestic outsourcing cannot be improved any further due to high labor costs and the significant amount of manual processing required for receivables management.

With clients demanding more savings and productivity, debt collectors are looking offshore. RMA has responded to this market need. At the request of one of its largest credit card customers, the company began operations in India in 2001 for collections of early-stage delinquencies. It established a multiyear partnership with eFunds Corporation, a provider of electronic payment and risk management.

eFunds, a business unit of Deluxe Corporation, uses its resources in India to provide telephone support for RMA's accounts receivable clients. eFunds operates two facilities in India — a 50,000-square-foot, 350-seat center in New Delhi and a 32,000-square-foot, 300-seat facility in Mumbai. These facilities are equipped with the latest technology and telecom systems and provide 100% infrastructure redundancies to ensure the systems are operational 24x7.[14]

Challenges of Offshoring Collections

Despite the tremendous potential, collecting U.S. debt overseas can be fraught with pitfalls. It can be difficult to find good overseas partners and to train foreign collectors to call U.S. customers. Cultural differences and foreign accents also present hurdles in offshoring debt collection. Lastly, it's challenging for offshore debt collectors to remain competitive while maintaining quality. Overpromising clients and then being unable to deliver on those promises is not uncommon.

RMA has struggled with the last of these pitfalls in particular. It is finding that cost savings overseas don't necessarily translate into higher profits. With offshoring, clients will demand price reductions; the amount of the discount demanded often depends on the size of the client. RMA passes the savings on to the client when it provides these discounts. The company hopes to retain its margins, but will lose money from the top line as total revenues shrink.

Thus far, RMA has sent easy work overseas. The calls are early-stage collections or reminder calls that do not require a lot of experience to handle. The main reason for delegating these kinds of calls to India is that India has a very polite society unfamiliar with the aggressive nature of collections calls. With experience, RMA likely will begin sending the really tough work overseas, that is, the late-stage delinquencies. We expect the first step in offshoring debt collection to be the migration of inbound/outbound calling offshore. Eventually, we expect the more complex pieces of the process, such as skip tracing, to be shipped offshore as well.

How to Create a Business Case for Offshoring F&A

Now that you have read what British Airways, Alpha Industries, and RMA have accomplished in the F&A offshore area, it is time to ask yourself what your organization's strategy for F&A processes is. Does F&A offshore outsourcing make sense for your organization?

The Strategic Context: Challenges Facing Your Firm

Four major changes are taking place in the finance function. First, processes are being embedded in enterprise applications like SAP. General ledger, accounts payable, and accounts receivable processes have been digitized and standardized. Now they can be managed around the world seamlessly. Even the higher-order processes, such as forecasting and budget planning, are being automated.

Second, technology is allowing finance organizations to become virtual. Financial staff do not need to be in the same city any longer. Companies can have multiple locations, all of them interconnected.

Third, management of information is becoming critically important. Digitization, globalization, and process standardization have increased the speed of business so dramatically that CFOs must understand their businesses better. This is a major initiative among CFOs: a stronger grasp of the information their companies possess.

Fourth, finance is strengthening its fiduciary role to manage risk and opportunity. Companies are confronting increasing regulatory scrutiny. They are less concerned about general ledger and more concerned about compliance. In the past, CFOs were the controllers — the cops — ensuring that the books were right. Now, technology fulfills this role, so CFOs must ensure that the controls are right, not only for the assets on the books but also for the assets off the books.

In this networked economy where shareholder value is critical and it is easier to handle the financial work outside the boundaries of the firm, CFOs are realizing that outsourcing and offshoring can play a role in managing the financial health of their companies. In order to reduce costs, they must offload some financial work to specialists. The next step in your offshore journey is to determine which F&A processes you consider core and noncore.

Which F&A Processes to Retain and Which to Offshore

Within the area of F&A, no one task is best suited for offshore outsourcing. The tasks that companies should start with are those that would bring them the most immediate benefits. For one company, the process could be in accounts receivable where managers know quality improvements would improve their DSO (days sales outstanding). For another company, it might be accounts payable that could benefit from offshoring. For yet another company, it might be reconciling accounts born of multiple acquisitions. The starting places are endless.

Having said that, typically the first functions firms set aside to be offshored are commodity processes, such as accounts receivable and payable, which entail minimal company-specific knowledge and do not differentiate the company from its competitors. Some companies that have gained confidence in offshoring are starting to outsource management reporting. Budgeting and forecasting are activities that are still not quite ready to be offshored.

Executives are more comfortable outsourcing repetitive, generic finance processes than operations requiring higher level analytical thinking. Where companies tend to draw the line, however, is at outsourcing finance policy setting and management judgment. Strategic finance decisions will always remain in-house

Figure 6.5 describes the finance and accounting processes as a pyramid with four tiers. The first tier covers transactional activities such as accounts receivable and payable; the second handles financial and management accounting; the third covers financial decision making; the fourth is responsible for strategy and policy.

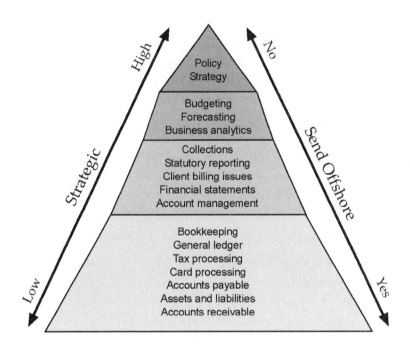

Figure 6.5: Core versus Noncore F&A Processes

Tiers one and two often account for 80% of a company's finance head count. Most of the first tier is outsourced, whereas the activities of the second tier — cash management, reconciliation of cash, and statutory reporting — are run through a shared services center. Many companies have considered offshoring the first and second tiers, but have not yet embraced sending the third and fourth tiers offshore. The logic is based on the reality that companies cannot outsource or offshore the thinking, but they can outsource the high-volume, repetitive, vanilla type of transactions to get economies of scale.

There are always exceptions to the rule. Pioneers such as GE are pushing the boundaries past basic accounting transactions to include budgeting, forecasting, and business analytics. In order to reap offshoring's benefits, companies need to plan and source carefully. Making the transition to an arrangement that reduces costs over the long term often requires substantial management commitment and time.

After a core versus noncore capability and application assessment, a detailed cost benefit analysis of the functions being offshored is key to any successful business case.

Developing the Financial Justification

Once you have identified the F&A processes or tasks that are candidates for offshoring, you need to generate a proposal for outsourcing based on gaining definite, measurable business benefits. Let's look at the benefits, costs, and risks of F&A offshore outsourcing in more detail.

Tangible Benefits of Offshore F&A

Offshore F&A delivers two distinct tangible or measurable benefits: operating cost savings and lowered capital investment.

Cost Reduction. Many corporate, back-office cost reduction initiatives first seek to consolidate activities to achieve economies of scale. This consolidation is normally associated with business process re-engineering (BPR), or reducing the number of unnecessary processes and resources. However, with BPR, only gradual cost reductions are normally possible through careful resource optimization by skilled process managers. With lower labor wages, offshore outsourcing could offer savings of 25% or more on existing processes and payback well within the first year. Several companies have opted to sell their shared services centers and switch to an offshore outsourcing strategy.

Reduced Capital Investment. Offshore outsourcing providers have state-of-the-art shared services centers that are designed to service international clients. The centers utilize good connectivity, workflow solutions, and 24x7 delivery capability. By outsourcing to such providers, companies can expect to save significant investments necessary to set up shared services centers.

Intangible Benefits of Offshore F&A

Some benefits of offshore F&A, such as service quality improvements, an increased focus on core competencies, skilled, qualified staff, and improved productivity cannot be measured directly but indisputably contribute to the case for offshoring.

Service Quality Improvements. Offshore outsourcing providers focus on using technology to provide cutting-edge processes. They add technology to their industry experience, process knowledge, and outsourcing operational practices to deliver a superior service solution. Staff members are well versed in process improvement techniques such as Six Sigma. Their culture is customer service–oriented, resulting in an organization that is committed to delivering world-class services that enhance customer profitability and control.

Core Business Focus. Financial executives should focus on strategic issues facing their companies, but in reality, they spend much of their time on administrative details such as budgeting, cash flow management, and transaction processing tasks. In fact, we estimate that CFOs spend 80% of their time on the day-to-day operations, leaving only 20% for the strategic planning and decision making that is imperative to company growth. Offshore outsourcing gives F&A managers the freedom to focus on core competencies and strategic issues rather than on routine, time-consuming activities.

Qualified Staff. Management responsible for existing shared services centers often encounter trouble recruiting and retaining staff. This is especially true in locations populated by many shared services centers where tight labor markets and salary pressure are a fact of life.

Offshore outsourcing providers attract and motivate skille employees. They support teams with employees of all types — technical, data entry, and administrative; thus, clients have access to accountants dedicated to operating and improving their processes.

For example, most Indian providers dealing with F&A outsourcing have a base of skilled professionals. The minimum entry standard is graduates, usually with a Bachelor of Commerce degree. These graduates speak English and are familiar with U.K./U.S. Generally Accepted Accounting Principles (GAAP). In addition, most supervisors have chartered accountant (CA) qualifications which is the equivalent to a U.S. CPA.

Improved Productivity. Offshore outsourcing can help improve productivity of existing staff. Take U.S. CPA firms, for instance, which are constantly looking for ways to both improve the productivity of their highly skilled personnel and reduce costs. Tax return preparation is a challenge for them. It is a highly seasonal and low-margin service. During the tax season, CPA firms work their permanent tax staffs 80-plus hours each week and employ temporary personnel who often have little or outdated knowledge of current tax law.

Offshore outsourcing can help CPA firms survive this hectic period. The tax preparation process involves three activities: consulting with the client; entering disparate pieces of information and records provided by a client into a tax software system; and reviewing the information for accuracy, completeness, and compliance with the law. Today, temporary personnel and overtime-working regular tax staff perform the second activity, but sending it offshore would free junior staff members to apply their knowledge more meaningfully, reduce costs, improve morale, and enable firms to deliver a higher quality of service.

Instead of spending long hours engaged in populating tax returns, staff members could apply the tax laws and their analytical skills, and consult with clients in a more meaningful, less frenzied manner. The quality of offshore work is commensurate with or better than onshore alternatives. Lower labor rates enable double- or triple-checking for errors. Therefore, a firm's reviewers in the United States can focus on substance instead of checking for and correcting data entry errors.

Strategic Benefits of Offshore F&A

Offshore outsourcing can also provide the following strategic benefits.

Business Process Transformation. Business process offshoring is a vehicle for achieving the greater target of business process transformation. Consider the benefits of offshoring: economies of scale of the shared services center, the technology and experience of the vendor, and higher-quality service. Is it any wonder that companies see outsourcing as a strategic weapon for change? The key to successfully offshoring F&A appears to be re-engineering processes before venturing offshore.

While the majority of early F&A outsourcing deals centered on transaction processing, customers now want BPO providers to manage the business process from soup-to-nuts. They realize outsourcing can take them beyond what they can achieve themselves.

Outsourcing brings an outsider's discipline to reviewing and reshaping entire business processes, helping companies execute ambitious improvement and growth plans.

Costs of Offshore F&A

In addition to the benefits we outlined, there are, of course, costs involved in offshoring your F&A processes.

One-Time and Recurring Transition Costs. When you send your financial processes to an offshore provider's shared services center, expect to incur one-time transition costs. They include lease terminations, employee severance, disposal of current assets, and connectivity costs. In addition, there are ongoing costs for telecommunications, operations, and program management.

Coordination Costs. A common misconception is that once the service providers are chosen and the contract is complete, the bulk of the work is done. Although correctly choosing a vendor and developing a solid contract is critical, the importance of the company's role after the first phase is often underemphasized. Coordination issues could arise as a result of insufficient direction, cultural differences, lack of communication, inadequate management of projects, and differences in the way projects are structured.

Hidden Costs. Hidden costs also lurk within F&A offshoring. The most important problems stem from relationships that are not well thought out before the deals are sealed. The CFO, for example, should have a clear understanding of what her company will owe if it decides to exit the relationship or move some of the work to another vendor. Companies should also consider their intellectual property rights.

Summary

Finance and accounting processes, often relegated to a supporting role, are suddenly in the spotlight. The reasons: Investors are demanding a higher level of transparency; the SEC is asking for accelerated reporting; and internal stakeholders are seeking better decision support information. As a result, there is renewed energy around better management of costs, information timeliness and accuracy, and working capital improvement.

To address the demands of these internal and external parties, finance organizations should consider offshore outsourcing as a key element of their overall strategy. Examples of F&A offshoring include cash management, mortgage origination, and lending in banking; trade support and settlement, custody, and accounting in capital markets; and claims processing, policy administration, and sales and marketing in insurance.

F&A offshore strategies have helped many companies such as British Airways and Citibank sharpen their focus on core capabilities. Collaborating with the right global BPO partner will allow companies to reap the benefits of offshoring and fend off competitive challenges.

Finally, thanks to the relentless pressure to cut costs, reduce capital outlays, and maximize operational efficiencies, we expect the demand for F&A offshoring to exceed that of many other processes for the foreseeable future. Technology and telecommunications advances are constantly reducing the barrier of physical proximity for outsourcer and provider, fueling the growth and evolution in offshore delivery of F&A services.

Chapter Seven

Human Resources
Offshore Outsourcing

*"Every organization of today has to build into its very
structure the management of change."*

— Peter Drucker

Introduction

Human resources (HR) is a complex but necessary business function
that consists of many processes such as payroll, recruitment, hiring,
training, change management, career development, benefits management,
employee assistance programs, executive compensation, as well as health,
safety, and regulatory compliance. More sophisticated firms have begun
migrating some of the commodity HR tasks offshore as they look to
concentrate on functions central to their corporate mission.

Many executives think that HR is not core to their business. They are
looking for ways to stop investing costly internal resources on time-
intensive HR transaction processing. Sending HR tasks offshore can
reduce in-house costs and boost the bottom line. Companies tend to
favor offshoring repetitive, generic, commodity HR transactions rather
than ones requiring more analytical thinking.

The practice of HR outsourcing and offshoring is gathering momentum.
The reasons for this trend are simple: In many organizations, employee-
facing processes are fragmented; HR application integration is weak;
and there are multiple points of failure. Many structural and process
problems need to be fixed before HR is streamlined and digital. One

way to cope with these structural problems is to selectively outsource different HR functions.

With outsourcing, the objective is still the same: cost savings and increased worker productivity. HR providers such as Exult, India Life Hewitt, and Accenture pledge to perform back-office HR functions more cheaply and efficiently than companies can do on their own, thanks to economies of scale, standardized processes, and advanced technology. For many businesses, the equation of high-quality HR processes at lower prices is irresistible, particularly when HR offshoring allows them to devote their energy to core competencies.

Our objective for this chapter is to give you better insight into HR processes that are being sent offshore. We explore the market and industry forces reshaping the modern HR organization. We illustrate the steady evolution of HR processes from transaction HR to human capital management to outsourcing. The unique trend we highlight using best-practice case studies is that in HR, outsourcing vendors like ADP and Affiliated Computer Services (ACS) are actually the early adopters of the offshore model. Lastly, we outline how you can create your own HR offshoring strategy.

Why Are Companies Offshoring Their HR Operations?

While outsourcing basic HR processes, such as payroll, HR call centers, and recruiting, has been an accepted best-business practice for decades, it is only in the last few years that the necessity to shed entire noncore functions such as benefits management have moved to the forefront of the outsourcing discussion.

As more companies accept the notion of HR outsourcing, we are starting to see mega-deals as large as the ones that occurred previously in IT outsourcing. A case in point is Procter & Gamble (P&G) and IBM's ten-year, $400-million global agreement for human resources services. In January 2004, IBM assumes operational responsibility for three HR shared services delivery centers in Costa Rica, England, and the Philippines. About 800 P&G employees will be absorbed by IBM.

Under the agreement, IBM will support 98,000 P&G employees in 80 countries, providing services that include payroll processing, benefits administration, compensation planning, expatriate and relocation services, travel and expense management, and HR data management. IBM will also provide application development and management of P&G's HR systems, including P&G's existing, leading-edge global SAP implementation and employee portal. The agreement should enable P&G to improve employee services and reduce HR costs through process transformation, technology integration, and best practices.[1]

Companies outsource HR for one or more of the following three reasons: to reduce costs, to obtain new processes they do not have, or to acquire technology. Companies first want cost savings. To achieve those savings, they need productivity gains, so they turn to process reconfiguration. Then, to achieve more, they move to technology innovation.

Taking care of employees is costly. HR-related expenses account for nearly two-thirds of some corporate budgets; thus, reducing HR costs makes good business sense. This is especially true when it comes to commodity tasks. For instance, at most companies, changing an address or transferring an employee is a multistep process that includes downloading a form, filling it out manually, placing it in an envelope, and mailing it to HR. An HR employee then opens the envelope and types the information into the human resources system. It usually takes two employees well over an hour to make an address change. Clearly, HR processes are time-consuming, costly, and repetitive.

It's hardly surprising that a top priority for management is to reduce overall operating costs while increasing workforce productivity. HR managers are quite familiar with the resulting conundrum: They must not only help reduce workforce costs, but their own overhead costs as well. They also are asked to maintain or even enhance services while cultivating a more productive and motivated workforce.

To improve productivity, companies are reorganizing the HR function in new ways in response to globalization, technological, and economic pressures. Firms are moving from a functional perspective to a process perspective and need to quickly acquire new process management skills to support the new organizational structure. Processes that build employee-oriented enterprises and make it easier for the workforce, full-time, part-time, temporary, or contract, to do its job are essential. Balancing these conflicting objectives — achieving cost savings in the near term while enhancing productivity in the long term — is the challenge facing almost all areas of HR.

The complexity and costs of HR are rising. We are beginning to see high-cost activity being replaced by lower-cost technology in some cases and lower-cost labor in others. HR technology is becoming central to improving productivity. Even as companies adopt employee self-service, they continue to look for ways to become more cost-effective.

This is where offshoring enters in. While self-service is a mega-trend, there will always be a need to support the conventional channels such as telephone, mail, and face-to-face. Utilizing technology, self-service, and low-cost offshore resources is the ultimate cost-effective HR solution.

A Brief Overview of Human Resources Practices

Some companies are using outsourcing to radically restructure their businesses. An advanced case in point is British Telecom (BT). BT is using outsourcing to create a unique business model. Its outsourcing partners are Accenture HR Services (for HR functions); Computacenter (desktop IT); HCL Technologies and Progeon (call center); Telereal and Monteray (property and facilities management); and Xansa (financial transaction processes).

In 1991, BT had more than 250,000 employees almost all in the United Kingdom organized around 61 geographically based areas. HR was a disparate, multifaceted department sprawled across 26 sites. Employing 14,500 employees to serve the needs of BT's staff, HR used 26 separate systems, 30 different help lines and was not only costly to run, but also unable to keep up with the rapid changes happening within the business.

BT, in an attempt to become more effective, restructured operations from the geographic focus to customer-centric functional units. The HR business unit followed suit with a similar rationalization of its services to nine sites with a consolidated HR system portfolio. BT made massive efforts to streamline HR by automating its HR functions in the late 1990s. Its new e-HR portal reduced administrative costs by 45%, increased staff efficiency by 5%, and led to a huge reduction in both paperwork and staff by e-enabling such functions as payroll, annual leave, expenses, and even training.[2]

In 1998, BT decided on an entirely new approach to HR — outsourcing its transactional HR functions. In August 2000, the telecom company outsourced its entire HR function in a 50-50 joint venture with Accenture called e-peopleserve. BT transferred 1,000 of its HR people to the joint venture to create a full-scale, end-to-end HR transactional solution that covered the complete employee lifecycle. The e-peopleserve model combined the management of BT assets, systems, and processes related to its HR functions with highly efficient, global solution centers.

Interestingly, the e-peopleserve joint venture was dissolved in 2002, with Accenture buying BT's stake, taking the operation in-house, and rebranding it Accenture HR Services. The Accenture unit continues to serve BT and supports 103,000 employees with just 600 HR staff.[3]

The point of the BT example is to illustrate the changes taking place in the HR landscape, especially at leading firms. HR technology coupled with outsourcing are leading to some new, low-cost alternatives for companies hoping to radically restructure their HR operations.

The Evolution of Human Resources

Over the past two decades, HR practices have steadily evolved. The closed-loop (technology changes processes, processes change technology) phenomenon has resulted in HR processes and applications evolving in many different directions. Despite the advancement of HR applications, the business fundamentals driving them have not changed much over the years. The two basic, long-term goals of HR applications remain intact: control HR administrative costs while boosting employee productivity, and direct the HR personnel and other managers to value-creating functions by reducing the number of mundane or unproductive administrative processes.

As figure 7.1 shows, the transformation of HR is taking place in a series of steps, from core HRMS transaction automation systems to more advanced HR market places, such as those seen in the areas of benefits management and business process outsourcing (BPO). Now we are pushing the BPO envelope further with offshore outsourcing. To get a better perspective, let's examine HR offshoring in more detail.

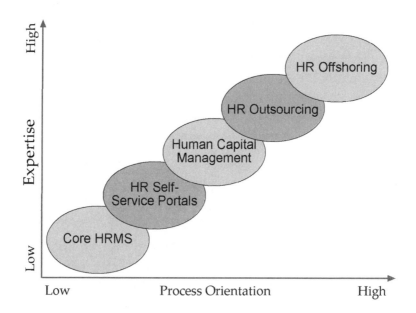

Figure 7.1: The Evolution of Human Resources

Human Resources Management Systems

Until a few decades ago, HR kept employee records on index cards and everything was handled on paper. Thankfully, those days are ending with human resource management systems (HRMSs). These applications are finally streamlining administrative transactions and eliminating variation, resulting in substantial time, staff, and budget savings.

The goal of an HRMS is to reduce costs by digitizing nuts-and-bolts tasks such as payroll or employee record management. The first step of this process is often putting employee records online. The scope of HR applications is quite amazing. PeopleSoft has a module for everything an HR manager could potentially want. From simple task automation in the early 1990s to massive integrated suites in the early 2000s, the evolution in application features and functionality has been stupendous.

HR Self-Service Portals

The next phase was Internet or Web-enabled HRMS. These solutions were aimed at providing portals that enabled employee self-service.

Why self-service portals? As more employees use the Web in their daily lives, they are raising the HR expectation bar. Employees are asking questions such as: If I can manage my personal finances online or pay my taxes online, why can't I do the same with time tracking and other data entry applications on the corporate intranet? Why do we need endless amounts of paper for everything?

As technologically savvy employees become familiar with self-service applications, they begin to ask for more features so they can address their daily needs. Self-service portals are mushrooming to provide alternative methods for managing and communicating human resources, benefits, and payroll information. Portal functionality ranges from 24x7 self-service to e-learning. The common theme is supplying employees with access to company information, policies, and online learning, enabling them to manage their workdays, as well as allowing businesses to monitor individual performances.

Human Capital Management

The market has evolved from simple online transactions to more complex process management. The challenge is not features or functionality, but value capture and extraction — understanding what needs to be done and integrating the various modules together to solve an employee problem. This is driving more investment in workforce management or human capital management (HCM).

HCM centers on giving employees the tools they need to access and manage the work-related information important to them. For instance, from a single portal, new employees can enroll in and manage their healthcare and benefit programs. They can easily initiate job requisitions for open positions, plan staff salaries, conduct performance appraisals, and create development plans all through a portal. The focus is more on the business processes and less on the transactions.

Best-practice HCM companies include IBM, Accenture, and Cisco Systems. Accenture, a global technology consulting firm with 75,000 people in 46 countries, illustrates the productivity improvements possible with HCM portals. The company has eliminated paper and digitized almost all employee-centric processes. Take manager self-service processes for instance. Instead of filling out paper forms and forwarding them to HR for approval and processing, managers can initiate and complete HR workflows on their own. Process digitization has led to lower costs and the ability to support revenue growth without increasing head count.

Despite its potential, HR process digitization is constrained by the vagaries of application integration. Employee-centric process digitization is often hindered by a lack of integrated data, which are usually housed in disconnected systems such as payroll, recruiting, and time management. The ability to capture the full range of data found in legacy and custom applications is essential for employee satisfaction. Vendors like SAP that promise a "complete suite" of integrated, prepackaged applications are racing to solve this complex issue.

HR Outsourcing

HR outsourcing (HRO) is an alternative to in-house HR technology investments. Executives increasingly are turning to outsourcing to reduce costs and boost efficiency. Outsourcing vendors such as Hewitt Associates, Watson Wyatt, ADP, Exult, ACS, and Accenture promise to perform back-office HR functions more cheaply than companies can do on their own, thanks to economies of scale, standardized processes, and advanced technology.

For many companies, the equation of high-quality HR service at lower prices is irresistible, especially when outsourcing allows them to focus on their core businesses. The reasons managers frequently recite for outsourcing HR are the following: they want to concentrate on core competencies, cut costs, and free up time and resources.

How does the HRO model work? Vendors apply their human resources, payroll, and benefits expertise and employ integrated technology systems to administer clients' HR programs. For instance, in benefits outsourcing, vendors provide services that include the management of health and welfare plans (medical), defined contribution plans (401(k)), and defined benefit plans (pension). Vendors take over and automate the processes required to manage client benefit programs and provide online tools and information that support decision making and transactions by clients and their employees.

In pursuing an HRO strategy, companies can choose to outsource a few functions, such as payroll and recruitment, or all services. Outsourcing all HR functions means relying on a professional employer organization (PEO). A PEO offers an end-to-end suite of HR solutions designed to share the responsibilities associated with being an employer. As co-employer, a PEO assumes many of the legal burdens, such as health benefits, workers' compensation, unemployment insurance, payroll, and tax compliance. The PEO industry began to emerge a decade ago and has grown to accommodate more than 2,000 PEOs. Administaff, ADP, Randstad, Paychex, Manpower, and Ceridian all compete in this sector.

The growth of HRO is also in part a response to the rising costs of regulatory compliance and the accelerating pace of technological change. HRO companies can provide cutting-edge technology and greater expertise on compliance with new HR regulations. They also can spread the cost of new technology over multiple clients, reducing the need for capital investments.

Some of the results from HRO have been very encouraging. Credit Suisse First Boston estimates that it has saved $115 million since 1994 by outsourcing most of its transactional HR functions. Kellogg, the cereal maker, reported that outsourcing had reduced the time it took to fill employee vacancies from 67 days in 2000 to 39 days in 2001. Over the same period, the cost per hire was cut in half, from $7,905 to $3,784.[4]

HR Offshoring

As HR outsourcing begins to include more functions, leading providers are taking it to the next level. They are systematically sending many discreet HR subprocesses offshore to provide even more savings. The ability to lower costs and provide better standardized services is fueling this trend.

In order to comprehend how offshoring is reshaping the delivery of HR, it is important to understand the three main HR offshore delivery models:

1. Captive offshore shared services center.

2. Third-party offshore outsourcing.

3. Blended global delivery model.

Captive Offshore HR Shared Services Center. Exult, a leading HR BPO provider, provides us with an example of this model. Exult has moved offshore with the establishment of its Indian subsidiary operations, Exult Client Services (India) in Mumbai. The captive center will be its fifth client service center and will focus on HR transaction processing, daytime "off peak" processing, and call center work.

Exult plans to leverage this offshore center by serving customers such as the consumer electronics retailer Circuit City. The retailer handed off the management of its human resources administration for 38,000 employees to Exult. Under the seven-year agreement, Exult will provide payroll, benefits administration, compensation, and employee contact center services. The BPO provider will manage the services from facilities in North Carolina and India.

Third-Party Offshore Outsourcing. This model centers on transferring an internal HR function that is performed in-house to an offshore provider that will perform the function from a low-wage country. Crossdomain Solutions, an employer and accounting services firm based in Bangalore, India, exemplifies this model. Crossdomain provides employer-employee services to a variety of companies in the United States and Europe. The process areas include payroll processing, travel expense management, claims administration, and retiree benefits administration.

Blended Global Delivery Model. The Motorola and Affiliated Computer Services (ACS) relationship typifies this model. Motorola took a bold step in converting its HR functions from a cost-center model to a profit-center model when it outsourced them to ACS.

In December 2002, Motorola signed a ten-year HR outsourcing contract with ACS valued at $650 million. According to the contract, Motorola transferred 600 employees and a substantial part of its HR systems, software, and process capabilities to ACS.

ACS will combine the capabilities of Motorola with its BPO abilities to create a new, wholly owned ACS business that will do two things: support Motorola and provide HR BPO solutions to other customers worldwide. Over the course of the agreement, which begins in 2004, Motorola has the potential to share in the financial performance of the new business unit, that is, receive commissions based on predetermined revenue target growth by ACS Global HR Solutions.[5]

ACS operates global facilities in Mexico, Guatemala, Jamaica, the Dominican Republic, Ghana, Spain, Fiji, and India. ACS Global HR uses these offshore centers to provide HR information systems, benefits administration, global relocation, employee assistance programs, HR selection and assessment, learning services, employee call centers, as well as compensation, staffing and performance management systems and processes. As the HR needs of companies expand, ACS Global HR Solutions is positioned to expand the breadth and depth of its offerings.

Offshore HR remains the fastest growing part of the HR BPO market. A significant number of HR BPO companies, such as ADP, are pursuing the offshore option. Tasks that are being sent offshore tend to be lower-level administrative and technical commodity tasks. This focus makes sense as we estimate a typical HR department spends more than 80% of its time managing tactical and transaction-oriented operations.

Offshoring HR Processes

Which HR processes are companies offshoring? Initially, companies and vendors are offshoring repetitive, generic HR processes rather than operations that require a higher level of analytical thinking. These processes include compensation services, employee relations, benefits administration, and workforce management.

Compensation Services

Compensation services include managing payroll, time and attendance reporting, on- and off-cycle pay, wage garnishments, tax calculations, tax reporting, and administration of salary, bonus, and stock option programs. By offshoring these functions, a global company will reduce its investment in internal resources.

Cisco Systems, headquartered in California, is the worldwide leader in networking. Cisco offshored payroll processing and employee query resolution issues to Crossdomain Solutions. Cisco employees can also use the Crossdomain intranet to log in online and check their investment and tax-related information. Crossdomain specialists take care of payroll, reimbursement processing, queries, and remittances.

Employee Relations

Employee administration includes the capture, tracking, modification, and effective reporting of employee-related data. Learning solutions include performance review, learning planning, skills evaluation, and performance assessment.

In December 1999, BP Amoco, one of the world's largest companies and a leading provider of energy and petrochemicals, signed a seven-year, $600 million contract with Exult. BP Amoco asked Exult to create and operate a comprehensive, global HR services organization that would transform the way in which HR administrative, transactional, and information services were provided to BP's 56,000 employees.

BP outsourced compensation, benefits, payroll, performance management, training, employee development, recruiting, staffing, sourcing, expatriate administration, relocation, employee relations, policy and legal compliance, employee record management, and vendor sourcing. The only function that remains in-house is BP's U.S. learning and development program.

The goals for BP Amoco were to reduce associated management costs, improve the quality of service to employees, fulfill the strategic objective to be online, and to release time for HR staff and line managers to concentrate on managing the performances and careers of employees. In 2000, Exult established an offshore contact center in Glasgow, Scotland, specifically to accommodate BP Amoco and other U.K. and U.S. customers. It selected Scotland because of its accessibility, educated, English-speaking workforce, relatively low cost of doing business, and European Union membership.

Despite some initial transition problems, BP has benefited from the arrangement: Payroll processing is more timely and accurate; employees get their benefits questions answered sooner; HR processes have been standardized across the company; and, for the first time, BP has measurable data on which HR activities are effective. Because BP is no longer handling routine transactional work in-house, many of its HR employees were deemed unnecessary. As a result, it cut its core HR staff by 65% — from 100 to 35 people.[6]

Benefits Administration

Benefits services include managing health, medical, 401(k), pension, and life insurance plans; distributing healthcare and retirement plan information; managing eligibility; overseeing vacation schedules; tracking leave; maintaining retirement earning histories, enrollments, and retirement or vested rights estimates; and terminating benefits.

In February 2003, Convergys Corporation agreed to provide outsourced health and welfare benefits and leave of absence administration services to Office Depot for five years. Office Depot sells office supplies, technology products, and furniture to businesses in the United States, Canada, and 20 other countries.

Convergys will support approximately 37,000 of Office Depot's U.S. employees with employee care specialists, Web-based self-service capabilities, and technology from Convergys's multi-channel service centers. Convergys, a leader in integrated billing, employee care, and customer care services, headquartered in Ohio, employs more than 48,000 people in 49 customer contact centers and data centers in the United States, Canada, Latin America, Europe, the Middle East, and Asia.

Workforce Management

Functions in workforce management include recruiting and new hire services that process and manage workforce changes and help effectively develop and deploy human capital. Recruiting services include needs identification, candidate sourcing, resource selection, resume screening, interviewing, assessment, offer procedures, and hire administration.

The need for better workforce management for its 130,000 employees prompted Bank of America (BofA) to outsource its HR functions to Exult for ten years. In November 2000, Exult assumed responsibility for BofA's payroll operations, accounts payable, benefits administration, general benefits management, and performance evaluation. Per the outsourcing agreement, BofA transferred hundreds of its employees to Exult.

In 2001, Exult, to further reduce HR-related IT costs, offshored HR technology work to two software companies in India.[7] It also moved some back-office functions to provide 24x7 nonstop service and maximize the price and performance ratio. The BofA contract was expanded to include expatriate administration services and regional staffing services.

The migratory trend to offhsore HR marks new chapter in HR outsourcing. Let's see how ADP and GM are approaching this new era.

Offshore HR Case Study: Automatic Data Processing

Automatic Data Processing Inc. (ADP), incorporated in 1961, is a pioneer in business process outsourcing. ADP offers employer, brokerage, dealer, and claims services. The company targets financial services companies, motor vehicle dealers and manufacturers, and insurance companies as customers.

Figure 7.2 illustrates the evolution of ADP's employee service offerings. The complexity and cost of providing these services is steadily going up.

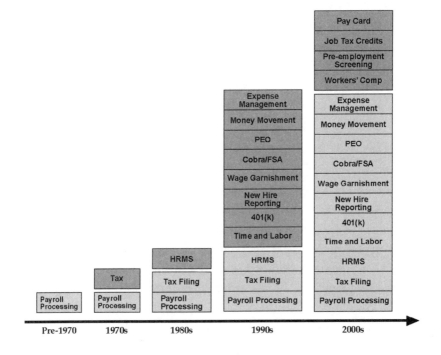

Figure 7.2: Evolution of ADP's Employee Services

At the same time, ADP cannot increase the price of these services due to strong competition from the likes of Paychex and others. The only way to provide low prices to customers and yet grow profits is to cut costs using a blended onshore and offshore model.

The unique trend that we highlight in this case study is that of outsourcing firms like ADP adopting offshoring to create a blended model that lowers their cost structures.

Offshore HR and Transaction Processing

Companies offering HR outsourcing services are vulnerable to economic downturns, too. According to ADP's 2002 annual report, its employee services division suffered from stagnating sales in the weak economy, client loss due to bankruptcy, and fewer employees on client payrolls (companies like ADP usually bill for their services on a monthly, per-employee basis). The same HR outsourcing companies that businesses seek out for cost savings have had to search for ways to cut costs themselves. One of the ways is to transfer operations overseas either to a third-party vendor or to in-house international offices.

With 2003 sales of $7.1 billion, ADP has established itself as a major player not only in employee services (comprehensive HR, payroll, and benefit administration solutions), but also in security brokerage (securities processing and investor communication services), auto/truck dealer (computing solutions for auto/truck dealers and manufacturers), and insurance claims services (auto repair estimating and claims processing solutions). Nearly all of its businesses have been touched by the troubled economy. Employee services was affected by companies cutting staff, brokerage services suffered as the financial industry continued to stumble, and claims services remained largely unchanged. Dealer services alone seem to have weathered the storm, reporting 12% growth in its fourth-quarter 2003 earnings release.

In the same release, management reiterated that it does not predict significant improvement in fiscal 2004 either. The mid-single-digit revenue growth forecast is a break from its consistent record of double-digit growth. Growth in general has been hard to come by and has led the company to exit or restructure lagging businesses. ADP doesn't intend to stop there.

Offshoring operations are part of ADP's restructuring plan. In June 2003, ADP announced that it was opening a 40,000-square-foot global technology center in Hyderabad, India. The center, which will support more than 500 clients, was ready for business barely one month later, perhaps a reflection of the priority the company has placed on the project. At the time of the announcement, 400 employees supported ADP's operations in India. This number is slated to more than double to 1,000 in a year's time. ADP's actions in India contrast directly with its actions in the United States, where the company has been downsizing or consolidating unprofitable operations, such as the Rockville, Maryland, medical claims unit.

Structure of Offshore Operations

The offshore operations are housed in a captive subsidiary called ADP Wilco. ADP Wilco, based in Hyderabad, India, is the international offshore center of ADP that provides development and support services for the international financial services sector, outsourced securities data management services, and BPO services across ADP.

The offshore center houses personnel such as customer service representatives and production operations staff for functions such as payroll processing, benefits administration, training, and information technology support and maintenance. These client service centers also contain systems and technology, such as contact management systems, imaging and workflow, and HR application software and databases. Offshore centers are designed to give efficiencies and economies of scale by leveraging the functionality, staff, and technology of centralized processes and services across many business units for multiple clients. They also provide redundancies for service continuity purposes.

ADP can communicate with the service centers online through its own intranet systems or by phone, fax, or e-mail. The offshore operations are connected directly to the United States via a 2 Mbps international private leased line circuit (IPLC) and Internet bandwidth of 2 Mbps. The infrastructure permits clear, easy interactions between ADP staff and global clients. It also allows ADP to offer clients a blended service delivery model — part of the work is done in the United States, part of the work is done in India.

We expect that as ADP gains experience with offshore centers it will ship much of its work offshore since processing back-office transactions can be done almost anywhere in the world. As ADP Vice President and General Manager, Malcolm Thorne, said, "India has all the advantages — location, quality manpower, time zone differential, higher productivity, IT infrastructure, and supportive regulatory environment. All these factors compelled ADP to expand our high technology backbone operations."[8]

Value and ROI of a Blended Service Model

In HR, ADP has two offerings that leverage proven platforms:

1. Managed payroll services (payroll administration and processing) and

2. Enterprise 3000 Services (HR, payroll, benefits transaction processing, and call center).

To support its vision of becoming the leader of IT-enabled services for HR applications and the provider of choice for a broad range of services to small, midsize, and large employers, ADP is executing a blended service bureau model — partly onshore and partly offshore. Like many other companies that turned to offshoring for cost-containment relief, ADP will benefit from cheaper labor rates and improved productivity.

Eventually all HR BPO providers will need a strategy for global delivery of their services, and many will choose to leverage offshore sites in countries such as India, the Philippines, Ireland, Canada, Mexico, and the Eastern European states.

Offshore HR Case Study: General Motors

Europe is the hotbed for HR outsourcing innovation. In November 2003, Affiliated Computer Services (ACS) and General Motors (GM) teamed up to overhaul some of GM's noncore HR processes for its European operations.

GM employs 341,000 people globally in its core automotive business and subsidiaries. Founded in 1908, GM has been the global automotive sales leader since 1931. The company has manufacturing operations in 32 countries, and its vehicles are sold in more than 190 countries. In 2002, the automaker sold more than 8.6 million cars and trucks, nearly

15% of the global vehicle market. GM's global headquarters are in Detroit, Michigan, and its European headquarters are in Zurich, Switzerland.

Outsourcing HR in GM Europe

The contract between GM and ACS had its origin in a $100 million deal between GM and Arthur Andersen that stipulated Andersen would provide finance and accounting transaction processing (including billing, accounts payable, disbursements, accounts receivable, and various accounting activities) for GM's European operations. The service agreement signed in May 2000 was an extension of a $250 million agreement signed in November 1999 under which Arthur Andersen provided financial transaction processing and U.S. payroll services for GM's operations in North America.[9]

After Andersen got into trouble, ACS acquired the GM finance and accounting outsourcing contracts in May 2002. ACS also acquired Andersen's shared services center in Barcelona, Spain. Because of this project, ACS was attuned to GM's business culture and the way it operated, which eliminated some of the introductory discussions and meetings that normally takes place between vendor and client.

The HR outsourcing deal was announced in November 2003. Under the new HR contract, ACS is supporting HR services for GM's European operations, which is no small task considering that the multinational corporation has 75,000 active and 35,000 inactive employees scattered across ten European countries — Austria, Belgium, France, Germany, Poland, Portugal, Spain, Sweden, Switzerland, and the United Kingdom.[10]

Handling recruitment, personnel administration, time keeping, payroll, expatriate payroll, travel and expense, training, reporting, and data archiving in nine different languages is no doubt keeping ACS and its small army of subcontractors extremely busy.

This contract marks the first-ever Pan-European payroll consolidation with an outsourcing provider. ACS is also responsible for deploying PeopleSoft HR across Europe and utilizing SAP in order to support European payroll. ACS is using its Barcelona, Spain, office as its home base and developing a network of support offices in the United Kingdom, Belgium, Germany, Spain, and Sweden.

Understanding GM's HR Process Requirements

What is GM looking to achieve by outsourcing HR to an external service provider? Based on our experience, we found that GM and every other company is looking for six elements from their HR service provider:

- Standardization: The HR solution has to be customized from a standard platform of assets and capabilities that implement company-wide processes and procedures.

- Centralization: Using specialized services centers, the goal is to deliver consistent, high-quality HR services to the entire workforce.

- Integration: The client and vendor must work together to provide services using a "one-stop" HR contact center with a single point of coordination for third-party products and services.

- Self-Service Technology: The vendor must support and implement new HR tools that use workflow technology to support fast, efficient service provisioning while enabling employees and managers to serve themselves.

- Labor Cost Reduction: HR outsourcing relies on reducing labor costs. The service provider helps in this quest by seamlessly handling the administration of thousands of transactions in the most efficient, professional, and compassionate manner possible.

- Best Practices: The client and vendor must work closely on applying rigor and discipline to HR. This includes service level management and quality practices throughout the operation, with established transparent financial charges for all HR services.

These requirements are multifaceted and very difficult to achieve. That is one of the reasons why HR outsourcing contracts tend to be spread over seven to ten years.

Dynamics of the GM-ACS Partnership

The underlying assumption behind this deal was that GM's HR employees would be afforded more time to concentrate on strategic issues such as organizational development, human performance, change management, and resource planning. However, the distance from the day-to-day HR operations can come at a price. Once companies get used to outsourcing the bulk of their HR tasks, the process knowledge can disappear along with it, which can make implementing new HR strategies difficult.

Another problem that executives who employ strategies similar to GM's routinely mention is that service providers sometimes cobble together a patchwork of solutions from the various HR departments and subcontractors and never attain a tight, truly integrated HR solution.

Another key issue that GM has to keep a close eye on is integration. ACS delegates some of the HR work to subcontractors, such as ARINSO International, which helps ACS with the PeopleSoft deployment and the SAP payroll applications. ACS, as the main service provider, bears full responsibility for service delivery, overhauling the HR processes, coordinating the new technology, and integrating the subcontractors.

GM did not publicly state whether its European HR staff would be cut because of the new partnership, but it's likely. Offshore outsourcing, however, does not always result in significant layoffs. Some companies seize the opportunity to retrain insiders and deploy them elsewhere. Some build into the outsourcing agreement a provision to transfer a certain number of employees over to the service provider. And some find it too difficult to let employees go at all and, thus, never realize all of the savings originally built into their business cases.

The blueprint of the GM/ACS deal is worth reviewing for executives who are considering going ahead with comprehensive HR outsourcing initiatives of their own.

How to Create a Business Case for Offshoring HR

Imagine you are the head of the HR function in a multibillion-dollar, global company. Your CEO mandates that you have two years to slash your costs by 30% while improving service levels. What would you do?

Welcome to the cost management world of most HR executives. They quickly are figuring out that there are three ways to reduce HR costs: centralize, standardize, or outsource HR operations. Some companies have centralized their HR operations into shared services centers. Others have found centralization difficult and have encountered resistance from powerful business units that do not willingly relinquish control over their

HR operations. The standardization option is also troublesome if firms are not willing to invest in requisite, large-scale HRMS applications.

That leaves the third option. In contrast to the "do-it-yourself" approach of the first two, outsourcing, particularly offshore outsourcing, is becoming more appealing to HR executives. Despite making good business sense, offshore outsourcing is not a simple undertaking. Companies can become consumed by the activities that it comprises: documenting internal processes, evaluating potential offshore vendors, transitioning infrastructure and employees to an outsourced arrangement, and monitoring the contract on an ongoing basis.

To ensure that HR BPO delivers on its promise, we recommend a three-step approach to prepare for outsourcing an HR business process. The first step, before engaging a vendor, is to understand what your core and noncore HR processes are. Second, evaluate your costs. And third, understand the necessary service levels from the employees' perspective.

Which HR Processes to Retain and Which to Offshore

Determining which HR processes you should outsource and which you should keep is always a thorny question.

Consider this: When AT&T opted to outsource HR for its 70,000 employees based in the United States, AT&T's finance and HR departments developed an atypical process for determining which HR functions would be best served by outsourcing. Rather than ask managers to prove why a particular function should be outsourced, the team asked them to provide evidence that a particular HR function should be retained in-house. In doing this, AT&T's managers became more analytical about the benefits of outsourcing, less threatened by the strategy, and better able to communicate the value of outsourcing to the employee population. Ultimately, managers designated nearly every HR function for outsourcing. The outcome: a seven-year, end-to-end outsourcing agreement with Aon Consulting.

The business rationale behind a decision to outsource HR processes varies from industry to industry and organization to organization depending on the perception of what the core and noncore HR processes are and the vendor's ability to undercut or outperform the organization's own internal

HR function. How suitable it is to outsource all or part of the HR function requires addressing multiple questions such as:

- Is this function or process strategic to our company? Is it core or noncore? Is it critical or noncritical?

- Is this function or process customized or standardized? Is there a low or high variation in demand? Is it an administrative task? Is it low volume or high volume?

Core versus Noncore. Organizations regularly struggle with separating core (differentiating) activities from noncore (commodity) activities as a prelude to HR outsourcing. A core process distinguishes a company from its competitors; a noncore process does not directly contribute to shareholder value and the ability to distinctively compete in the market place.

The view companies have of what constitutes core processes in HR is often very different. In some instances, companies feel that HR reflects values that are too important to outsource. Marriott International, Southwest Airlines, Disney, or MBNA America are shaped by specific core values in their culture and service delivery. For them, HR is an essential ingredient of their differentiated business model. For example, at Disney and Southwest, hiring and training are kept in-house to create a continuing lifeline between the company's founding values and every corporate associate, whether she is a Disney greeter or a Southwest ticketing agent. HR via organizational and personnel development processes can have great impact on the way the company works, how the culture feels, and the type of talent attracted and hired.

Another factor affecting the core versus noncore analysis is HR innovation such as employee self-service. Human resources has received an infusion of technology that is tremendously affecting the way service is delivered to employees. HR lends itself well to self-service, and increasingly companies are looking to exploit emerging technologies as a way of providing a higher level of service at lower costs. However, front-end employee self-service also requires a robust, automated, back-end transaction processing capability.

Areas like payroll, training, benefits enrollment, and healthcare claims all have a combination of self-service and transaction processing. For larger companies, many of the employee self-service HR processes tend to be transaction-intensive. The leverage that an outsourcing company can achieve by running processes for many companies on a similar technology platform can produce compelling economics to a client.

Critical versus Noncritical. Another distinction that should be made is between critical (essential) and noncritical (useful) activities. Some companies may label the HR back office noncore but critical, that is, they run the HR back office exceptionally well as a minimum requirement to compete. Payroll processing, for example, is noncore but critical.

Figure 7.3 shows a framework for analyzing HR activities. The processes that are low in strategic value are candidates for offshoring. The processes that are high in strategic value such as HR strategy, policy, executive compensation, and labor relations do not make good candidates for offshoring. We encourage you to look at the core and noncore HR processes in your organization.

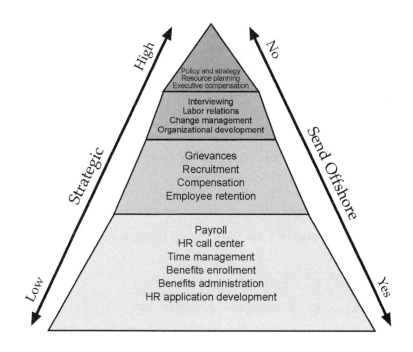

Figure 7.3: Core versus Noncore HR Processes

Do Your Homework

Once you are sure that HR BPO is right for you, carefully examine each HR process. Before you outsource, you need to benchmark internal processes and compare them to your peers, so that you know how well you are performing and at what cost. Otherwise, you have no way of really knowing whether performance has increased and costs have decreased.

If you can't measure it, you can't outsource it. Internal process benchmarking allows you to gather and provide extensive, validated, internal process data to the vendor. This is important. Time and again contract negotiations run into trouble when serious pricing and service level questions arise because the vendor has no confidence in the client-supplied data made available during negotiations and the due diligence process. Contracts are all about binding commitments. When internal data is not available or is of questionable validity, experienced outsourcers will not commit to binding service level agreements.

Due diligence also applies externally. Assess prospective outsourcers and the value they can bring to your company. Look for both process and industry expertise and a proven track record of the service the outsourcer will provide. If you anticipate growth, look for an outsourcer that can grow with your needs. Most importantly, talk to existing customers and find out what problems they have had and how they were resolved.

Offshoring is time- and effort-intensive. You don't want to discover after the fact that your processes were not right for outsourcing or your service provider was not right for your processes. So take a step back and do your homework.

Understanding the HR Service Level Requirements

What service levels are you providing to your employees today? What are your employees' expectations?

Before you sign any offshore outsourcing contract, hammer out the details of the acceptable service levels. In particular, establish a service level agreement (SLA) that specifies exactly what you expect from your outsourcer specific to the business process you are outsourcing. Service level agreements should be detailed and based on measurable, process-specific metrics. If you are outsourcing recruitment, the SLA should specify metrics such as time to hire, cost of hire, appropriateness of new hires, and how long new hires stay with your company.

In addition, establish penalties for poor performance and incentives for performance that exceeds targets. That way it's win-win, and the objectives of both parties are aligned. The result is a much higher probability of success. But be sure service levels promote not just performance but also results. Service level agreements should not be limited to technical criteria such as calls answered per hour or average hold time. They need to be backed up with business value. Are you increasing employee satisfaction?

Moreover, reserve the right to make changes later in the relationship or to cancel the contract if the arrangement isn't meeting your needs. Specify in your contract the ability to renegotiate service levels at a later date. The BPO market is still developing. A deal that seems attractive today might not be competitive next year.

Remember, outsourcing HR hinges as much on re-engineering service delivery as it is does on reducing costs. Getting HRO right is important but difficult. The promise of HRO is captivating, but in practice it can be perilous. When it works, HR outsourcing allows companies to process employee transactions swiftly, and increase employee support by providing customized information and services. But when HRO doesn't work, it can lead to sizable debacles.

Summary

The market for HR outsourcing is very large. According to *FORTUNE* magazine, Global 500 corporations employed more than 47 million people in 2002. The median number of employees for a Global 500 corporation was 63,000. The companies are operating in multiple locations, countries, languages, and regulatory environments. Satisfying an employee base of this magnitude presents enormous complexities.

At the same time, fragmentation and geographical dispersion of work results in redundancy and inefficiency. In addition, the large number of third-party vendors typically used by an HR department to handle discrete functions complicates HR process management. So by necessity, HR departments devote most of their resources to administrative functions rather than strategic planning and initiatives.

As a result, HRO has become popular because external vendors, through technology and economies of scale, can provide more cost-effective HR services than in-house departments. Despite the momentum behind HR outsourcing, it is relatively early in the evolutionary cycle. HRO is where IT outsourcing was 20 years ago. There are not yet statements of work or service levels in place. HRO is still more in the proof-of-concept stage with some pioneers pushing the envelope.

With HRO, the job of the HR professional is changing. Transactional work is giving way to more strategic workforce management. As a result, the demand for HR strategists is growing for several reasons. First, although vendors have proven their ability to handle routine transactional work, internal HR consultants will be needed to determine what combination of pay, benefits, and learning opportunities are necessary. Second, even if outsourcing does remove all the transactional work, someone with a solid understanding of HR and business will be needed to manage the multimillion-dollar vendor contracts.

Finally, companies need a robust HR function that is responsible for ensuring the speed and accuracy of employee transactions, regardless of who is doing the work. In today's competitive markets, flexibility, and quality of HR are critical to gaining a winning edge. Rapid deployment of new HR capabilities is equally crucial to attain this goal. Onsite, onshore, nearshore, and offshore HR combinations, if used with care, will help companies obtain that edge by functioning as an extension of their in-house capabilities.

Chapter Eight

Transaction Processing Offshore Outsourcing

*"If you can't describe what you are doing as a process,
you don't know what you're doing."*

— W. Edwards Deming

Introduction

How much is back-office transaction processing costing your organization? On some level, every business must cope with transaction processing. For example, whenever someone uses an automatic teller machine to withdraw cash, transfer money, or deposit checks, the action spawns a series of back-office transactions that have to be processed by a variety of systems. Transactions are essentially time-stamped records for purchases, sales orders, deposits, withdrawals, time cards, and paychecks.

Until this point, when we talked about business processes and transactions we organized the discussion based on general transactions — finance transactions such as accounts payable and receivable or human resources transactions such as payroll and benefits administration.

In this chapter, we focus on vertical-specific BPO transactions such as claims processing and credit card processing. We have found that as the BPO market matures, services are becoming more vertical-specific. For instance, insurance companies are outsourcing claims processing and policy administration while healthcare companies are outsourcing medical records administration and medical diagnostics.

Offshore transaction processing is growing. Many third-party, general outsourcing companies are currently concentrating on providing lower-end services such as medical and legal transcription services, digital conversion of physical documents, e-mail response centers, and lower-level business processing services. Since such "low-level work" has few barriers to entry, many vendors specializing in transaction processing have sprung up in countries such as India, China, the Philippines, Malaysia, and Mexico.

In fact, when asked to comment on the future of offshoring over the next 18 months, Prakash Gurbaxani, CEO of TransWorks, a CRM/BPO provider based in India, made this prediction: "In terms of growth rates, while customer care will continue to be the largest and perhaps where the current growth rates will continue, the finance and accounting, as well as transaction processing areas (claims, mortgages, rebates, and orders) will see significant growth in the next 12–18 months."[1]

Why Are Companies Offshoring Transaction Processing?

Organizations in a variety of industries — credit card, insurance, mortgage, retail banking, and telecom — face the tedious task of processing countless transactions, which results in the need to generate, manage, and document data in an organized, accessible manner. This task, though critical, is time-consuming and forces organizations to devote resources to activities that may not be core to their businesses. Outsourcing transaction processing allows companies to either lay off employees or reassign them to more important tasks.

Companies outsource transaction processing for a variety of reasons. Foremost among the drivers are the goals of focusing on the core business, improving service levels, and reducing implementation costs. Other drivers include:

- The high cost of processing transactions,

- Few best-practice processes in-house,

- Difficulty in hiring or retaining transaction processing staff, and

- Lack of timely or accurate reports.

Functions such as data entry that require little interaction between the customer and the vendor are ideal for offshore outsourcing. Customers can ship paper forms, invoices, or other documents or transmit electronically scanned paper-based data offshore to vendors for processing. After information entry and editing, computerized data can be sent back via telecom lines. Examples include workers in China who transcribe U.S. telephone numbers from printed directories onto CD-ROMs or workers in India who process the used tickets and boarding passes of international airlines.

Types of Transaction Processing

Some companies consider transaction processing core. First Data Corporation (FDC), the world's largest provider of processing services for credit card, debit card, money transfer, and other payment transactions, is one example.

FDC has market-leading positions in each of its three main segments.

1. Payment services consists primarily of Western Union, which dominates the person-to-person money transfer market through 151,000 agent locations in 195 countries and territories.

2. Merchant services provides credit card, debit card, and check transaction processing services to 3 million merchant locations directly and through extensive alliances with bank partners.

3. Card issuing services supplies credit, retail, and debit card processing services to more than 1,400 card-issuing financial institutions and retailers. This unit has more than 325 million card accounts on file.

FDC processes billions of transactions in each of these areas every year. Since a significant amount of money is involved, these transactions have to be audited and reported for regulatory purposes. Given the labor-intensive nature of these tasks, FDC and its competitors — National Processing, NOVA Information Systems (U.S. Bancorp), and Concord EFS — are increasingly turning to offshoring for cost management.

Driving down the cost of transaction processing is smart because it helps companies keep pace with their peers. The functions that are most easily and profitably sent offshore depend on the industry and the specific business processes. In general, they can include:

- Data entry of any paper applications or documents,

- Processing of credit card applications, transfers, or payments,

- Account reconciliation and records management,

- Legal and medical transcription,

- Document processing, and

- Order processing, which spans application forms, information verification, authorization, and confirmation.

Better IT and communication infrastructures have enabled back-office transaction processing work previously done in large, developed cities to venture offshore. We list the most popular types of transactions that are migrating offshore in table 8.1. To better understand the underlying mechanics of transaction processing, let's look at some common processes that are moving offshore today: mortgage processing, insurance claims processing, medical transcription, and content management.

Type	Industry	Task
Residential and commercial mortgage processing	Banking, Insurance	Spans information capture, verification of information on applications forms, and screening application against predefined criteria.
Insurance claims processing	Insurance	Refers to electronic information capture, information verification, eligibility determination, and reporting.
Medical transcription	Healthcare	Involves transcribing medical records dictated by doctors from an audio format to a hard copy or electronic format.
Content management	Information Healthcare	Includes the processing of paper and electronic documents (newspapers, magazines, or journals) into searchable catalogs and archives.

Table 8.1: Transactions Commonly Sent Offshore

Mortgage Transaction Processing

The mortgage loan processing business is a data-intensive operation, so it's not surprising that companies are considering offshoring select functions including application processing, direct sales, credit scoring and approval, and verification of title.

Other functions, such as insurance tax, escrow processing, early collections calling, and most of the customer service center functions, can be offshored along with at least part of loan-service setup, post-closing documentation, manual payoff processing, account balancing, statement printing, and refinancing. The savings from offshoring these functions can be 10%–15% of overall overhead costs.

Some of the mortgage firms leading the way in offshoring data-intensive administrative work are: GE Financial Services, Ocwen Financial Corporation, IndyMac Bank, and GreenPoint Mortgage.

To improve profit margins, these firms are adopting a two-pronged strategy.

1. They are automating front-end processes to deliver self-service to their customers and thus improve their margins on low-margin products and services.

2. They are offshoring back-office processes to improve efficiency and lower overall operational costs for both low- and high-margin products.

In this section, we present an overview of the mortgage industry, and the factors shaping it. We also provide a quick primer on the mortgage processing workflow. Using several examples, we explain how offshore outsourcing fits into the overall execution plan. We end with a discussion of ROI in offshore outsourcing for mortgage companies.

A Brief Overview of the Mortgage Industry

The U.S. mortgage industry is around $4 trillion in outstanding loan balances. The purchase of a home is typically the largest purchase consumers make. Most consumers do not have the financial strength to make the purchase outright; therefore, they obtain a real estate loan or a mortgage to finance the transaction.

The mortgage industry was born when the first bank of the United States received its charter in 1791 from the U.S. Congress. The industry began to change in 1937 when banks began utilizing keypunch machines and manual feed verifiers. They did this to adhere to regulations and data requirements. Mortgage computerization accelerated in the 1960s as the mainframe entered into banking and batch processing was implemented.

The bleak economic landscape of the late 1970s and early 1980s presented many challenges for the mortgage industry. The high interest rates forced companies to look for ways to increase efficiency in the loan process. Determining that they could reduce their paperwork through technology, companies moved to scalable, flexible, mid-range systems, such as the IBM AS400, which enabled them to build automated systems to lower costs, enhance efficiency, and make the home loan process more seamless for customers.

In the mid-1980s, the demand for mortgages began escalating. *Faster, better, cheaper* became the servicing mantra for mortgage processing. The legacy applications were no longer able to keep up with the processing that needed to be done. They were fast becoming too expensive to maintain and operate. Many businesses opted to replace core mainframe applications and implement networks and personal computers that allowed less people to provide more services. Loan files were computerized and available in real time to computer users throughout the company, precipitously reducing the cost to service a loan.

In the early 1990s, outsourcing became prevalent in the mortgage industry. Many mortgage processes that were done internally were transferred to external vendors. In the late 1990s, mortgage processing and technology became synonymous. New products like electronic mortgages, or e-mortgages, emerged with the Internet. E-mortgages became possible with the passing of the Electronic Signatures in Global and National Commerce Act (E-SIGN) in 2000. The first online mortgage closed that same year.

Recent Mortgage Industry Dynamics

The external forces driving change in the mortgage industry include demographic changes, market dynamics, evolving regulatory and legal requirements, mergers and acquisitions, and online mortgages.

- **Demographic Changes.** The two biggest population sectors, aging baby boomers and their offspring (the group known as "echo boomers") are creating a surge in housing. A wave of immigration in the 1990s also contributed to the growth.

- **Market Dynamics.** A slowing economy triggered a drop in interest rates, and the lowered rates spurred a refinance wave. (Refinancing is the repayment of a debt from the proceeds of a new loan using the same home as security.) In addition, a new point of sale (POS) model allowing the immediate processing of loans came into effect.

- **Evolving Regulatory and Legal Requirements.** If new proposals such as the Real Estate Settlement Procedures Act (RESPA) were passed, mortgage brokers would be required to provide concrete cost information to borrowers to enable them to truly shop for a loan among various lenders.

- **Mergers and Acquisitions.** There has been a blizzard of merger activity in the mortgage industry. Acquirers inherited diverse products and processes, business partners, and technology platforms and have had to re-engineer their mortgage processing platforms.

- **Online Mortgages.** More customers are shopping, initiating, closing, and refinancing mortgages from the comfort of their own homes. Utilizing the entirely paperless process saves customers the $750 loan origination fee and reduces the mortgage cycle from 45 days to 5 hours.[2]

The compression of the mortgage processing cycle has become a competitive differentiator. The pressure to process mortgages more quickly and at a lower cost has led to the industry moving offshore.

For example, one of the largest commercial mortgage companies decided to offshore financial statement analysis to TransWorks, a BPO company headquartered in India. The mortgage company received the physical financial statements customers sent to its shared services center, grouped them, scanned them, and forwarded the statements to TransWorks in India via FTP.

The scanned statements were uploaded into the TransWorks workflow application and then reviewed and recast into standard templates based on the type of mortgage. TransWorks then analyzed the recast statements and computed certain ratios to evaluate the loan servicing capability of the business. The BPO provider uploaded its completed analysis to the FTP site for the client to review and take the necessary action. By offshoring financial statement analysis to TransWorks, the commercial mortgage company reduced data processing costs by 55%, decreased turnaround time by ten days, and managed peaks in volume that occurred during the quarterly financial reporting period.[3]

A Primer on the Mortgage Processing Workflow

Before we delve into what is being outsourced, we should give you a quick primer on mortgage processing. Mortgage processing has two components: loan origination processes and loan servicing processes.

The loan origination process is pretty much the same for the different types of loans — real estate lending covers first and second mortgages, construction loans, land-only loans, investment property loans, home improvement, and equity lines of credit. These loans may occur in a variety of shapes and sizes — fixed and adjustable, normally amortizing, interest-only, single-payment, and balloon.

From start to finish, the complete mortgage process spans disclosures, prequalification, origination, document preparation, processing, loan tracking, underwriting, commitment, and closing. The participants include the applicant, the mortgage loan processor, loan originators, underwriters, closers and shippers, and real estate agents.

After hopeful homeowners complete their mortgage loan applications, the work of the processor begins. A processor accumulates the detailed paperwork required for loan approval. Tasks include reviewing the file for accuracy and completeness, qualifying the borrower, and knowing initial documentation requirements. The "order out" process is the review of the verifications of employment, deposit, and mortgage or rent.

A few days after ordering out the documents, the loan file exhibits begin arriving on the processor's desk. These exhibits include the preliminary title report, the credit report, appraisal, property inspections, and the flood hazard determination. The processor's role is to complete the loan file for review by the underwriting department. The responsibilities of the underwriter include risk analysis, property evaluation, and proper documentation requirements.

Underwriters send the loan decision to "closers" who prepare legal documentation, close, and fund the loans. The closer's role is, as the name implies, to close the transaction, or formally transfer the ownership of the property from one person or entity to another. The closer ensures that the title is free from encumbrances (that the property can be legally transferred from one individual or entity to another).

Once the loan closes, the back-office processing work begins in earnest. Loan servicing involves the processing of mortgage loan payments and the administration of mortgage loans.

Offshoring the Loan Servicing Process

Figure 8.1 illustrates the detailed business process that is behind mortgage loan servicing, which includes payment processing, tax tracking and payment, monthly statement disbursement, escrow and insurance analysis, collections, and loss mitigation. Offshoring loan servicing began in the late 1990s and is likely to gain momentum as firms gain experience with it. Offshore loan servicing involves business process management services such as financial statement analysis, investor reporting, and customer services.

A case in point is GreenPoint Mortgage (GPM). According to S.A. Ibrahim, president and CEO of GPM, "The first driver [for offshore outsourcing] is that our business is a fast-growing one."[4] The value of mortgages originated by the firm went from $10 billion in 1999 to $33 billion in 2002. To help its offshore activities, GPM signed a five-year, $30-million deal with Progeon to provide mortgage loan servicing. As part of the contract, Progeon established an Extended Process Operations Center (EPOC) dedicated to GPM.[5] Offshore outsourcing helped the GPM team support the growth in loan origination volume by shifting the back-office loan servicing processes from Columbus, Georgia, to Bangalore, India.

Loan servicing also involves significant call center interaction. U.S. and European firms are using offshore resources to answer status questions like "Did you get my payment?" or "How much do I owe to pay off this loan?" By leveraging the 9.5-hour time difference between the U.S. and

India, mortgage companies can provide support for their customers and mortgage brokers on a 24x7 basis.

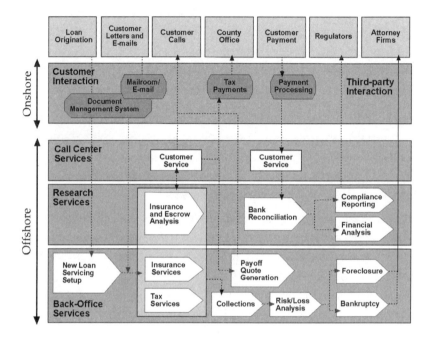

Figure 8.1: The Loan Servicing Process

Loan servicing call center reps can perform the various collection tasks necessary to maintain contact with the borrowers in order to obtain repayment. Early-stage delinquency processing and late-stage collection activities can be supported from an offshore location. The case study of Risk Management Alternatives in Chapter 6 illustrates this process in detail.

Tasks that are connected to loan servicing such as tax administration, online investor reporting, fraud detection, or regulatory compliance document processing are also being offshored. Functions such as payment processing and payment collection are not good candidates for offshoring. The cost differential between processing a task onsite versus offsite will eventually dictate which tasks will migrate offshore and how fast.

The Return on Investment

By shaving loan servicing costs 20%–50% through offshore outsourcing strategies, innovators are beginning to put a lot of competitive pressure on the rest of the industry. The cost savings are primarily due to lower wages. Employees handling back-office tasks in India earn about $300–$500 per month as compared to the $3,000–$4,000 employees are paid in the United States.

Beyond the cost arbitrage, mortgage companies are realizing improvements in operational performance such as timeliness, quality, and adherence to compliance requirements (audits and regulations).

Finally, the innovators in the mortgage industry are proving that automating front-end loan origination and offshoring back-end loan servicing can lead to increased internal efficiency. In general, for companies looking to improve profit margins and compete in low-margin product markets, offshore outsourcing can complement self-service projects and vice versa.

Insurance Claims Processing

Not so far removed from the mortgage industry is the insurance industry. The world of insurance — auto, life, home, and health — is undergoing significant change with mergers and acquisitions, deregulation, increased competition, and product development. To remain competitive, insurance companies are developing strategies to increase their customer bases, expand into new geographic areas, and extend their product offerings. One major industrywide initiative is to focus more on customers and increase product sales by reaching out to them through multiple channels (agents, direct mail, telephone, e-mail, and Web site).

Following are some examples of companies that are offshoring insurance claims processing or of vendors leading the charge.

- Aviva is the largest U.K. insurance company and one of the top five life companies in Europe. Aviva operates under the Norwich Union brand in the United Kingdom. According to its offshore plan, the insurer will send 2,350 jobs (350 call center staff and 2,000 back-office administration and IT roles) that service its general insurance and life insurance businesses to India. Aviva also plans to transfer to India 150 administration roles that support its general insurance business in Canada.[6]

- Swiss Re created a captive center in Bangalore, India. It is offshoring various administrative activities, including technical reinsurance accounting, contract administration, claims settlement, current account management, and the development of special business reports for external and internal needs.

- WNS Global Services, a leading BPO company, acquired Town and Country Assistance Limited, a U.K.-based automobile insurance claims management company. This acquisition gave WNS a 150-seat center in Ipswich, United Kingdom, which acts as a transition location for U.K. and other European clients. In addition, WNS acquired ClaimsBPO, a provider of BPO services to the U.S. healthcare industry in September 2003.

To understand how offshore insurance claims processing works, we turn to ICICI OneSource, a BPO player specializing in transaction processing and contact center services. ICICI OneSource is working with a leading U.K. motor insurance company to provide inbound customer service and sales for motor insurance. Specifically, ICICI OneSource processed policies, sold breakdown insurance, and e-mailed quotations to clients.

Key factors in the project's success were call quality and hitting the sales target. Agents handling the insurer's customers have decreased the average handle time (from a target of less than five minutes to an actual average of 3.47 minutes); lowered the average wrap time (from a target of less than one minute to an actual average of .21 minutes); increased the number of call answered in less than ten seconds (from a target of 90 to an actual average of 96); and reduced the abandon ratio (from a target of less than 4% to an actual average of 2.3%). Estimated annual savings for the U.K. insurer stand at $1 million.[7]

Auto and life insurers are not the only ones in the insurance industry to embrace offshore outsourcing. One of the largest dental insurance companies in the United States outsourced its claims processing to WNS Global Services. The dental company wanted WNS to cost-effectively process and adjudicate about 1 million dental claims yearly. The outcome: an offshore center capable of processing more than 18,000 claims and 3,000 documents daily with a turnaround time of 24–48 hours.

Different Types of Insurance

To understand the scale and scope of the insurance industry, it is important to get an overview of the different types of insurance policies. Some insurance concerns itself strictly with healthcare, while some centers on providing for your family in case of an accident. There is also insurance that is designed specifically to protect companies. Regardless of the type, the processes necessary to support the policy and the possible claim are paper-intensive and ripe for offshore processing.

A partial list of the many insurance options people and businesses have available today follows in table 8.2. Managing them is complicated and time-consuming.

Health and Disability	Property and Casualty	Business
■ Health insurance ■ Dental insurance ■ Long-term and short-term disability ■ Life insurance, such as whole life, universal life, or variable insurance ■ Accidental death and dismemberment (AD&D)	■ Auto insurance ■ Homeowners insurance ■ Condominium insurance ■ Renters insurance ■ Personal articles insurance ■ Crop protection ■ Flood insurance	■ Employment practices liability (EPLI) ■ Directors and officers liability ■ Errors and omissions liability ■ Cyberspace liability

Table 8.2: Insurance Coverage Available to People and Businesses

Historically, the insurance industry has not been a primary beneficiary of technology. The processes that existed between the insurance agent and carrier have remained largely unchanged for the past fifty years. Over the last decade, however, these antiquated, traditional processes have undergone significant transformation, leveraging technology to create new efficiencies and channels for customers to access directly. Let's look at one insurer that has embraced technology to become more efficient.

Offshore Insurance Claims Case Study: MetLife

MetLife is one of the biggest insurance and financial service companies in the United States. MetLife has a full menu of products including property and casualty insurance, life insurance, and financial services such as retirement and savings.

As a large insurer, one of MetLife's core activities revolves around processing claims filed by its many policyholders. Millions of claims pour in monthly and tens of millions yearly. The claims process is one of the main interaction points between insurers and customers and a major factor in how customers view their insurers. The timeliness, quality, and operational costs of processing claims affect customers directly. Taking ten days to process a claim due to a manual, inefficient system is unacceptable to many customers.

At MetLife, the claims management process is an integral part of its operations (see figure 8.2). An efficient process can generate a high level of customer satisfaction and lower costs whereas an inefficient process can result in the loss of customers and higher operating costs.

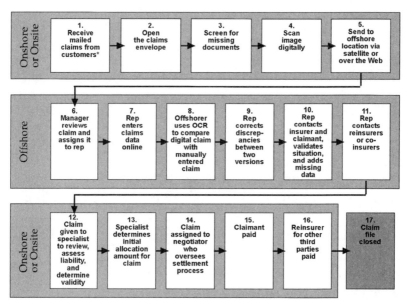

* If claims are received electronically, claims processing can begin offshore.

Figure 8.2: The Insurance Claim Process

The Offshoring Solution

MetLife knew it had to take steps to automate the claims process, and it began searching for a vendor with expertise in that area. MetLife outsourced to Affiliated Computer Services (ACS). For MetLife, one of ACS's largest draws was its experience in the insurance industry. At the time MetLife evaluated ACS, the company was processing claims for eight out of the top ten global healthcare providers.[8]

ACS and MetLife's relationship began in 1999 when ACS signed a five-year contract with MetLife to support its dental claims processing unit through digital imaging of dental claims, image storage, and teleresearch services. In 2003, MetLife renewed and expanded its contract with ACS. ACS agreed to handle MetLife's disability claims processing, long-term care, small business center, brokerage, annuity, and group and individual areas. The services that ACS provides include mailroom, data capture, data cleansing, and imaging.

How the Process Works

ACS's services begin once a claim arrives in the mail in Kentucky, the location that policyholders are directed to use for filing claims. First ACS opens the claim by sanding off the edges of the envelope. Next employees check to see if any required documents are absent. Then it sorts the claim. Finally, the claim is scanned and beamed offshore, and the data is captured through ACS's own satellite network. (Although MetLife uses ACS for paper claims, ACS can receive client data in other formats, such as by voice, over the Web, or via fax, and digitize and distribute it via satellite.) The network distributes the digital claims among ACS's offshore operations in China, Guatemala, the Caribbean, Mexico, and Ghana.

Once a digital claims is received offshore, two employees will independently enter the data from the claim, and the system will compare the two versions to make sure that they are identical. After the data is entered, ACS uses optical character recognition (OCR) — a method for converting scanned text into electronic text — on the digital claim and compares it with the manually entered data.

After the verification step, claims that have errors or are missing material are sent to the MetLife dedicated call center operation on ACS's premises. Call center agents then take steps to correct the errors or omissions by phoning policyholders or doctors who can provide the necessary information. Once a claim has been processed, ACS can either send it back to MetLife's claims processing system or archive it.

MetLife's Return on Investment from Offshoring Insurance Claims

As a result of its partnership with ACS, MetLife states that it has cut costs by 50%, improved customer satisfaction exponentially, and garnered a huge ROI.[9] Confronted by slashed IT budgets and pressure to reduce operating costs, many insurance companies are following MetLife's lead and are heading offshore for transaction processing, application development, and legacy maintenance.

For those companies seriously considering processing claims offshore, it should be noted that some parts of the claims process are more easily offshored than others. Many of the initial steps in claims processing such as receiving claims, gathering information, and opening a claims file are offshorable. Call center activities such as collecting claim information and contacting involved parties are also offshorable. However, processes related to negotiation, settlement, investigation, or valuation (such as assessing liability or evaluating fraud) of a claim are not easily offshored.

Medical Transcription Services

Along with claims and mortgage processing, the third type of transaction processing commonly sent offshore is medical transcription. Physicians in the United States, Canada, and some European countries are required by law to maintain computerized records of patient information. These records can support risk management initiatives and reduce malpractice exposure by ensuring accurate, legible, and defensible charts. Thus, medical transcription is simply transcribing records dictated by doctors or other healthcare providers from an audio format to a hard copy or electronic format. Physicians dictate the patient information, which is converted into a voice file and transmitted to offshore centers via satellite links. It is then transcribed, and the document is sent back to the hospital.

Some organizations that are offshoring medical transcription include the Children's Hospital of Wisconsin, which sends transcription work to India through Heartland Information Services of Toledo, Ohio, and the

University of Pennsylvania Health System (UPHS), which utilizes A+Network.

In the United States, the medical transcription industry is worth about $6 billion and is growing at the rate of 20% annually. As there is a shortage of medical transcriptionists (professionals who listen to and transcribe the document) in the United States, companies are setting up their facilities in other countries or asking offshore third-party vendors to provide this service.

Why Are Companies Outsourcing Medical Transcription?

Quality of medical documentation is critical to the success of a healthcare facility due to external and internal regulations and requirements. External forces such as government regulations — the Health Insurance Portability and Accountability Act (HIPAA) — and insurance company documentation requirements continue to drive the need for quality medical documentation.

Internal forces such as reductions in staffing levels, capital expenditures, and a shortage of qualified medical transcriptionists can hinder a hospital's ability to provide quality medical documentation, which in turn can result in a decrease of overall receivables. Offshoring medical transcription services is a growing trend in the health management industry that has been shown to be successful due to cost reductions, improved quality of work, and increased availability of resources.

By outsourcing medical transcription work, hospitals can save money in numerous ways. They can eliminate or reduce the cost of IT equipment needed for an in-house transcription department. They can decrease fixed employment related costs such as payroll and benefits by not having transcriptionists on staff, thereby freeing up office space. They can also reduce the cost of transcription by utilizing offshore resources at a reduced price. In addition, by moving to an outsourced business model, hospitals can minimize variable costs because the transcription costs occur in direct proportion to the physician's dictation requirements: You only pay when the service is needed.

Another substantial challenge for health information management personnel is managing the end-to-end workflow of the dictation and transcription process. Most facilities are forced to deal with multiple vendors, some focused on the dictation equipment and the rest focused on the transcription process.

The medical transcription industry is highly competitive and fragmented, pitting literally thousands of small local and regional service providers against a few large national transcription vendors. A typical large medical transcription provider might have a 200-seat center with a dedicated team of doctors and editors capable of transcribing 100,000 lines per day with a turnaround time of one to four hours for emergency dictations and an accuracy rate of 98.5%. In line with the hospitals they serve, offshore medical transcription providers truly never sleep — they run a 24x7 operation 365 days a year.

As the need for transcription services grows, along with increasingly demanding physicians, payers, and consumers, it will continue to put pressure on the limited pool of highly skilled practitioners. This shortage of qualified transcriptionists puts upward pressure on wages and benefits, causing a higher-than-normal turnover rate as institutions and services compete for these prized resources. These factors are contributing to the demand for offshore transcription vendors.

Offshore Medical Transcription Case Study: UPHS

The University of Pennsylvania Health System (UPHS) includes four hospitals, the Penn medical school, and about 100 outpatient practices scattered throughout Philadelphia. In 2003, UPHS decided to take a new approach to medical transcription and partnered with CBay System's joint venture A+Network.

Founded in 1998, CBay Systems specializes in healthcare BPO services, particularly the offshore medical transcription industry. CBay provides transcription to hospitals, integrated healthcare facility networks, and medical clinics. In 2001, the company formed a joint venture called A+Network with Arrendale Associates that aims to provide customizable, end-to-end transcription services. CBay customers can choose to outsource part or all of their transcription, as well as decide what method of dictation they would like to use.

Medical Transcription Workflow

Throughout the transcription process, all tasks must conform to HIPAA (electronic transfer and security) regulations. Let's examine a typical offshore transcription workflow (see figure 8.3).

Data Capture. UPHS elected to try CBay's handheld option to record dictations because the devices that CBay offers are portable and hold about 5 hours of dictation. Handhelds also eliminate the possibility of lost tapes and save physicians from having to punch in long strings of numbers when phoning in their dictation. Doctors upload their dictations by docking the handheld in a universal serial bus (USB) cradle that is attached to an Internet-capable PC with a secure connection to CBay.

Document Routing. Documents can be routed via different types of connections, including Web, modem to modem, LAN, and WAN. Data can be stored in a central repository that interfaces with legacy systems and keeps all data gathered from dictators, transcribers, and other sources linked so they can be tracked. Security is important to consider with document routing.

Transcription. After a UPHS dictation is uploaded, the voice files are downloaded and saved at the offshore center. The file is then distributed to one of CBay's 2,500 transcriptionists who begins transcribing it. When finished, a first level proofreading is done. The report is further quality checked by more experienced staff including physicians. CBay promises that completed transcribed reports are 98% accurate.

Document Delivery. After the quality check, the transcribed report goes through an internal editing and formatting process. The text files are then uploaded back to the hospital server. CBay guarantees hospitals a 24-hour turnaround for most reports. Industry standards for transcribed reports are as follows: about 3 hours for stat reports; 12 hours for history and physical reports, operative reports, and emergency room reports; and 48 hours for discharge summaries.[10] The company is able to make its 24-hour guarantee by taking advantage of the time zone difference and running a 24x7 operation. CBay bills UPHS per line of dictation transcribed, which is standard practice in the industry.

One of healthcare providers' main concerns (other than cost) is HIPAA compliance, and CBay seems to have covered that base via an "unbreakable technology platform" that includes 128-bit and triple DES encryption.[11] CBay also has redundant hardware to guarantee uninterrupted dictation, transcription, and document management availability.

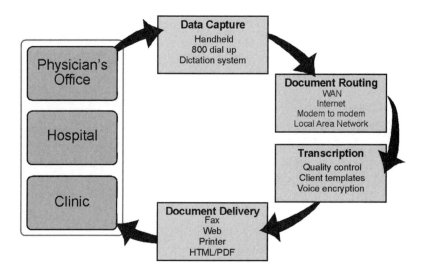

Figure 8.3: Medical Transcription Workflow

The Results

One of the primary reasons UPHS selected CBay as a service provider was undeniably the lure of reduced costs. The company claims it can deliver an average savings of 30% over other transcription strategies healthcare providers have tried. However, with much competition among service providers in the industry, vendors will need to differentiate their services on something other than a low-cost basis. CBay has started down this path by developing transcription software and marketing itself as an end-to-end transcription solution.

Finally, it will be interesting to note how the steadily advancing speech recognition technology affects the industry. Opinions are divided as to whether it will eliminate the need for medical transcriptionists all together or whether it will simply contribute to their productivity.

Offshore Content Management

Unstructured data processing is also making its presence felt in offshoring. A significant part of document management involves the electronic conversion of source documents (newspapers, magazines, or journals) through physical data entry or through computer-assisted data capture using the optical character recognition (OCR) or intelligent character recognition (ICR) techniques.

Some examples of offshore unstructured document processing are:

- Litigation support services (or pretrial coding) cover document coding and indexing, as well as online document management. Typically these support services are used for class action, oil spills, and securities litigation.

- Content conversion involves transferring traditional content (usually in print form) to digital formats.

- Medical image processing involves analysis of x-rays, ultrasound, and magnetic resonance imaging (MRI) images.

LexisNexis: Offshore Content Management

LexisNexis knows a lot about unstructured documents. Headquartered in Ohio, the company, a member of Reed Elsevier Group PLC, is the world's largest provider of online information with more than 1.6 million subscribers worldwide. LexisNexis provides digitized information to professionals globally in the legal, corporate, government, and academic markets.

LexisNexis offers subscribers searchable access to more than 3 billion documents from thousands of newspapers, magazines, trade journals, industry newsletters, and public records. It adds more than 9.5 million documents each week to the existing 3 billion online documents. The company collects the documents from more than 11,000 different sources.[12]

Paper to electronic document conversion and transformation is the heart of the LexisNexis business. To keep the costs of document conversion low, LexisNexis has outsourced a substantial amount of document-conversion and data-transformation services offshore to several external vendors in China and India. For instance in India, LexisNexis worked with Datamatics, a Mumbai-based IT company, to analyze the documents and then convert them to the LexisNexis proprietary format before they are loaded onto the mainframe systems.

As more structured (catalogs) and unstructured (documents) information moves online, data conversion, cleansing, and cataloging are emerging as critical functions. Converting reams of paper catalogs, data from back-office and legacy computers, and numerous other computing systems that store information about products into searchable, easy-to-navigate, electronic catalogs is not a trivial task. We expect that firms will be forced to use offshore resources to manage costs associated with digital assets.

TeleRadiology: Content Management in Medicine

Another example of content heading offshore can be found in the field of radiology. Radiology is the use of radiation (such as chest or dental x-rays) or other imaging technologies (such as ultrasound and magnetic resonance imaging (MRI)) to diagnose or treat disease. These images are really digital content that can be examined anywhere in the world. Consider the following examples:[13]

- Massachusetts General Hospital uses Wipro's staff of twelve radiologists in India to convert 2-D images into 3-D images, so that they are more easily discerned by surgeons.

- Infinity Radiology, based in Dallas, is using radiologists in South Korea for reading and processing x-rays.

The shortage of trained radiologists is partially driving this offshore content processing trend. The huge differences in incomes earned by U.S. board-certified radiologists compared with imaging practitioners elsewhere in the world also are encouraging some of the offshore activity.

The average annual salary offered to candidates for U.S. radiology positions in 2002–2003 was $317,000. Interviews conducted by *Diagnostic Imaging* magazine with radiologists in India showed that a typical Indian radiologist earns between $15,700 and $21,000 annually. Radiologists skilled enough to read CAT scans, MRIs, and ultrasounds earn about $26,000.[14]

With such a dramatic difference in costs, it should come as no surprise that the pressure is growing to leverage offshore resources in medicine. The offshoring of medicine is barely a trickle today, and regulatory restrictions are likely to keep it from growing rapidly. It is a sign of things to come. Other candidates for medical offshoring are the analysis of tissue samples, the reading of electrocardiograms, and the monitoring of intensive care units.

Summary

More CIOs and business leaders are asking, "Is transaction processing something we're good at, or should we outsource or offshore it?" Lately, the inclination has been to do the latter, which accounts for the boom in offshore transaction processing in the banking, insurance, brokerage, retail, medical, credit card, and mortgage industries.

On a global scale, organizations are being forced to address the traditional inefficiencies — manual and time-consuming processes — that plague back-office transaction processing.

Industry-specific transaction processing BPO has emerged over the last few years to fill specific niches. They include:

- Mortgage banking — servicing, processing, and origination outsourcing;

- Medical transcription — medical billing, transcription, scheduling, data entry, customer service, and related medical administrative tasks; and

- Financial — credit card, medical, and retail collections; mortgage servicing and processing; investment clearing services; banking transaction processing and data entry.

We anticipate that by utilizing automation and standardization, the transaction processing market will eventually become very specialized based on industry-specific knowledge. The transformation will not happen overnight, but, as this chapter suggests, it is not far off. Transaction processing, one of the leading success stories of offshore outsourcing, is definitely here to stay.

Chapter Nine

Creating Your Offshore Strategy

"Don't ever take a fence down until you know why it was put up."

— Robert Frost

The Offshore Journey: Where Should You Begin?

Is your company being forced to do more with less money and fewer resources? Are your service levels below the industry average? Are your competitors' products cheaper partly due to their offshore strategies? Do you want access to new technology and capabilities without increasing your budget? If you answered "yes" to any of these questions, then your company is a candidate for offshore outsourcing.

Many C-level executives and managers have either contemplated or begun offshore outsourcing projects. Those that have taken the plunge often make the same discovery: The offshore savings envisioned and the savings achieved in reality are not aligned. Despite the enticing tales of Ph.D. engineers who will work for $15 an hour and vendors that promise Six Sigma quality, the risks of offshore outsourcing projects are complicated and deserving of serious consideration.

Still interested, but wondering what you should do? A disciplined process will improve your chances for a successful offshore venture. The outcome of an offshore outsourcing project depends not only on the strategy a company selects but also on the discipline with which the strategy is implemented. The experiences of the many pioneers show that offshore projects are more successful if upfront planning is in place, project management methodologies are used, and team members understand their roles and responsibilities. Poor offshore implementations are typically the result of the "let's do something quickly" mentality. The ensuing rush to execute can be harmful.

Immediate success is rare in any field and offshore outsourcing is no exception. In this chapter, we walk you through the key steps of formulating a disciplined offshore strategy. We discuss the following:

- How to create a business case for offshoring,

- Issues to consider when evaluating and selecting an offshore vendor,

- Critical success factors for managing an offshore service level agreement, and

- The project management issues that offshoring will create.

Creating an Offshore Strategy: A Seven-Step Roadmap

Let's say your firm has decided to offshore a single business process or some elements of information technology. What are the steps that will help your endeavor to meet with success?

Classic project management advocates a seven-step methodology that will help you avoid costly mistakes. We have adapted this methodology specifically to realize the benefits and minimize the risks of offshore outsourcing.

To create an effective offshore strategy, management should perform the following seven steps:

1. **Analyze your offshoring goals and set the strategy** — establish your reasons for offshoring and what value you expect to receive.

2. **Create the offshore delivery model** — assess the make-versus-buy decision. If you intend to buy, conduct strict due diligence on your potential offshoring vendor.

3. **Negotiate the offshore contract** — draft a contract that specifies the general, financial, and legal framework of the relationship.

4. **Design service level agreements** — make sure your contract defines the SLAs clearly, such as what will be measured and when, as well as the penalties the vendor faces if it fails to meet SLA metrics.

5. **Manage the transition** — transitions can make or break the contract, and a transition plan is critical. Keep track of SLA agreements and check metrics carefully.

6. **Manage the relationship for maximum value** — prioritize relationship management to make the link between the vendor and your company friction free. Plan for changes.

7. **Measure performance improvement** — nonstop service quality measurements and audits are necessary to show that customer needs are being met and steady progress in terms of quality is being made.

All these steps are important and critical. According to Phaneesh Murthy, CEO of iGATE Global Solutions, "Companies often make three mistakes when they go offshore. The number-one mistake is not enough upfront planning and analysis to try and figure out what are the right processes to offshore, and how to do it well. The upfront analysis is key because C-level management is concerned with risk management. The risks increase if you pick the wrong set of processes. Two not paying enough attention to the whole process of transition management: How do you control risk during transition management? The third mistake is when companies go offshore for the wrong reasons. You're going offshore because your neighbor went offshore, not necessarily because it benefits your business. Therefore, you make decisions that are not necessarily the right ones."[1]

Figure 9.1 summarizes the seven steps we just discussed. For more detail on each of the steps, read on.

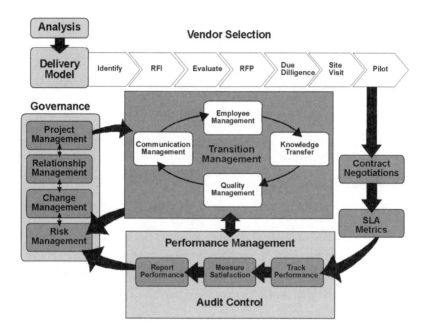

Figure 9.1: Seven-Step Methodology for Creating an Offshore Strategy

Step 1: Strategy Analysis: Objective and Scope

The first step of your journey is defining the objective, scope, and time frame you have in mind for your offshoring initiative. Without a clear understanding of the strategic goals for offshoring, your hard work could be wasted. Many firms have started offshoring projects with hazy strategies and unclear ROI expectations. In order to avoid that scenario, your company needs to decide several issues upfront.

To Offshore or Not to Offshore

Is offshore outsourcing right for your organization? Which areas or functions? The sober truth is that cutting costs is the preferred route to profits these days. Most costs, directly or indirectly, are related to labor or technology. The ability to cut costs through conventional means — productivity improvements and layoffs — is reaching its limits. Offshoring is a viable approach for reaching the next level of sustainable cost reduction.

Every offshore outsourcing initiative begins with a decision to change, to either reach certain cost milestones or enable changes in the business model. As a result, it is critical to evaluate the advantages and disadvantages of keeping a business process or IT function in-house or sending it offshore. The importance of the "why offshore" question cannot be emphasized enough. If you are unable to fully answer this question, then you are bound to run into problems downstream.

Companies frequently offshore for the wrong reasons. Sanjay Kumar, founder and CEO of vCustomer, a provider of customer contact and back-office processing solutions, states, "In customer service, the challenge today is that most offshore decisions are driven by tactical rather than strategic issues. If nobody takes a strategic interest in outsourcing, then it's driven by a budget. What happens is the CFO will come and say, 'I heard XYZ company cut its costs by 40% in customer service by offshoring to India. Why can't you guys do it?' So then the pressure is on to achieve 50% savings enabling the manager to look good for his CFO. The decision turns out to be not as strategic as it could be since the focus becomes cost not quality."[2]

It is also important to recognize that different people have different motives for offshoring. According to Somshankar Das, CEO and president of e4e, a business process and technology solutions outsourcing company, "Different people have different perspectives and reasons for offshoring. CFOs are trying to figure out how they can reduce fixed costs, make the costs more variable, [and] how they can achieve some of these things without having volatility in the earnings. From the perspective of the VP of engineering, he's a little less interested in the cost reduction, but more interested in the availability of skills and the pool of engineering talent. From the CEO's perspective, it is about strategic point of view because they are trying to see how offshoring can help them get a better position in the market place."[3]

After you determine why you are offshoring and what your organization hopes to accomplish, analyze your current costs and prioritize areas or functions that could be a match for offshore outsourcing. For each opportunity, clearly state your objectives. What benefits would you like to achieve? What improvements are needed and why? How would offshoring affect operations? How would it affect your customers?

Once you have decided that your business can benefit from offshoring, it is time to evaluate the scope of the process selected and the ROI. Before you invest time and money developing an RFP, choosing a vendor, and negotiating a contract, you need to be certain that the business case for offshoring is airtight.

Defining the Scope of an Offshore Outsourcing Project

Begin with the end state in mind. Figure out the capabilities the company needs to align offshore operations with business strategy. Which divisions, functions, or processes of your organization should be involved in your initial offshore outsourcing scope? Offshore outsourcing has its fair share of success stories, but it's important to realize that some functions or processes should never be sent offshore. For instance, pharmaceutical companies should not send their research offshore if they are worried about intellectual property (IP) issues.

Picking a process to offshore. Keeping your culture, customers, and employees in mind, determine what processes you want to send offshore. Inbound calls or outbound calls? Telemarketing? Catalog sales? Technical assistance? Early-stage payment delinquency? Processes should be selected based on savings potential, labor attributes, interdependencies, and regulatory constraints. Classify them into three categories: probable, possible, and unlikely to be offshored.

Some criteria to consider in selecting a process to offshore are:

- If the process has a large cost base

- If the process is labor-intensive

- If it has interlinkages that would be violated by relocation

- If the skills to complete the process are available offshore

- If a significant wage level differential can be created by offshoring

Perform a gap analysis. For the processes that are considered probable, you need to carefully measure current state. You cannot improve what you do not know. If you don't know what the current internal costs are for accomplishing tasks you plan to send offshore, how can you know how much you will save? Perform a gap analysis to define current state costs, business processes, quality metrics, and procedures. Understanding and articulating what you want to do and what you need from a potential outsourcing partner is a key step. Thinking about the feasibility of sending a particular process offshore is critical.

Define the process scope carefully. If the process scope is not clear, the offshore project will be doomed. Functions, processes, locations, third-party agreements, or projects that will be part of the outsourcing agreement are termed in-scope; those that are not are called out-of-scope. Part of the scope definition includes establishing an appropriate baseline, which outlines the current service delivery costs, service levels, and benchmarks and serves as a guideline for the future or desired state. We cannot overstate the importance of defining your scope carefully.

Define the financial justification and ROI. Every offshore project needs careful financial justification as part of the business case. Because so much of the benefit of offshore projects lies in the future, it is hard to know when or if they are going to pay off. This creates enormous stresses in the resource and budget allocation process. Given finite resources, how can managers choose between onshore projects that have a near-term and quantifiable outcome and offshore projects whose returns are hard to estimate? Developing a well-researched financial model with assumptions clearly stated is a mandatory step.

Part of every financial model is a cost-benefit analysis. Offshore outsourcing cost-benefit analysis takes each task of a business process and defines its value and the basis for measuring its benefits or effectiveness. Then the costs of performing each task are reviewed, taking into account labor, technology, and other cost variables. In the effort to improve a process, care must be taken to evaluate alternatives on the same "cost" and "benefit" bases. This is where most companies have trouble. They do very little detailed analysis of their current state and costs. The tendency to "wing it" and not be data-driven leads to poor strategic choices.

At the end of step 1, you should have a clear picture of what you want to achieve through offshore outsourcing. You should understand the scope of processes to be offshored and avoid the classic trap of rushing into offshoring without understanding the current and future state. Why is this important? Without knowing how your current processes are performing, how will you be able to set up metrics for the offshore provider? How will you know when customer satisfaction improves?

Step 2: Create the Offshore Delivery Model

What offshore business and delivery model will help you accomplish your stated objectives? If you need a refresher on offshore delivery models turn to Chapter 2, otherwise we will summarize some basic decisions regarding the business model that you need to make.

The Relationship Decision: Build versus Buy versus Lease

Will you build your own operation offshore (insourced or captive centers), buy into an existing one (joint venture), or create a sourcing relationship (outsource to a third party)? Building your own offshore location enables you to maintain quality control and ensure culture transfer, but joining forces with an existing operation — either through a joint venture or an external service provider — will save you a number of headaches, from clearing bureaucratic hurdles to having to learn the nuances of conducting business in a specific country (see figure 9.2).

Raja Gopalakrishnan, head of U.S. operations for ICICI OneSource, one of the largest third-party BPO services companies in India, predicts, "We can expect to see more hybrid operating models combining both captive and third-party resources, as well as an increase in offshore deals involving 'insourcing,' where after two or three years into a contract, the outsourcing company will have the option of taking over the offshore operations from the third-party provider."[4]

Another factor that affects the relationship decision is the level of experience your company has. If you have no prior experience with offshoring, start with a well-documented process requiring very little day-to-day interaction like data entry or legacy application maintenance. Gradually move to higher value-added processes. Our advice would be to wait on more complex models such as captive centers, joint ventures, or a build-operate-transfer.

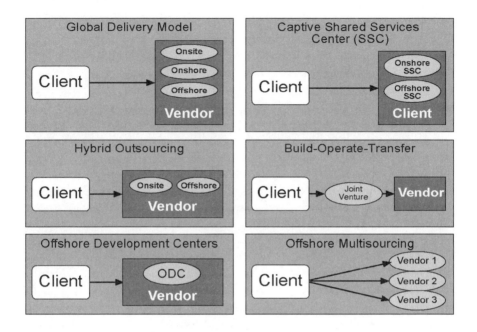

Figure 9.2: Offshore Business Models

The Location Decision: India versus China versus Russia

A critical aspect of any business model decision is the location. Many firms tend to offshore for cost but stay for quality. In order to limit their exposure to the risks associated with offshoring, such as faulty infrastructure and geopolitical instability, many businesses take a multivendor, multisite, or multicountry approach. That way, if there is trouble wherever their operations are based, companies can promptly transfer their processing or programming work to another location within that country or to another destination altogether.

Managing location risk may require multiple vendors. New York–based Guardian Life Insurance, which outsources application development and maintenance, thought so. Guardian contracted with Patni Computer Systems of Mumbai, India; NIIT Technologies of New Delhi, India; and Covansys of Farmington Hills, Michigan. As Shelley McIntyre, vice president of technology services at Guardian, said, "We didn't want to put all our eggs in one basket. We went to three to lessen risk."[5]

Every location has a certain risk profile. Evaluate the location based on distance, time zone differences, cultural differences, language barriers, quality of suppliers, legal framework, and geopolitical stability. Selecting a country can be an intimidating task, so we dedicated an entire chapter (Chapter 11) to this subject.

The Governance Decision: Your Way or the Vendor's Way?

Are you comfortable managing an offshore operation? In the past, you may have taken advantage of a time and material (T&M) contractor to supplement your staffing needs. Bringing on contractors and putting them to work is a process many managers understand. You tell the contractors what is needed, when it is due, and how it needs to be done. You control project management, resource planning, and scheduling. In an offshore project, however, the vendor is expected to assume responsibility for the complete development and delivery of the final product, which means that he also handles project management, resource planning, and scheduling. Offshore outsourcing requires a different type of preparation, approach, and relationship than T&M contracting does.

The Vendor Decision: Infosys versus Keane versus Accenture

Selecting a vendor is like diving into a swimming pool: Once your feet leave the diving board, you are fully committed. Before you dive in, make sure that the water is more than a few inches deep. According to Richard Swanson, director of BPO services at Patni Computer Systems, "There are a lot of pure player providers who haven't been doing it very long. There are a lot of vendors that have just four walls, some lights, some desktops, and some fancy brochureware, and they're in the offshore outsourcing business. So due diligence is really critical."[6]

Given the relative immaturity of the offshore industry, selecting a vendor can be quite tricky. Thousands of companies have sprung up in India, Canada, South Africa, and Ireland to provide offshoring services. Due to the sheer amount of work involved in picking an offshore vendor, we decided to devote a separate chapter (Chapter 10) to this topic.

At the end of step 2, you should have completed the due diligence on your business model, location, relationship characteristics, and vendor that will help you achieve the goals set forth in your business case. You should have created a request for proposal (RFP) and evaluated proposals from potential service providers.

Step 3: Negotiate the Offshore Contract

Once the delivery model and vendor are selected, the contract negotiations begin. Negotiations lay out a rational framework that specify the general, financial, and legal aspects of the offshoring relationship. Contract negotiations are an important step in avoiding problems downstream. All services and costs must be clearly defined, so that both parties have the same expectations about what services will and will not be included in the contract.

Alignment of expectations with vendor capabilities is vital. Nothing will create distrust and dissatisfaction quicker than misalignment between what you expect the vendor to perform and what the vendor is actually providing. Several key issues that warrant extra attention follow.

The General Contract Framework

Forging the right master agreement is critical. When negotiating, make sure you have a strategic view of what you want to achieve and the goals that are important to you. Think about the incentives and rewards for both your company and the vendor. Make sure that anything that is important to you (meeting deadlines or getting your offshore project operational as soon as possible) is part of the contract. You also must make an effort to understand what is important to the vendor. When both companies understand each other's goals, they have the basis for a sound relationship.

Price, quality, and deadlines, however, are not the only things that need to be negotiated and agreed upon. There are many other aspects to a good outsourcing contract.

Flexibility. Outsourcing agreements are often long term — one year, three years, and even ten years — so the contract needs to be flexible enough to change with the times. Expect significant revisions to your BPO contract every two years — you may want to expand or limit the scope of your project or accommodate new risks and technologies.

Payment Terms. It is essential to clearly define the payment cycle and terms — the period within which you make the payment after receiving the invoice (such as 30 days). Vendors can be paid after they reach milestones, or they can be paid regularly on a weekly or monthly basis.

Conflict Resolution. As is expected, many outsourcing relationships periodically encounter problems that can stem from unclear requirements or missed metrics. Be sure to document the procedures for reporting and resolving problems.

Term, Expiration, and Renewal. Explicitly define the duration of the contract and spell out the terms under which it will expire or the terms under which it can be renewed. It is better to require a formal renewal in writing rather than specifying conditions for automatic renewal.

Statement of Work. Draft a statement of work that will help to keep the arrangement on track by clarifying your needs and the vendor's responsibilities. The statement of work should define the scope and objectives of the services to be provided and include a time line and deliverables.

Performance Measurements. Define the cost reductions with the vendor — will savings come from people reduction (make sure to define which people) or re-engineered processes (make sure to define which processes). Document and understand the details and do not accept generalities. Do not allow the outsourcer to only define metrics for the first year and gloss over improvements for the remaining years of the contract. Add achievable improvements year after year and change your baseline as you go. Build a review process into the contract that will look at the costs and savings the vendor promised in the beginning.

Service Level Agreements (SLAs). It is crucial to discuss key objectives and measurements of success. Without clearly defining key metrics in the beginning, confusion could arise about responsibilities, which in worst-case scenarios leads to finger pointing and dissatisfaction. You must spend time on this step. Upfront requirements definition and careful planning can save time and eliminate rework. Time spent on contracts and SLAs during negotiations will save much confusion and unhappiness down the road.

Financial Framework

How much is offshore outsourcing going to cost you? This phase of the contract negotiations is aimed at ensuring that the contract is being executed within the approved cost parameters. It consists of pricing, price stability, and hidden costs.

Pricing. Outsourcing arrangements with offshore vendors can run from thousands of dollars to millions of dollars over the course of a multiyear agreement, depending on the size and complexity of the contract. When the relationship involves purchasing assets such as infrastructure or data centers, hiring staff, or integrating client facilities, the provider makes a substantial investment. Accordingly, price setting itself is both complex and iterative.

Familiarize yourself with supplier pricing and margins. Contracts can be written on a fixed-price or variable-price basis. With fixed-price engagements, the vendor assumes the risk of absorbing cost variability. When set too low, fixed-price arrangements diminish the vendor's flexibility and motivation to respond to changing business conditions or emerging technologies. While variable pricing allows for increased risk sharing, it may also create misunderstandings if and when costs exceed expectations, especially if scope and accountability are poorly defined.

Price Stability. In long-term outsourcing arrangements, it is important to understand the price stability. Some vendors may increase their prices by more than 30% per year, so you need to ensure that you discuss the annual percentage rise before signing the contract.

Hidden Costs. Some offshore vendors advertise low-labor costs while promoting their services until they get you to sign the contract. Later they produce an invoice with billing for separate services like documentation, overtime, or project management. Make sure you discuss hidden costs with the offshore vendor and ensure all costs are documented in your contract.

Many companies do a good job of estimating costs for the vendor but fall short when estimating their internal costs. An often-overlooked cost of offshore outsourcing is the required investment in management time and travel. Project management takes on new complexity with offshore work and can eat up money and management time while sinking quality if it's not done right. You should reserve 5%–15% of your total budget for the internal management team to oversee the outsourced process. Depending on the offshore location, travel costs can quickly accumulate and tend to be woefully underestimated.

Legal Framework

Warranties, liability, and confidentiality are a few of the legal issues that you will need to address. Other issues include:

- Protecting your trade secrets (processes, source code) and intellectual property (IP).

- Ensuring the security and privacy of your data. Who maintains ownership of information? Is the ownership of data or source code clearly defined?

- Being aware of local regulations, such as labor and taxation laws.

- Responding to a vendor that fails to perform its duties.

- Terminating the relationship. Does your contract have termination stipulations? Are you protected? How do you or the vendor initiate termination? What fees apply?

- Enforcing your contract rights from the United States and the chosen offshore country.

Drawing up a legal framework before launching an offshore outsourcing project is similar to drafting a prenuptial agreement before marriage. Although some would argue that a prenuptial agreement is not romantic and means that the marriage is doomed to fail, if there is a lot at risk, it is essential to involve a legal document. The same legal precautions need to be taken before signing an offshoring agreement.

At the end of step 3, you should have negotiated a general term sheet, pricing, and other financial details, as well as the overarching legal framework. You should have worked with the appropriate legal counsel to negotiate and structure the contract. This will help avoid a common misstep — the contracts are drawn up in a hurry and problems stem from a relationship that is not well thought out before the deal is sealed.

Step 4: Design Service Level Agreements

Designing a detailed service level agreement (SLA) is a difficult and somewhat overlooked step of the offshore roadmap. SLAs define the level of performance the vendor promises to deliver and your rights if they fail to do so. SLAs and key performance indicators (KPIs) are determined in the contract negotiations and transition periods. They are generally finalized at the end of the transition period, although they may be re-examined at an agreed upon time if new processes or technologies are implemented.

Effective SLAs identify the expected results and the measures by which both parties will evaluate performance. It is important to put in writing what the vendor is expected to deliver, as well as the roles and responsibilities of both parties. Avoid statements such as "to be defined or specified later" or "to be agreed upon later" at all costs. Do not leave anything undocumented. If the vendor says, "It was not in the SLA..." you can safely assume that there will be an extra cost associated with getting that task completed.

Elements of an SLA

A well-designed SLA describes the start and end dates for the service, the schedule for reviewing performance, and the documentation to be used in measuring the service. Other important questions to be answered in the SLA include:

- What types of service levels are customers and end users expecting?

- How will you measure the service level? Will it be user satisfaction surveys, errors in work, or automated software methods such as system availability?

- What is the measurement period? Is it daily (24x7 or 9 to 6), weekly, or monthly?

- What is the minimum quality of work? What are the provisions and penalties for over- and underperformance? Missing minimum levels can result in breach of contracts requiring some form of make-good actions.

- What is the escalation process for issue resolution? What provisions are made for special or emergency issue resolution?

An SLA should always be mutually agreeable to you and the vendor. Both parties should discuss the requirements and desired outcomes and negotiate an SLA that can be implemented with attainable goals.

Our research indicates that SLAs often lack effective performance penalties and incentives. Be certain to attach specific penalties for performance levels that were not met, such as hold time for customers or problem resolution time. Remember that you cannot measure what you cannot define, so if it is not clearly defined in the SLA, then there will be no way to measure the performance of the vendor.

According to Tim Barry, vice president of outsourcing at Keane, "When outsourcing deals have problems, it's typically because client and supplier expectations regarding performance and service levels are misaligned. Regardless of the type of outsourcing deal, it's critical that both parties create and approve statements of work and service level agreements that support the client's business needs."[7]

At the end of step 4, you should have a carefully designed SLA that measures whether or not a provider is delivering the needed results. This step refines the cost and value of each metric and defines the reporting process, the process for changing metrics, and which metrics will be part of the SLA. Metrics should be unambiguous. Document contract terms for failures to deliver or penalties for missed metrics. Do not wait until after you sign the contract to agree upon the cost of each metric.

Step 5: Manage the Transition

Despite rigorous due diligence, vendor reviews, and test projects, the real work begins once the contract is signed. Smooth transition management is the next issue to tackle. This is considered to be a critical success factor of offshore initiatives. Transition management is defined as the detailed, desk-level knowledge transfer and documentation of all relevant tasks, technologies, workflows, and functions.

Tim Lavin, senior vice president for operations at Ambergris Solutions, a leading Philippine-based provider of customer care solutions, explains,

"Once the contract is signed and it's time to move the business over to the operation, it's important that you have an operations team who is experienced in the implementation of new accounts, specifically in the implementation of new accounts offshore. That's the biggest pitfall. If you do have a resource that has the expertise and attention for detail and project implementation, your rifts and worries are minimized."[8]

The transition period is perhaps the most difficult stage of an offshore endeavor, taking anywhere from three months to a year to complete. There are many issues to consider when moving to the new vendor. For example, current employees must be a willing part of the process. This takes some effort if employees' positions are at risk, so communication is critical. Let's look at some key aspects of transition management.

Knowledge Transfer Between Organizations

Knowledge transfer is the tricky task of bringing the vendor's employees up to speed on your internal procedures and processes. Before you can begin transferring knowledge though, you have to establish what knowledge has to remain in-house and what should be transferred. Job shadowing may be part of the methodology to help train the vendor employees for day-to-day operations.

Consider the case of Otis Elevator, the world's largest manufacturer of elevators headquartered in Connecticut. In 2001, Otis moved from a project-by-project service delivery model to having Wipro set up a dedicated offshore development and maintenance center in Bangalore, India. This dedicated center had a permanent team that worked on nothing but Otis application development and maintenance projects.

An effective transition plan was a priority for Otis. According to David Wood, director of systems development at Otis, "The first big issue was knowledge transfer. We were sitting on a large inventory of applications built by a variety of vendors." Wood and the Wipro project leader spent a month developing a transition plan that included writing technical documentation that outlined file-naming standards, hardware, and software specifications; creating a high-level project plan; identifying the best onshore and offshore managers; and providing opportunities for knowledge transfer, such as job shadowing. "The transition period requires bringing a few people who will eventually be working offshore onsite to go through the application, get an understanding of it, and create the documentation that's required," says Wood.[9]

Otis spent $420,000 on the transition and didn't recoup that investment and start saving money for a year. Wood estimates Otis is saving $1.4 million a year on application development and maintenance, a nice complement to the annual $7 million it has been saving by using its own captive development center in Pune, India.

Knowledge transfer also involves technology transfer and documentation. If the vendor will be assuming licenses or operations of client-owned applications or infrastructure, then all in-scope systems must be identified and documented. Licenses, maintenance agreements, hosting, and telecom infrastructure may be part of the transition. If separate entities will manage applications or hosting, protocols must be established to ensure roles and responsibilities are clear.

Documentation also figures prominently in knowledge transfer. Make sure the vendor has documented training manuals and escalation procedures for recurring problems.

Communication Management

Communication management describes the processes required to enable appropriate and timely generation, collection, and dissemination of outsourcing information.

There are two types of communication management: strategic and operational.

Strategic communications apprise all employees within your company of your offshore outsourcing intentions and the reasons behind them. Employees want to know what is happening, why, and how it affects them. Problems occur when leadership does not inform middle management and lower-level employees of the offshoring plan. When business units are not kept informed, they become frustrated, and the vendor transition is slowed down.

Too often, outsourcing is treated like a dark secret, and corporate rumor mills breed fear and distrust. Companies must step forward and clearly state their objectives such as to save costs, become more competitive, give customers better service, or provide a better return for stockholders.

Your employees must understand why their company is putting so much effort into launching and managing an offshoring initiative.

Managing communication can be the difference between a successful offshore transition with limited disruptions and shattered morale among the remaining employees. Ron Glickman, CIO at DFS Group, a subsidiary of Louis Vuitton Moet Hennessy, advises companies to move fast to spread the word once a decision to outsource has been made.

DFS Group outsourced to Cognizant, an IT services firm with an offshore presence, and eliminated three out of four IT jobs inside DFS. There was discontent among those who lost their jobs, but Glickman's goal was to avoid turning the process into a unproductive waiting game of staff wondering who would be laid off next. According to Glickman, "Moving as quickly as possible with the change process helps minimize morale issues. Speed is really important."[10] DFS eliminated the tension involved in the transition by making sure employees were aware of what was happening and were paid bonuses for staying on through the transition.

Operational communications are the day-to-day communications between you and the vendor. You will need to develop a communication plan that addresses issues such as the time difference between different locations, the language and cultural differences, whether videoconferencing capabilities exist, and when to schedule status meetings. Such a plan should specify how often you communicate, what is on the agenda, who will initiate the discussion, how the meeting will take place, and who should be involved.

Richard Jones, CTO of mortgage lender Countrywide Financial, first gained experience working with offshore outsourcers before Y2K. The CTO thinks that poor operational communication is the most common reason work sent offshore fails to meet project specifications. "To make communications tight, you need to have an onshore element [of the outsourcer]," he says.[11] Countrywide turned to Keane for its application development work. Keane's onshore presence allowed Countrywide IT managers to better communicate project requirements to the vendor.

Communication tends to become more complicated as more parties, countries, and time zones are involved. We recently worked on a project for a California company with a presence in India. Scheduling a status meeting and coordinating East Coast, West Coast, and Indian time zones added a layer of complexity to what should have been a straightforward task. When working offshore, simple problems become exacerbated. Having the processes and experienced management in place to address such issues quickly guarantees you greater success.

Employee Management: Redeploy, Transfer, or Let Go?

Companies underestimate the importance of the human side of offshoring. According to Ilya Billig, vice president of marketing at LUXOFT, a software offshoring company based in Russia, "Companies need to communicate by clearly stating the goals, the course of actions that will be taken not to lose people or how many people may lose jobs, and what people can do to avoid losing jobs. That is the most important thing to do for any company that is considering outsourcing. The companies need to be very honest...[and] open in their outsourcing approach."[12]

Your employees should be a major focus for the leadership of your company during the transition phase. Many of those affected by offshoring attribute their dissatisfaction to poor communication. The communication effort should begin before any potential vendors are involved. You must have a strategy for letting all employees know, especially those who may be at risk of losing their jobs, the reasons for outsourcing and the process that is going to occur. It will not be an easy task, but it is a necessary one.

One sensitive subject that has to be discussed is redeployment or other options for existing staff. Redeployment should be included as part of the transition costs, as it may involve severance payments and possible employment court settlements if it is not handled correctly. It is important to maintain business continuity during the period when an offshore initiative is announced and when it is implemented. Expenses for retention and severance packages have to be taken into account.

With the strong feelings offshoring engenders, there is also a need to include a media and PR plan that keeps stakeholders properly informed regarding reasons for outsourcing and that protects your brand and image.

Quality Management During Transition

Quality management describes the processes required for making sure that the contract is fulfilling the business objectives for which it was undertaken. It consists of quality planning, assurance, and control.

In January 2003, Delta Air Lines moved part of its reservations call center to service centers owned by Wipro Spectramind in India. Dedicated voice and data connections tie the Mumbai, India, operations to Delta's U.S. operations. Initially, the airline was concerned about quality because revenues could be lost if customers were frustrated with the offshore service provider, so it decided to monitor operator performance remotely.

To control quality that is thousands of miles away, Delta uses contact center management software from Witness Systems Inc. The vendor's eQuality Suite automatically creates voice and screen data captures from individual agents workstations that can be viewed in real time or archived. "It's a tremendous coaching tool, and nobody knows when they're being monitored," says John Jacobi, a vice president in Delta's technology unit.[13]

To guarantee quality, many companies are emphasizing certifications such as ISO 9001 or Six Sigma. Possessing these certifications puts many companies at ease because they know the quality of the vendor's work is high. The vendors are expected to deploy a consistent, high-quality process for analysis, design, development, quality assurance, reporting, project monitoring, and management.

At the end of step 5, you should have performed the transition work associated with offshoring. To minimize chaos, spend some time creating a transition plan, which maps out the processes and includes project management, communication, and education plans, as well as metrics. From people to processes, all aspects of your transition process should be well thought out, documented, and, most importantly, communicated.

Step 6: Manage the Relationship for Maximum Value

After you have begun managing the transition, it's time to turn your skills to governing the offshore relationship — captive center, joint venture, or external vendor. This goes beyond the mere monitoring of contractual obligations. It focuses on proactive and collaborative management of the relationship, the evolution of services provided, ongoing communication processes, performance review standards, and overall project management.

Governance is another one of those areas of offshoring that can make or break a project. The reality of managing functions and people that aren't right outside your office door is often not understood until it is upon you. You have to establish the three levels of a governance relationship (see table 9.1):

1. The strategic level, often the executive steering committee, aligns the processes, projects, and goals with business requirements. It also directs the client and vendor's relationship.

2. In complex organizations, you have program offices that are tasked with making tactical decisions on program costs, project priorities and milestones, expected ROI, and risk management.

3. The operational level, often called the project office, handles the day-to-day management of offshore projects to ensure that processes are running smoothly.

Steering Committee	Program Office	Project Office
■ Define overall strategy ■ Establish IT, business, HR, legal, audit, and compliance support ■ Provide necessary funding ■ Charter program management office ■ Report to board	■ Vendor evaluation ■ Relationship management ■ Process selection ■ Best practices benchmarking ■ Staff retraining and redeployment plan ■ Communications ■ Performance reporting	■ Weekly check-ins ■ Quarterly operations review ■ Biyearly site visits ■ SLA monitoring ■ Document internal processes for further improvements

Table 9.1: Levels of Governance

Reporting needs to occur at all levels with a combined scorecard that can be reviewed at the executive and manager levels so that any red flags can be resolved quickly. For both the strategic and operational levels, you will need to clearly define the roles and responsibilities for each team member and then identify the competencies for each person.

Offshore Project Management

Building an offshore partnership requires much effort and delicate handling by management. Any business model that distributes work across multiple locations involves many hand-offs and requires close coordination to manage service levels. It's difficult enough managing a project onsite; that difficulty is amplified when a project is undertaken on another continent. Now, ask yourself: Do we have an appropriate management and administrative structure to effectively coordinate onsite and offshore resources?

In offshoring, even if the vendor does the day-to-day project management, you still have to communicate with, collaborate with, and monitor the vendor. The distance between you and the vendor puts a greater importance on project management to ensure deadlines are being met and reporting is timely and accurate. Structured communication processes will decrease risk and increase efficiency.

Working out cultural differences is also critical. Even with simple tasks, such as sending e-mail, you must allow for cultural and time differences. For example, Americans usually think "yes" means a person agrees with a statement, while in other cultures people say "yes" to confirm that they understand, not that they necessarily agree. Because of the potential for misunderstandings, onshore project managers need to prepare their own staff for working with offshore vendors.

Many managers underestimate the cost of offshore project management, and some do not even consider it when they estimate ROI. Our experience tells us that when you outsource a major business process, you should allot between 5% and 15% of your budget for managing the outsourced process. If the process is strategic or transformational in nature, your offshore project management costs could rise to 20%.

Offshore Relationship Management

Your offshore project may require new organizational processes to properly manage the ongoing offshore relationship between team members. Relationship management is necessary to compensate for the loss of direct interaction between stakeholders, managers, and team members. Informal meetings that take place in hallways or in the breakroom often help with communications. Without these channels, the project manager must allocate dedicated resources to maintain appropriate levels of communication and coordination. Regular formal and informal communication in the form of teleconferences, videoconferences, and e-mail exchanges is essential for success. Don't underestimate the difficulties of remote management and time differences.

Consider the case of Sony Electronics, which struggled initially to get offshore call center employees to understand the service demands of U.S. customers. Sony outsourced call center functions to India and the Philippines. Maureen Read, vice president and general manager of Sony's customer service center, says she regularly visits the Indian call center and spends a lot of time explaining Sony's customer service philosophy. "I learned early on that you cannot expect an Indian company to teach their Indian employees how to [understand] Americans," she says. Read says that with customer service in particular, people from your company have to provide "an ongoing influx of American viewpoints."[14]

In long-term, complex engagements, both parties should have relationship managers. These individuals ensure that changes occur in a timely manner and that issues are resolved appropriately. Your relationship manager should have liaison skills, knowledge of the organization, business case expertise, analytical skills, and a good reputation within your organization. They should also be senior enough to make decisions within defined boundaries without waiting for further approval.

Contract and SLA Change Management

A key activity for every project office or manager is change management. The general rule of thumb says that changing competition or consumer preferences render a significant amount of process design obsolete every five years. The goal of change management is to ensure that standardized procedures are used for efficient, prompt handling of all changes.

What happens when technology changes mid-contract? Rapid changes taking place in technology add to the challenge of offshoring and require an equally swift ability to adapt. Striving to reach low-cost milestones also tends to drive contract and SLA changes. According to Sanjay Kumar, CEO of vCustomer, "…once companies reach a certain threshold in terms of cost savings, they should be shifting their focus to quality and process improvement. Companies should be focusing their efforts on telling vendors to deliver a higher level both in quality as well as service delivery metrics. Strategically, companies should be building in an incentive for the vendors who do deliver on the quality and process improvements."[15]

Given the likelihood of external changes, one area that will have to be amended is the scope of the contract. You need to define in your contract how changes in service scope or content are provided for. You will also need to think about the process for changing the SLAs and contract. How can you modify the agreement to be more responsive to your needs? What threshold operating levels should trigger the change process automatically? What must be done to change the agreement? What are the limitations on change posed, for example, by the economics, term, or technology requirements of the offshoring relationship?

Many offshore companies are known for their change management process quality. Burlington Northern Santa Fe Railway (BNSF) based in Texas offshored some software development to Infosys Technologies in Bangalore, India. According to Jeff Campbell, vice president of technology services and CIO at BNSF, "Communication and collaboration are key to success. Infosys was world-class in change control and methods of delivery. They have a program office at our headquarters. They have full-time people here that manage the flow through methodology and communications."[16]

Managing the change process safeguards against companies and vendors disagreeing over what the vendor is providing. Once operations begin, change management needs to monitor change orders and work orders. Without this strict process, confusion and redundancy of work may occur.

Risk Management Assessment and Adjustment

During the course of a contract, things change. Risk management describes the processes concerned with identifying, analyzing, and responding to outsourcing partnership risks. It consists of ongoing risk assessment, impact analysis, and risk mitigation mechanisms. You should use detailed scenarios to attempt to understand new or potential risks and develop procedures and contingencies to mitigate them.

Why is this necessary? The goal for companies today is to achieve a state of business continuity in which critical business processes are always functioning and mission-critical services are always available. In light of various threat levels and geopolitical instability, business continuity is becoming an increasingly important subject for companies that are offshoring.

To attain and sustain business continuity, companies must engineer availability, security, and reliability into every offshore process. Companies must also examine existing processes with offshore exposure to determine the criticality of such processes and the completeness of business continuity plans. Companies should create scenarios that focus on contingencies for situations in which political, social, or military emergencies develop. The probability of such an event is low, but the potential impact to a business can be significant. Many CTOs are asking offshore vendors about their disaster recovery and backup plans.

Security is the most often cited concern among companies that are considering offshoring. Problems with security — a breach that fosters customer distrust or a catastrophic event that affects data, processes, and customers — can cost companies money and credibility.

There are some standard issues that should be addressed such as business continuity, data recovery, and data security, as well as some things unique to overseas work such as data privacy and intellectual property rights. Insurance coverage may need to go beyond standard liability to insure potential disruptions.

At the end of step 6, you should have established the framework to govern offshore outsourcing and overcome the common misconception that once vendors are chosen and the transition is complete, it is smooth sailing. History repeatedly has taught us the importance of governance — well-defined processes and procedures for project management, relationship management, and contract and SLA management — should not be underestimated.

Step 7: Measure Performance Improvement

As offshore outsourcing becomes viable for multiple business processes, the types and complexity of contracts and sourcing alliances are bound to explode. With organizations outsourcing almost every aspect of their operations, multiple vendors participating in sourcing deals, business users and governance teams residing in separate locations, and activities occurring 24x7, it's a nonstop challenge to coordinate interactions, manage performance, monitor contract terms, track financial metrics, and maintain alignment. A disciplined, continuous improvement program is a necessity for long-term success.

Continuous Performance Reporting

Communication, monitoring, and reporting of SLA metrics is an ongoing responsibility that should be taken seriously. Using well-defined reports and schedules makes communication easier. Some questions to answer are: How is performance monitored and reported? How are targets established? Who is responsible for reporting? What is the schedule for client reviews? What is the time frame, content, and format of standard reporting? When and how are exceptions to be reported?

It is a good idea to put into place audit controls such as:

- Are SLA deadlines being met and adhered to?

- Is reporting timely and accurate?

- Is the quality of work consistent with the defined SLAs?

- Invoice checks — Is the number of people on the project accurate?

- Does the vendor have valid software licenses in place?

Auditing takes a significant amount of time, but it works to ensure that vendor invoicing is correct. Consider the case of DHL Worldwide Express, a shipping subsidiary of Deutsche Post World Net. DHL outsourced development and maintenance work to Infosys, based in Bangalore, India. At DHL, a project manager audits the time sheets from the vendor and rolls the figure into an invoice, which has to be audited against the overall project and then funneled to finance for payment.

Ron Kifer, vice president of program solutions and management for DHL, said "We knew there would be invoicing and auditing, but we didn't fully appreciate the due diligence and time it would require."[17]

Many companies use a dashboard report to summarize SLA metrics. The dashboard report can easily highlight what is going well and what needs to be escalated. Using a color-coded system of red, green, and yellow allows managers to quickly see those problems in red that need to be resolved immediately or areas that are green that do not require action.

Continuous Learning and Recalibration

Many companies start by outsourcing processes "as is" — basically, "take my mess and automate it for less." They prefer to wait until processes are transitioned and things settle down before entering into a phase of re-engineering and streamlining processes using quality management methods such as Six Sigma.

Six Sigma is a quantitative method that relies on statistics to identify and correct process defects. For instance, in call centers, Six Sigma process improvement methods can help in developing new decision trees, changing the orders of the screens, and altering the decision rules so that calls do not have to be escalated. By eliminating steps in processes or changing the scripts for the agents, calls can be resolved more quickly.

The core activity in learning and adjustment is constantly looking for ways to benchmark and make changes if problems are unearthed. Because of the physical distance between you and the offshore operations, gathering data for performance improvement might require frequent site visits. The questions you want to answer include:

- How much did my organization save from offshoring?

- What offshore operations, data, or activities are not performing according to plan?

- How is our current business model — captive center, sole sourcing, or multisourcing — performing?

Answering these questions with detailed data allows you to recalibrate your strategy. At the end of step 7, you should have a well-defined offshore outsourcing model. You should have the learning framework in place for continuously improving the overall strategy.

Summary

Offshore outsourcing can save time and money, but only if companies do it right. Many managers become excited as they uncover the potential benefits of going offshore and, shortly thereafter, discouraged once they consider the practical difficulties of shifting traditional in-house operations to an offshore model.

In this chapter, we did not minimize any of the difficulties you will encounter during the journey. Nonetheless, we strongly believe that any company can overcome the obstacles if two crucial ingredients are present: careful planning and project management.

Firms that jump on the offshore outsourcing bandwagon without paying attention to external planning — negotiations, vendor selection, and due diligence — will struggle with their offshore projects. Careful planning allows you to address issues that invariable arise as a result of cultural differences, lack of communication, inadequate management of projects, and differences in the way projects are structured.

Similarly, firms that don't pay attention to project management — organizational changes, complex cultural dynamics, and inertia toward status quo — will also struggle to benefit from their offshore strategies.

Change is always hard. Table 9.2 lists the top ten reasons why offshore outsourcing projects fail to produce the desired change.

1. Misaligned client and vendor expectations regarding scope of work
2. Bargain shopping — vendor selected on the sole basis of cost
3. Undefined service level agreements
4. Shoddy day-to-day project management
5. Vague accountability — too many cooks in the kitchen
6. Low or ambiguous performance guarantees
7. Badly managed project time lines or budgets
8. The absence of a change management process for change requests
9. Vendor is unable to understand its client's industry or unique processes
10. Very little or nonexistent buy-in from employees and middle management

Table 9.2: Top Ten Offshore Mistakes

Make sure that you address these issues in your offshore venture. The reality is that many members of the Global 1000 will not succeed in making a timely transition to the offshore model. Keep in mind that successful offshore outsourcing relationships must be win-win situations for both clients and vendors.

Chapter Ten

The Vendor Decision

"Uncertainty will always be part of the taking charge process."

— Harold Geneen

Introduction

If you decide to offshore to a third-party vendor, one of the most important tasks you will face is vendor selection. Many offshore partnerships are long-term in nature with benefits and ROI accruing the more time is invested. With all of the upfront work that outsourcing to an offshore third-party vendor entails, from contract negotiations to employee reassignment, it behooves companies to make doubly sure the vendor they select aligns with their goals and corporate culture.

How you select your vendor will have a significant impact on your success, so taking the time for due diligence at this stage in offshoring is well worth it. How do you decide? How do you go about the painstaking fact gathering and analysis process? How do you determine how much industry knowledge vendors have? How can you gain a sense of their processes and methodologies? Will cultural diversity inhibit effective communication? You will need to answer a host of questions.

The search for good vendors can be long and tedious. Many of the vendors that meet a defined set of criteria will be unsuitable for a variety of reasons. Months of studying potential prospects, visiting companies, and negotiating costs may result in frustration and a temptation to close a contract too quickly that could end in dissatisfaction.

The key to success, hard as it may seem, is maintaining discipline throughout the process. You should be aware that the offshore vendor selection process is different from outsourcing to a company within your own country. The difference in performance between the best offshore vendor and the worst offshore vendor is considerably larger than the differences among the performances of U.S. outsourcing companies.

In this chapter, we highlight a vendor sourcing methodology that can help you find the right vendor for your company. The first step is identifying what type of vendor fits your needs.

Types of Offshore Vendors

To choose a service provider, you must first understand your environment and the level of service that you expect. You should have pinpointed which processes you want to outsource and if you want to transfer assets to the vendor. You should have some idea of how deep and broad you would like the relationship to be. Having this knowledge at your fingertips will help you narrow down your vendor list.

In general, there are three types of vendors available.

- **Transaction providers** offer a narrow scope of process to outsource, such as data entry or payroll. They perform the task efficiently but do not usually transform or re-engineer the process. Transaction outsourcing is the quickest and easiest, but it is so narrowly defined that it fragments processes since certain activities are handled by third-party vendors and others are still handled internally. The typical transaction contract value is $1–$5 million, and the average contract length is one to two years. SLA metrics are usually based on the number of transactions. Examples include payroll (ADP), call center (Sykes), and customer billing (Convergys).

- **Process providers** focus on multiple, related processes, such as call center or tax accounting, and take responsibility for the processes they manage. SLA metrics are usually based on process outcomes. The typical full-service provider contract value is $5-$10 million per year, and the average duration is three to five years. Examples include call center (eTelecare), accounts payable (Ephinay), and application development and maintenance (Keane).

- **Full-service providers** handle several business processes, such as human resources (HR) or IT. Comprehensive providers take full responsibility for the complete processes they manage and typically offer to re-engineer the process to make it more efficient. They often take over existing operations and hire hundreds to thousands of the client's employees. The typical contract value per year is $50–$100 million, and the average length is seven to ten years. Examples include HR (Exult, Accenture) and finance and accounting (Affiliated Computer Services, EDS).

Usually companies choose which type of vendor they want based on what they are trying to achieve. Will you be offshoring one well-defined task, several processes, or a total end-to-end process? If you are looking to improve a process, you are going to need to find a vendor that has expertise in that area and is willing to re-engineer the process.

To achieve cost savings, you will need a vendor that can achieve economies of scale and that manages similar processes for other companies. Understanding what you want to accomplish with offshore outsourcing will help you define the type of vendor you are looking for.

Selecting the Right Vendor

Selecting the right vendor for a long-term relationship is a critical task. According to Vellayan Subbiah, vice president of sales and marketing at 24/7 Customer, "The offshore industry is in its infancy — it's only about three-and-a-half years old — so there are a plethora of vendors just like in the dot-com boom. Out of these firms, fifty will survive and five will become great institutions. That's the way this space is going to shake out. So there is always a danger in the whole vendor selection process to go and pick somebody that may or may not be a survivor."[1]

A well-organized vendor selection process can take anywhere from six months to a year. When companies start the selection process, one aspect they do not consider is the expense, which can range upward of 2% in addition to the annual cost of the deal. For example, if your contract is estimated at $10 million, selecting a vendor could add expenses of $200,000. Associated costs include analysis and documentation of requirements, creation and dissemination of RFPs, evaluation of the

RFP responses, contract negotiations, and the development of service level agreements. In addition, project leaders, staff, outside consultants, and legal fees must be paid.

According to Ron Kifer, vice president of program solutions and management, DHL Worldwide Express, "There's a lot of money wrapped up in a contract this size, so it's not something you take lightly or hurry with. There has to be a high degree of due diligence making sure that the company can respond to your needs." Kifer devoted several months to vendor selection before engaging Infosys to handle a startling 90% of development and maintenance work for DHL.[2]

As with any decision, the process of selecting a vendor should follow a well-established methodology that spells out the criteria and steps for vendor selection. Let's look at each step in detail.

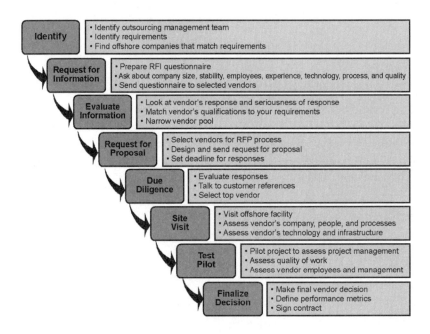

Figure 10.1: Vendor Selection Methodology

Identify: Assemble Your Core Team

As a first step, it is critical to form a core team that will participate in the evaluation of the vendor responses and in the negotiations. The team should consist of individuals pulled from various groups throughout the company, such as subject matter experts (SMEs) from the business units affected, legal staff, and human resources personnel. For example, if you plan to outsource a customer care process, the team should have a substantial faction of people who have many years of collective experience in customer care.

Each of your team members should be assigned defined roles and responsibilities. Forming your core team at the onset of the process assures that the outsourcing team is fully informed and can make the best decisions moving forward. The first task of this team is to learn from the experiences of other corporations that have offshored. The next step is external benchmarking to compare your current process to others in your industry.

Request for Information

Offshore outsourcing occurs when some or all of the responsibility for the provision of a service is transferred to an external vendor. A request for information, or RFI, provides material for the first rounds of vendor evaluations. This step sometimes is used as a "tire-kicking" effort to validate vendor interest and to evaluate what is going on in the outside world.

Outsourcing initiatives fall into two groups — sole negotiation or request for information/request for proposal (RFI/RFP). Companies take the sole negotiation route if they already know the vendor they want to outsource to and if they are not going to open up the bidding process to all vendors. Companies that want to learn more about vendor availabilities and options lean toward the RFI/RFP route. Often outside sourcing consulting firms such as neoIT, TPI, EquaTerra, or The Everest Group are used in this process to help define the important requirements and information needed.

For an RFI, it is in your best interest to define as specifically as possible the requirements that are important to your company. In order to receive comparable information back from multiple vendors, you should prepare a questionnaire to send to selected vendors. The questionnaire should explain your company's business goals, objectives, and the reason why you are looking for an offshore vendor. Potential questions to include in your questionnaire could relate to vendor size, stability, location, infrastructure, quality processes, and skill sets. A sample questionnaire might include some of these categories:

- **Business Profile** — How long has the vendor been in business? What is its business model? How large is the company? What is the financial stability of the company? How many locations does it have and in what countries? What are the vendor's onshore, nearshore, and offshore capabilities? What are its areas of expertise?

- **Customer Base and References** — Ask the vendor to provide the last three contracts they signed as references. Can the vendor provide long-term client references?

- **Management** — How many managers will be assigned to your account? What are its escalation procedures? What will the level of participation of senior management be in planning, development, and other aspects of the business development process? What experience does the management team have?

- **People** — What educational requirements does the vendor have? What employee retention initiatives does it have in place? What training programs are established? Will the vendor use subcontractors? Can the vendor scale up quickly?

- **Process** — What quality certifications has the company achieved? What experience does the vendor have in the same area or industry that you need? Does it have a defined project management methodology? Does it have quality control measurements in place?

- **Infrastructure** — Does the vendor have the facilities to deliver what you need? What do its telecom and infrastructure look like? Does it have formal contingency or redundancy plans in place?

- **Security** — What security measures will the vendor take to protect your company's intellectual properties in terms of information? What procedures does the vendor have in place to protect your data?

- **Delivery** — What are the vendor's reporting guidelines? What personnel will the vendor assign to coordinate and communicate reports and review performance?

Evaluate Information

Once your RFI has been completed and returned by each offshore vendor, match the responses to your requirements and weight the criteria based on importance. Eliminate vendors that do not meet your needs or have not responded to the specific questions.

The best way to choose the most legitimate and effective offshore vendor is by conducting an extensive evaluation to determine suitability. By suitability, we mean compatibility concerning procedures, quality assurance controls, infrastructure, and security. It is important to find an offshore vendor consistent with the parameters pertinent to your company's business objectives.

Throughout the entire process, it cannot be stressed enough how critical it is to select a reliable vendor. One important question to ask is if the vendor uses external subcontractors. If the answer is yes, you will also need to investigate the company that the vendor subcontracts to.

In the case of the University of California, San Francisco (UCSF), Medical Center, three separate subcontractors were involved in patient transcription. The first contractor was a Bay Area transcription service, which UCSF had worked with for many years. The Bay Area company regularly used about 15 U.S. subcontractors. One subcontractor, a woman from Florida, also used subcontractors. One of the Florida woman's transcribers, a Texan, sent his work overseas to Pakistan. The Pakistani transcriber threatened to post UCSF's patient files on the Internet unless it assisted her in resolving a financial dispute with the Texas man who had hired her. She attached actual UCSF patient records to her e-mail threat. After receiving payment from another subcontractor, the transcriber withdrew her threat.[3]

Request for Proposal

Once you have cut your vendor list, it is a good idea to prepare a request for proposal (RFP). An RFP spells out your requirements in detail — relevant skill sets, costs, language skills, security, business continuity, IP protection, infrastructure, and quality certifications — and gives prospective vendors the information they need to prepare a bid. Many companies create an ideal SLA that describes exactly what they would like to see in a contract. It spells out the processes they want to outsource, the type of contract they want to get, and highlights all the details that are important to them.

A good RFP includes sections on four elements: company, people, process, and technology. Let's look at the information each section should cover.

Assessing the Company

External service providers differ significantly in terms of performance, style, and experience.

Topic	Discussion Points
Company stability	Commitment, experience, year of establishment, size, company growth, and funding position.
Company vision	Vision and values
Management	Experience of management team.
Services	Areas of expertise, customers.
Culture	Openness, timing flexibility, learning, and communication.
Reputation	Project management, infrastructure reliability, and customer relationships.
Pricing	Cost of the agreement, any exception cost based on performance metrics, price stability, and hidden costs.
Location	Country, language, and time zones.
Legal	Contract agreement, indemnities, the transfer of people, and how the contract might be terminated.
Flexible contract	Schedules and deliverables, SLAs, guarantees, payment, conflict resolution, term, expiration, and renewal options.

Table 10.1: Topics to Cover in the RFP's Company Assessment

Simply offering nearshore or offshore resources does not guarantee that a company has the skills, processes, and management capabilities to support a true global sourcing model. Carefully evaluate a company's reputation, references, culture, and management style and whether it fits with your company.

The company section of the RFP details the stability of the vendor, the services the vendor will deliver, and its reputation. The vendor you are evaluating may be riding the new outsourcing wave and might not have developed adequate processes and relationships to stay in business for the long haul. Hence, it becomes crucial to try to gauge the stability of the offshore vendor.

Assessing the People

The people section of the RFP details resources assigned at each level: project management, middle management, team leader, and task level.

Topic	Discussion Points
People quality	Quality of resources, hiring policy, experience, education, skill set availability, frequency of employee background checks and formalized performance reviews.
Training	Training programs for new employees, accent neutralization training, documentation, and ongoing skills training.
Language	Languages used for oral and written communication.
Compensation	Compensation levels, industry compensation averages, and benefits.
Scalability	Manpower abundance, as well as depth and knowledge of employee resources.
Retention	Retention rate, policies for keeping employees, average employee tenure, country's average turnover rate, and frequency of employee satisfaction surveys.
In-house resources	Tendency of the vendor to use other companies for resources (if it does, you will also need to obtain information on that company).

Table 10.2: Topics to Cover in the RFP's People Assessment

As people-intensive businesses, outsourcing companies find attracting, training, and retaining skilled professionals, not to mention scaling, challenging in the fast-growth offshore markets; therefore, it is important to evaluate skills, hiring profiles, training programs, and retention capabilities.

For instance, people will play a significant role in the success of offshore call center projects. At the core of excellent customer care are dedicated customer service reps (CSRs). They must be trained to speak the language of your business. The vendor should have sophisticated training programs to ensure they can deliver world-class customer care that results in increased customer satisfaction.

Assessing the Process Capabilities

The process section of the RFP details project management, quality, and security. A few topics to include in this section follow.

Topic	Discussion Points
Project management	Project planning, risk management, communication, reports, supervisor-to-employee ratio, and presence of documented escalation procedures for problems.
Project quality	Standards, reviews, testing, certifications, and satisfaction measurements. The most widely known standards are ISO 9001 and the Capability Maturity Model (CMM). Most U.S companies have their CMM Level 1 certifications while many of the leading offshore vendors have Level 5 certifications.
Regulatory compliance	Compliance with the USA Patriot Act, Sarbanes-Oxley Act, the Health Insurance Portability and Accountability Act, and other regulations.
Physical security	Vendor location security procedures, such as an access card security system.
Intellectual property (IP) security	Vendor's policies on duplicating or misusing your project information, IP rights, noncompetition and nondisclosure terms, and history of piracy.

Table 10.3: Topics to Cover in the RFP's Process Assessment

Assessing the Technology Infrastructure

The technology section of the RFP details the infrastructure stability and disaster recovery of the vendor. In this section, you may want to think about querying the vendor on the topics in table 10.4.

Topic	Discussion Points
Technology	Domain, applications, and infrastructure expertise.
Software infrastructure	Availability of all your software environments, such as your operating system, databases, and application servers.
Secure networking infrastructure	Network's security, safety, and reliability for remote access.
Power backup	Availability of additional resources for power outages.
Internet and communication	Multiple levels of Internet connectivity, such as a leased line, broadband DSL, or ISDN.

Table 10.4: Topics to Cover in the RFP's Technology Assessment

Once you receive the responses to your RFP, you need to evaluate each of them. In many cases, vendors will propose a slightly different delivery approach, so comparing apples to apples might be difficult. Take the time to review each proposal. If there are aspects in one proposal that you want the other vendors to include in their pricing, go back to the vendors and ask for a revised proposal that includes that feature.

The offshore vendor responses to the RFP should be evaluated based on their project management processes, delivery approach, quality performance, resource allocation, and pricing. Evaluate based on which qualities you had ranked as the most important success criteria. If it is technical skills you need, look at the technical expertise of the proposals before you look at the costs. You want to be sure the vendor will be able to deliver what is important to you as opposed to just focusing on price.

Many companies new to outsourcing will engage a consultant or legal firm to help them think through these issues. The larger the contract, the more it makes sense to bring in outside counsel. Many BPO agreements are structured for five to ten years and millions of dollars are at stake, so utilizing the expertise of a consultant to help with vendor evaluation and legal issues can be a good idea.

Due Diligence: Sweat the Small Stuff

Your due diligence should validate or invalidate client-supplied information on process and financials. There is a significant opportunity for disconnects here unless clear definitions of in-scope processes, as well as direct and indirect expenses are documented.

Get to know the management team. Many companies have emerged recently due to the demand for offshore resources. Familiarize yourself with the backgrounds of the management team members, their experience, areas of expertise, the culture they want to instill in the company, and their goals for the company. Also look at the vendor financials to assess their ability to invest in further growth.

Make sure there is a fit between your company and the vendor's management team. According to Tim Lavin, senior vice president for operations at Ambergris Solutions, a leading Philippine-based provider of customer care, inbound sales, and technical support solutions, "There's a lot of companies offshore that are doing a wonderful job with delivering excellent service, but there's also a lot of companies that are jumping on the bandwagon. My advice would be to first check out the experience levels of the executives that are principle in the organization and ensure that they have credible backgrounds."[4]

Look at the vendor's success record and references. It is important to examine the vendor's record with its recent clients. Don't just ask for the references; ask for detailed histories on the last three clients, then talk to the vendor and the client separately. Ask what went well and where there was room for improvement. Ask what lessons were learned and how they were applied. This will reveal whether the vendor is learning from experience, the importance of which is frequently underrated.

As Derek Holley, president of eTelecare, a Los Angeles–based company with operational contact centers located in the Philippines, explains, "The whole idea behind evaluating outsourcers is to find the facts and not the story. If you look for stories, you'll end up hiring the company that has the best storytellers."[5]

In addition to checking references, evaluate project management competency, the level of success achieved, the quality and standards of work delivered, adherence to contract terms, and the communication process. Vendor differentiation is very difficult, and many offshore vendors make promises they are unable to deliver. Careful due diligence to uncover potential surprises is your company's job and will be critical to the success of the relationship.

Site Visit: Look for Show-Stoppers

No contract should be signed without a site visit. Just as you would not hire an employee without interviewing them in person, you certainly should not hire a vendor without visiting them in person.

Spend a couple of days at the vendor site and sit down with as many people as possible: team leaders, project managers, customer service agents, and upper management. If you are outsourcing a call center or any function that will have the vendor's employees speaking directly with your prospects or customers, you will want to interview some of the employees that will work on your project. Try to talk with agents and team leaders separate from upper management. Make sure that the story they tell you about culture and processes is consistent.

While you are at the site, assess whether the vendor has the following:

- Reliable voice, data, and power systems,

- The ability to scale up to meet your growth requirements, and

- Experience with the exact process or task in question.

Once onsite, ask about the recruiting process and the interviews. Sit in on a coaching session. Review the vendor's processes. Evaluate how the vendor's technology works. Bring your technical personnel to interview offshore developers and technicians. Check out the infrastructure redundancy and performance. Make sure the vendor's facilities provide a comfortable working environment for employees with air conditioning or heat, adequate seating, and up-to-date telecom equipment.

Attrition is sometimes a significant problem with offshore vendors. Look for vendors that are able to retain employees successfully. According to Krishnaswamy Subrahmaniam, president and CEO of Covansys India and Asia, "We have almost no attrition amongst our most experienced employees (those with ten to 15 years of experience), and very little turnover within our project management ranks (all of whom have seven to ten years in the industry). At the team lead level, however, where employees usually have about three to four years of experience, retention is often a challenge. That's where most of the churn takes place."[6]

The site assessment will evaluate the vendor's technical infrastructure, work culture, security compliance, quality of human resources, and project experience. Listen to what the vendor is telling you and use your powers of observation to see if what the vendor's people are promising you matches with what is happening at the site.

Test Pilot: Reality Testing

Float some trial balloons — a pilot project is one strategy that many companies use to ensure a proper fit between their company and the offshore vendor. A pilot allows you to critically review the offshore vendor's project management process for efficiency and effectiveness. It is important for your company to determine if project execution is completed within guidelines, if the deliverables are timely, and if the offshore vendor has adhered to defined quality standards. This is an excellent way for your organization to check and recheck the facts before making a final "go/no-go" decision.

Depending on the scale and scope of the offshore initiative, a pilot program may be a good idea. You can evaluate with real experience the actual benefits before jumping into a long-term relationship. For instance, if you are planning on outsourcing 300 call centers agents, it is a good idea to start small and work out the kinks, along with the training programs, documentation, procedures, customized training materials, and technology, before sending all work offshore. Most vendors offer a program in which about 30 agents are trained, and operations are executed on a pilot basis for two to three months.

Finalize the Decision

If you have followed all the steps, then you are doing it right. You have taken your time and done the necessary vendor due diligence. In addition, the pilot should have allowed you to get a taste of the vendor's skills and the confidence to proceed. You didn't just blindly jump in to a relationship like some other firms have. At this point, you are ready to make the final decision of whether you want go with a single vendor or multiple vendors to diversify the risk.

To help you with the vendor selection process, we compiled information on the top offshore vendors in the different areas.

Leading Offshore Vendors in Information Technology

India is the epicenter of offshore information technology (IT) work today. While we expect global players such as IBM, Accenture, EDS, and Hewlett-Packard to be strong players in this space, currently, the Indian vendors that have long been providing these services rule the roost. In alphabetical order, the top five Indian IT services companies follow.[7]

	HCL	Infosys	Satyam	TCS	Wipro
Head-quartered	Noida, India	Bangalore, India	Hyderabad, India	Mumbai, India	Bangalore, India
Year Founded	1976	1981	1987	1968	1945
Number of Employees	10,000	19,000+	10,000 (excluding subsidiaries)	24,000	23,000
Revenues (2003)	$388 million	$754 million	$433 million	$1 billion	$902 million

Table 10.5: Top Five Offshore Vendors in Information Technology

HCL Technologies

Overview: HCL Technologies specializes in software-led IT solutions and services for midsize and large organizations. It has operations in 14 countries, which add to HCL's global reach and its vast rollout support capability. The company's clientele includes 370 organizations, including 40 Fortune 500 companies.

Verticals: Aerospace, pharmaceutical, automotive, retail, banking, semiconductor, funds management and securities, telecom, healthcare, transportation, insurance, travel, networking, and utilities.

Offshore Model: HCL delivers its services through 16 state-of-the-art software development centers in India, each of which focuses on specific technologies and business domains. HCL has taken measures to protect itself and its clients from events that could disrupt the flow of business. It has policies in place for disaster recovery, as well as data, network, and physical security. Dedicated T1 lines through local ISPs and international carriers, such as BT, AT&T, and Sprint, connect the company's various centers and offices worldwide.

Clients: Air Canada, Alcatel, BEA Systems, Cisco Systems, Credit Suisse First Boston, DaimlerChrysler, General Motors, Hewlett-Packard, Johnson & Johnson, LexisNexis, Lockheed Martin, Mercedes-Benz, NCR, Panasonic, Sun Microsystems, Toshiba, and the World Bank.

Infosys Technologies

Overview: Infosys Technologies provides consulting and IT services to clients all over the world. With more than 19,000 employees worldwide, Infosys uses a low-risk global delivery model to accelerate project schedules with a high degree of time and cost predictability.

Verticals: Energy and utilities, engineering enterprises, financial services, healthcare, life sciences, manufacturing, retail and distribution, technology, telecom, and transportation.

Offshore Model: Infosys's global headquarters and campus in Bangalore, India, hold the distinction of being the world's single largest software development facility among IT services companies. Infosys also has global development centers in other parts of India, the United States, Canada, the United Kingdom, and Japan. Thanks to its network of centers, Infosys can provide a wider range of services such as business consulting and technology architecture that involve high levels of client interaction over shorter engagement spans.

Clients: Schlumberger, Airbus, Boeing, Johnson Controls, First USA, GreenPoint Mortgage, Visa, Aetna, Aon Corporation, Dell, Eastman Chemical, Reebok International, and Visteon.

Satyam Computer Services

Overview: Incorporated in 1987, Satyam is a global consulting and IT services company that offers a wide array of solutions for a range of key verticals and horizontals. Satyam has a presence in more than 45 countries.

Satyam has established dedicated offshore centers for General Electric Appliances and Ford Motor Company, among others, and has devoted entire project teams to the respective companies.

Verticals: Automotive, financial services, utilities, government, insurance, healthcare, manufacturing, retail, and telecom.

Offshore Model: Satyam has development centers in India, the United States, the United Kingdom, the Middle East, Japan, Singapore, and Australia. The centers serve more than 290 global companies, including 80 Fortune 500 corporations.

Clients: Caterpillar, Ford, General Motors, General Electric, and Mitsubishi Motors.

Tata Consultancy Services

Overview: Tata Consultancy Services (TCS) belongs to the same holding company that owns India's largest business conglomerate, the $10.4 billion Tata Group. TCS provides end-to-end IT consulting and software services to Fortune 500 clients in approximately 53 countries.

Verticals: Financial services, insurance, telecom, manufacturing, retail, transportation, healthcare, government, and utilities.

Offshore Model: TCS pioneered the concept of offshore software development in India. TCS's offshore development centers (ODCs) conduct a range of IT-related activities for clients. Some of these client-specific centers house more than 2,000 consultants and engineers. TCS has set up ODCs for more than 22 client organizations, many of which are Fortune 500 companies.

Clients: Hewlett-Packard, Lucent Technologies, Nortel Networks, Prudential Insurance, Qwest Communications, Verizon Communications, American International Group (AIG), Citibank, Best Buy, General Electric, Boeing, and Morgan Stanley.

Wipro Technologies

Overview: Wipro is a diversified IT, consumer care, lighting, engineering, and healthcare business. Wipro's diversification into IT happened in 1980. The company grew from a small producer of cooking oil founded in

1945 to a colossus by Indian standards. Sales have increased by an average of 25% per year and earnings by 52% annually over the past four years.

Verticals: Utilities, financial services, government, healthcare, hospitality, technology, insurance, manufacturing, media and entertainment, retail, software, telecom, and travel.

Offshore Model: Wipro currently has one of the largest bases of offshore development centers (ODCs) — 35 ODCs scattered across the globe in India, the United States, Canada, Europe, Australia, and Japan. Wipro is even establishing a nearshore footprint in Canada. In 2002, Wipro Technologies opened a development center in Windsor, Ontario, Canada.

As an offshore outsourcer, Wipro specializes in infrastructure outsourcing, applications outsourcing, R&D outsourcing, package implementation, and business process outsourcing. With state-of-the-art communication facilities and infrastructure, the offshore centers work as a virtual extension of the client's development environment.

Clients: Best Buy, Delta Air Lines, Emerson, Compaq, Honeywell International, Otis Elevator, Microsoft, NCR, SANYO, Home Depot, Nokia, and Allianz Ireland.

Honorable Mention

The other major Indian and global IT service providers that deserve mention here include Patni Computer Systems, Covansys, Cognizant Technology Solutions, Syntel, EDS, Accenture, IBM, Affiliated Computer Services (ACS), and Computer Sciences Corporation (CSC). With these and others entrenched significantly or making strong moves to tap the vast IT talent pool in India, the battle for IT offshore outsourcing business has begun. We expect downward pricing pressure to grow and the vendor landscape to change significantly in the next few years.

Leading Offshore Vendors in Customer Care

Many companies are jumping on the customer care bandwagon. Five of the leaders in offshore customer care services follow.

	Convergys	Daksh	SITEL	Sykes	Spectramind
Head-quartered	Cincinnati, Ohio	Gurgaon, India	Omaha, Nebraska	Tampa, Florida	Bangalore, India
Year Founded	1998	2000	1985	1977	1945
Number of Employees	49,000	5,000+	23,000	16,000	6,500
Revenues (2002)	$2.3 billion	Private	$770 million	$453 million	$1 million

Table 10.6: Top Five Offshore Vendors in Customer Care

Convergys

Overview: Headquartered in Cincinnati, Ohio, Convergys employs 49,000 people, and provides clients with outsourced customer service, billing, and employee care. Its 46 call centers serve more than 1.7 million people each day.

Verticals: Telecom, cable, broadband, direct satellite broadcasting, Internet services, technology, financial services, and government. Convergys has cornered 80% of the telecom outsourced billing market.

Offshore Model: In October 2001, Convergys opened its first Indian call center, for e-mail customer service and technical support, in Gurgaon. The center employs approximately 2,500 agents. Convergys is planning to open two more overseas: one in Bangalore, India, and another in Manila, the Philippines. Its big push now is in HR benefits administration for customers such as Honeywell, Pfizer, and the State of Florida, with which it just signed a $280-million contract.

Convergys routes calls and data over privately leased E1/T1 circuits in the United States. The circuits integrate into the outsourcer's network to avoid unnecessary duplication and expense. Because of India's unreliable commercial power system, the Gurgaon call center has onsite diesel-driven electrical generators. These have enough fuel to run the call center for up to 20 days (compared to seven days for a typical U.S. generator).

Clients: Comcast, Rite Aid, Yahoo!, AT&T, AT&T Wireless, DIRECTV, SBC Communications, Sprint PCS, Bristol-Myers Squibb, General Electric, Lucent Technologies, Marriot, Pfizer, and Sodexho.

Daksh

Overview: Daksh is a leading Indian venture capital backed CRM company whose cosourcing model involves building dedicated service centers for clients. Daksh offers customer care services through channels such as e-mail, real-time chat, and call centers. Specific services include inbound customer service and technical support; outbound collections and telemarketing; back-office processing; and value-add or support services such as customer feedback, data analysis, and reporting.

Verticals: E-commerce and retail, telecom, banking, financial services, insurance, travel, and high technology.

Offshore Model: Daksh has four state-of-the-art customer contact facilities in two cities. These 24x7 facilities can support more than 6,000 customer care specialists. Daksh has a business continuity program to minimize the potential loss of time and resources, which includes a framework for recovery to complete operational levels.

The company is organized into independent business units with a common shared services function. The business units center on individual large clients or groups of smaller clients. This focus permits business unit heads to be better attuned to client delivery. They exercise direct control over operations, project-specific quality, client-specific training and transitioning, and recruitment.

Clients: Top Fortune 500 companies in North America and Europe including Amazon and Sprint.

SITEL

Overview: SITEL offers outsourced customer support services and manages in excess of 1.5 million customer contacts per day via the telephone, e-mail, the Internet, and traditional mail. Approximately 23,000 employees operate from more than 19,000 workstations in 77 customer contact centers located in 21 countries and provide services in more than 25 languages and dialects.

Verticals: Financial services, insurance, technology, consumer, telecom, and utilities.

Offshore Model: SITEL's offshore locations in Jamaica, India, Panama, and Canada service English-speaking customers, and its offices in Brazil, Colombia, and Mexico service Spanish language customers from the United States and Spain. Two of its contact centers — Montego Bay, Jamaica, and Mumbai, India — cover 30,000 square feet. The Mumbai center is a joint venture with Tata International.

Clients: American Express, Barclaycard, British Gas, Hewlett-Packard, Endesa, Cox Communications, GM, Home Depot, Sprint, Aegon Direct Marketing Services, Mitsubishi, AOL, and Philips Electronics.

Sykes Enterprises

Overview: Sykes Enterprises offers outsourced customer management solutions and services that encompass technical support, marketing support, and customer service. The company's 16,000 employees help to deliver these services through multiple communication channels including phone, e-mail, advanced speech recognition, Web, and chat.

Verticals: Technical, financial services, telecom, retail, and utilities.

Offshore Model: From its headquarters in Tampa, Florida, Sykes oversees 42 customer support centers with operations throughout the United States, Canada, Europe, Latin America, Asia, and Africa.

In 1995 Sykes established international operations, picking Amsterdam as the site for its European headquarters and 640-agent flagship center. Today, the countries in which it has support centers is too long to list, but we'll give you a few highlights: Canada – 4 centers; Costa Rica – 1; the United States – 27; Germany – 6; Hungary – 1; South Africa – 1; the Philippines – 2; China – 1; and India – 1. Sykes believes there are further opportunities to expand its offshore solution within certain markets, including Asia, Latin America, Eastern Europe, and South Africa.

Clients: SBC Communications, Microsoft, and Procter & Gamble.

Wipro Spectramind

Overview: Offering a full spectrum of BPO services keeps India-based Wipro Spectramind's 6,500 employees busy. Its customer interaction services span customer support, telemarketing, technical support, and IT help desk. The company was founded by Raman Roy in March 2000. Raman Roy and his team are credited with pioneering the remote services industry in India. Wipro Spectramind became a subsidiary of Wipro Limited in July 2002.

Verticals: Travel, technology, telecom, and utilities.

Offshore Model: Wipro Spectramind's headquarters are located in New Delhi, India. The company has established facilities in Mumbai, Pune, and Chennai, as well as global offices in the United States, the United Kingdom, and Canada. Wipro Spectramind uses dedicated international private leased circuits (IPLCs) over the Pacific and the Atlantic to route overseas voice calls and data directly to its facilities. An onsite dedicated satellite earth station functions as a backup for the IPLCs, and a direct link to international satellites bypasses domestic infrastructure.

Clients: Delta Air Lines, Microsoft, Sun Soft, and Thames Water.

Honorable Mention

There are many companies that offer expertise in customer care, in fact, too many to mention. A few of the better known companies include: eTelecare, Ambergris Solutions, ICICI OneSource, TransWorks (Indian Rayon), 24/7 Customer, HCL Technologies (HCL BPO), vCustomer, Tracmail, Minerva Network Systems, Cognizant Technology Solutions, SourceOne, Immequire, West Corporation, Spherion, MsourcE, Chasecom, and Customer Contact Center (C-Cubed).

Leading Offshore Vendors in Finance and Accounting

Offshore outsourcing in finance and accounting (F&A) is an emerging field. While the value proposition is clear and there is a lot of discussion on the topic, few vendors have ventured into this area. The F&A leaders are listed in table 10.7.

	Accenture	ACS	EDS	Ephinay	OPI
Head-quartered	Chicago, Illinois	Dallas, Texas	Plano, Texas	Charlotte, North Carolina	New York, New York
Year Founded	1989	1988	1962	2001	2001
Number of Employees	80,000	40,000	138,000	500+	700+
Revenues	$11.8 billion (2003)	$3.8 billion (2003)	$21.5 billion (2002)	Private	Private

Table 10.7: Top Five Offshore Vendors in Finance and Accounting

Accenture

Overview: Accenture is a global management consulting, technology services, and outsourcing company. During 2002, the corporate giant transformed its business model to blend consulting and systems integration services — areas in which it has decades of experience — with outsourcing services. Accenture offers a range of outsourcing solutions for managing business processes, applications, and technology infrastructure. The company is expanding its BPO capabilities in such areas as customer information, F&A, IT services, supply chain management, and HR administration.

Verticals: All.

Offshore Model: Accenture has offices in 47 countries around the world. The company is making a major push in India to provide technology and outsourcing solutions to clients at competitive prices. It set up software development centers in Mumbai and Bangalore focused on enterprise application development for Unix and other system platforms. Accenture employs 4,000 people in India and estimates that it will have 10,000 professionals in India by 2005.

It opened a European delivery center in Prague, Czech Republic, focused on business process outsourcing for F&A, customer care, and logistics for clients in manufacturing.

Clients: Avaya, Terasen (BC Gas), BellSouth, British Telecom, BankBoston, Barclays Bank, BBVA, Caterpillar, Dow Chemical,

Enbridge, EMC, KLM Royal Dutch Airlines, Thomas Cook, and the U.S. Department of Education.

Affiliated Computer Services

Overview: Affiliated Computer Services (ACS) provides commercial and government clients worldwide with diversified business process and IT outsourcing solutions. ACS supports operations in nearly 100 countries. The commercial BPO practice focuses on five major categories: F&A; HR; claims processing; loan processing; and document processing.

Verticals: Education, energy, financial, government, healthcare, retail, and transportation.

Offshore Model: ACS is a Fortune 500 company that comprises more than 40,000 people in 453 locations in the United States and 21 locations in nine other countries.

Clients: 7-Eleven, Alaska Airlines, the Florida State Department of Transportation, GlaxoSmithKline, Gateway Computers, General Motors, MetLife, Miller Brewing, Motorola, Office Depot, Southwest Airlines, and US Airways.

EDS

Overview: EDS was founded in 1962 by Ross Perot. EDS pioneered the ITO and BPO markets. Today, EDS uses its considerable experience to offer outsourced IT and BPO services to customers worldwide.

Verticals: Communications, consumer and retail, energy, financial services, government, healthcare, manufacturing, and transportation.

Offshore Model: In November 2002, EDS launched its "Best Shore" program, which involves rotating services for the same client among sites around the world so that the outsourced function is available 24x7. This approach follows a broader trend to diversify risk by moving work through low-cost facilities in multiple regions around the world. The program focuses on two broad types of services: business process outsourcing (mainly help desk) and application development and delivery. Best Shore facilities are located in Argentina, Brazil, Canada, Germany, Hungary, Mexico, South Africa, the United States, and New Zealand.

In May 2003, EDS opened a new offshore facility in Mumbai, India. Originally a 150-employee operation, the center is expected to have 700 employees by year-end 2003. When fully staffed, the center will provide help desk technical support services via phone, e-mail, and online chat. The center will also supply business process outsourcing services, including data entry, phone-based marketing, and management of financial (payroll, credit cards, loans, and mortgages) and administrative (medical and insurance claims) processes.

For companies looking for a nearshore option, EDS maintains about 7,400 personnel in Canada and books roughly $1.05 billion in U.S. dollars in annual revenues there.

Clients: American Airlines, General Motors, the U.S. Navy and Marine Corps, MCI/WorldCom, and US Airways.

Ephinay

Overview: Pronounced "F and A," Ephinay is a full-service finance and accounting BPO provider to Fortune 1000 and Global 2000 markets. Ephinay performs financial transaction processing and has the capability to manage clients' entire F&A departments. It prides itself on its proven delivery methodologies which can help its customers to improve quality, lower costs, and raise productivity.

Offshore Model: Ephinay has created a blended delivery model with service centers in Phoenix, Arizona, and New Delhi, India. The India service center was created in 2001 when AcFin Services, Ephinay's former name, was founded. AcFin later changed its name to Ephinay to indicate its plan to become the leading provider in that category of business services. The company then proceeded to acquire Core3, a Phoenix BPO company.

Clients: Fortune 500 companies, The Householder Group, National Dry Cleaners, and the International Academy of Design and Technology.

Outsource Partners International

Overview: Outsource Partners International (OPI) is a BPO firm specializing in F&A services. OPI's clients can outsource select portions of their internal accounting functions, such as accounts payable, accounts receivable, payroll, and financial reporting, or they can outsource all of them. Formerly known as itAccounts, OPI got its start when it acquired KPMG LLP's BPO practice.

Verticals: Professional services, distribution, nonprofits, import/export, manufacturing, financial services, insurance, healthcare, and higher education.

Offshore Model: OPI operates through six U.S. offices and a shared services center in Bangalore, India, with more than 700 associates. The company employs more than 100 certified public accountants (CPAs) and chartered accountants (CAs), the equivalent degree in India. The company's onsite/offshore model integrates its onsite personnel with its offshore processing. OPI's onsite staff handles day-to-day issues, such as reporting, analysis, and exceptions, and manages all interaction with its offshore personnel. Staffing often incorporates clients' current accounting personnel. OPI minimizes operating risks by gradually transitioning processes offshore.

OPI's Bangalore center is a state-of-the-art facility equipped with 125 computer workstations. The company uses an international private leased circuit (IPLC) to access data from its headquarters in New York City. This private line ensures security and speeds data transmission. The infrastructure also includes high-speed document scanners and Lawson accounting software.

Clients: KPMG.

Honorable Mention

There are other traditional and large, as well as new and upcoming outsourcing vendors that we have come across in our research and that deserve mention here. They include Cap Gemini Ernst & Young, Compass Connections, Computer Sciences Corporation, Deloitte Touche, EXL Service, FlexiInternational, IBM, Inaltus, SourceNet, and Unisys.

Leading Offshore Vendors in Human Resources

Similar to finance and accounting, offshore outsourcing in human resources (HR) is an emerging field. Few vendors offer these services. We list a few of the leaders in table 10.8.

	Cross-domain	Exult	India Life Hewitt	Ma Foi	Progeon
Head-quartered	Bangalore, India	Irvine, California	Bangalore, India	Chennai, India	Bangalore, India
Year Founded	1999	1999	1998	1992	2002
Number of Employees	200+	1,300+	200+	300+	1,000+
Revenues	Private	$420 million (2002)	$2.5 million (2003)	$10 million (2002)	$4 million (2002)

Table 10.8: Top Five Offshore Vendors in Human Resources

Crossdomain Solutions

Overview: Founded in late 1999, Crossdomain is funded by ICICI and specializes in employer and accounting services. Employer services cover every aspect of the employer-employee relationship, including payroll processing, claims administration, retiree benefits administration, and travel and expense processing. Crossdomain evolved as a division of Chartered Accountants based in Bangalore. The division was spun off during 1998 with the vision of focusing on BPO services.

Offshore Model: The company has offices in three cities in India: Bangalore, Mumbai, and New Delhi.

Clients: Bennett Coleman & Co., Cisco Systems, Citrix Software, DHL Worldwide Express, HP India, Honeywell, MphasiS BFL, Pizza Corner, Reuters, and Standard Chartered Bank.

Exult

Overview: Exult is an acknowledged leader in providing outsourced HR services to Global 500 corporations. It offers customers comprehensive, integrated HR process management through a service delivery model that includes HR process management expertise, shared client services centers, HR process consulting capabilities, Web-enabled applications, and management of third-party vendor relationships.

Offshore Model: Exult has shared services centers in North Carolina, Tennessee, Texas, Scotland, and India. The 31,000-square-foot Scotland center caters to its U.K. customers. The company anticipates that the Scotland center will play a significant role in service delivery to future clients in the United Kingdom, Europe, and other parts of the world, including North America. Exult began operations in its client service centers in India in May 2003.

Clients: McKesson, Bank of America, British Petroleum, International Paper, Prudential Financial, and Unisys.

India Life Hewitt

Overview: Specializing in payroll and benefits, India Life Hewitt was India's first HR BPO provider. The company's list of clients comprises more than 270 companies with more than 300,000 employee records. It is a joint venture of View India Enterprises (VIE) and Hewitt Associates.

Verticals: Financial services, insurance, engineering, manufacturing, pharmaceuticals, media, telecom, and technology.

Offshore Model: India Life Hewitt has offices in six Indian cities — Bangalore, Chennai, Delhi, Hyderabad, Mumbai, and Pune — that employ more than 200 professionals trained in the fields of payroll and benefits.

India Life Hewitt has taken pains to build a secure, reliable data center at its Bangalore location. It also has a customer interaction center with multiple self-service options to provide efficient access to the customer database. A communication network connects the Bangalore location to the other locations. India Life Hewitt has implemented a disaster recovery and business continuity plan.

Clients: Philips India, ICICI, Siemens, IBM India, Volvo India, SAP, Novell India, LG Software, Motorola PagePoint, Intel Asia Electronics, Sun Microsystems, Tata Communications, and Texas Instruments India.

Ma Foi

Overview: Established in 1992, Ma Foi Management Consultants Limited has built a reputation for a systematic, hands-on approach to HR consulting. With a network of 11 centers spread over nine locations in India, as well as three subsidiaries in London, Dubai, and Singapore, the company offers a global, one-stop shop to meet all HR requirements — senior-level search, database selection, turnkey recruitment, and HR consulting. Ma Foi's client base extends to 850 companies, including 90 Fortune 500 companies.

Offshore Model: In 2002, Ma Foi Management Consultants set up a wholly owned subsidiary, Ma Foi Outsourcing Solutions Ltd. (MOSL), to cater to the HR BPO needs of clients. The subsidiary handles outsourced HR processes such as payroll and résumé management.

Clients: Monsanto, AstraZeneca, GE Capital, Ford, Hyundai, Satyam, Infosys, Enron, Haldia Petrochemicals, and HSBC.

Progeon

Overview: Progeon was founded in 2002 to provide business process management services. It is a majority-owned and controlled subsidiary of Infosys Technologies with equity participation from Citicorp.

Offshore Model: Progeon's headquarters can be found on the Infosys campus in Bangalore, India. It has a fully secured and networked capacity of 1,000 seats spread over 100,000 square feet. Progeon plans to provide its clients with access to cost-effective talent pools in different geographies that meet their requirements and risk preferences. The company is establishing a center in Eastern Europe and two other centers in India. Progeon provides independent facilities for each client with 24x7 security, power backup, and redundant data and telecommunications links.

Clients: Cisco, Fidelity Capital, GreenPoint Mortgage, and British Telecom.

Honorable Mention

The HR offshore outsourcing market is immature. However, we see major players entering this space including U.S. HR outsourcing service providers Accenture HR, ACS, EDS, and Mellon HR. Accenture HR Services, a joint creation of British Telecom and Accenture, entered the outsourced HR market almost five years ago. ACS also went this route, teaming up with Motorola in a $650 million joint venture that the companies named ACS Global HR Solutions.

We also expect the BPO subsidiaries of Indian IT vendors such as Nipuna (Satyam), Spectramind (Wipro), and HCL BPO (HCL Technologies) to compete in this space. These subsidiaries, which offer HR as part of their BPO service portfolios, have access to the blue-chip clients of their parent companies, the same clients who could elect in the future to outsource their HR processes.

Summary

Offshoring is a marathon, not a sprint. Selecting a vendor has always been hard, but, in recent decades, it has become tougher than ever. The choices facing managers and the data requiring analysis have multiplied while the time for analyzing them has been compressed. So take your time and do the necessary due diligence. Never quickly pick a vendor and jump in to offshore outsourcing just to be the first or just because your competitor has already done so.

We end this chapter with some offshore outsourcing best and worst practices.

The Best-Practice Companies	The Worst-Practice Companies
Search for and benchmark information from multiple sources.	Listen to sales pitches and make decisions based on them.
Are analytical. They compare their current capabilities with the vendor's capabilities. (Value is only created if the outsourcer can complete the process better than you.)	Are ad hoc. They make offshoring decisions based on gut feelings and intuition.
Focus on the key questions in their RFPs.	Write 30-page RFPs that require 150-page responses from vendors.
Choose high-quality providers and negotiate the lowest prices from them.	Choose the lowest-cost providers.
Align incentives so that both parties work toward a common goal.	Treat their vendors like vendors rather than true partners.

Table 10.9: Best and Worst Practices

Choosing a service provider to manage your business processes and applications is a big step. Making the final decision means signing a contract that clearly defines the performance measures, team size, team members, pricing policies, business continuity plans, and overall quality of work standards.

Chapter Eleven

The Location Decision

*"A pessimist sees the difficulty in every opportunity;
an optimist sees the opportunity in every difficulty."*

— Sir Winston Churchill

Introduction

Where should you locate your offshore operations? Which country is right for you? Choosing where to locate operations is not a new problem.

In fact, there is even a science called location theory devoted to it. Location theory addresses the questions of which economic activities are located where and why. It has become a requisite part of economic geography, spatial economics, and regional science.

Traditionally, the location of economic activities was determined by broader factors, such as the characteristics of a particular region or metropolitan area, or narrower ones, such as the traits of a particular zone, city block, or individual site. With the advent of globalization, the Internet, and modern logistics, location theory is expanding to include remote countries.

When managers consider offshore outsourcing, one of the first things they wonder is should they decide on the offshore country first and the vendor second, or the vendor first and the country second. Some companies select the vendor first and then worry about the location. Others settle on the country and then attempt to pick the best vendor in that country.

Either way, managers have to understand how to decide which country is the right one for their operations. Even those managers who have operations in an offshore location need to know how to undertake geographic diversification of business process operations in an effort to manage long-term costs.

India, China, the Philippines, or Russia — choosing where to offshore is an important, long-term decision that can determine the skills and competencies, based on culture, education, and language, that are available for your project. Other critical factors affecting the location decision are the physical infrastructure, government regulations, legal policies, and political stability of countries.

In this chapter, we detail the prospects of eight countries and explore their positive and negative attributes. We also highlight risk factors for managers to consider when they evaluate offshore locations.

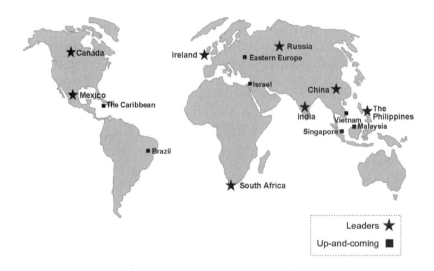

Figure 11.1: Top Offshore Locations

The Location Decision Matrix

Although vendors should be judged solely on the basis of their own merits, the fact remains that an offshore supplier's country determines the makeup of its workforce and wage structure, which influences the ability of companies to compete. Moreover, an offshore vendor's expertise and language skills are largely the product of its country's educational system and business culture.

Companies often have concerns about sending work offshore. Typically these concerns have been centered on contractual and legal matters such as intellectual property rights. As a result of events such as the Iraq war, the violence in the Middle East, and the September 11 attacks, companies are now conducting political and economic risk assessments when examining offshore options. For their part, vendors often attempt to alleviate client concerns by talking about disaster recovery capabilities, reliability of infrastructure, and security.

Virtually no detail is irrelevant in site selection. Geography, history, culture, language, and government policies contribute to the development and growth of every country's industries. To what extent do geographic and cultural issues influence companies' offshore decisions? At what point do the delivery model, cultural adaptability, and hourly labor rates of individual companies enter into decision processes? We'll answer these questions and many others in the ensuing pages.

Workforce Attractiveness and Economics

One of the major drivers of offshore outsourcing is the promise of cost savings from labor arbitrage. Although it is not the only reason why companies seek to locate their operations offshore, it is often the catalyst that leads companies to explore offshore outsourcing in the first place.

Labor arbitrage drives the immense cost savings. Compare the average salary of a U.S. programmer at $63,000 to a programmer in China at $5,000, India at $6,000, the Philippines at $6,500, or Russia at $7,500. With these variations, you can see why the offshore movement is growing.

Although cost savings may be the primary motive for offshoring, there are several other considerations companies need to take into account before signing on the dotted line. People are at the top of the list. The vendor's employees can make or break an offshore relationship. Some of the critical attributes related to employee quality are language skills, technical skills, educational levels, cultural compatibility, and quality management programs (see table 11.1).

Category	Includes
Labor	Size of labor pool, wages, skills and training, regulations
Cost savings	Costs that can be saved by utilizing this country
Language skills	Proficiency in English and other languages
Technical skills	Proficiency in IT tools, applications, and programming
Education	The quality of universities and colleges
Cultural compatibility	Compatibility of business practices and understanding of the American culture
Quality	ISO 9000, Six Sigma, CMM

Table 11.1: Location Decision Matrix — Workforce Attractiveness

Location Attractiveness and Risks

Table 11.2 summarizes the various factors that need to be considered in assessing the attractiveness of a country or city within a country.

Category	Includes
Infrastructure	Roads, electricity, telecom, and network stability
Stability (political, economic, medical	Political concerns: stability of current regime
	War: loss caused by invasion, civil war, or revolution
	Strikes: loss caused by riots, strikes, or civil commotion
	Terrorism: loss caused by malicious damage or sabotage
	Medical concerns: ability to respond to medical emergencies
Legal environment	Copyright protection, intellectual property rights
	Reporting issues (accounting requirements, taxes)
Regulatory environment	Government action: loss caused by the implementation of any discriminatory law, order, decree, or regulation
	Embargo: loss caused by the imposition of an embargo
	Cancellation of licenses and permits
Travel convenience	Ease of travel by plane or car
Time zones	How well do the time zones match?

Table 11.2: Location Decision Matrix — Location Attractiveness and Risks

When companies consider sending processes or data offshore, they must also think about the risks involved, such as the political, economic, and medical stability of a particular location. Other factors not to be overlooked are government regulations, taxes, and infrastructure.

Infrastructure — roads, electricity, and communications — is a huge consideration. Think about having your contact center set up in Bangalore, India, with thousands of calls coming in hourly. Power outages that occur for a few minutes every few hours are not good. In developed countries, availability of electricity is taken for granted. Rarely are companies confronted with the loss of power. The same cannot be said for developing countries. When your business success is dependent on computers or telecommunications, infrastructure evaluation is critical.

The Top Eight Offshore and Nearshore Locations

Many countries hope to get into the offshore game. Some have spent years preparing their infrastructure in anticipation of the offshore boom.

In the following pages, we review the top eight offshore and nearshore destinations — Canada, China, India, Ireland, Mexico, the Philippines, Russia, and South Africa — and discuss the competitive advantages and challenges that each country faces.

Destination: Canada

With similar business standards and the same time zones and official language as the United States, Canada is a haven for U.S. companies that do not want to stray too far from home. The Canadian centers for outsourcing include Halifax, Montreal, and Toronto.

Canada is consistently billed as one of the safest offshoring destinations. However, the country's reputation and proximity come at a price. Businesses that decided to outsource to Canada do not realize the cost benefits that they would if they ventured farther away to India, the Philippines, or China.

Competitive Advantages

The country has an excellent university system, comparatively inexpensive real estate, and well-established infrastructure in many areas. Labor rates are lower than those of the United States, and the exchange rate between Canada and the United States adds to their attractiveness. The cultural gap between Canada and Westernized countries such as the United Kingdom, the United States, and others is minimal.

Category	Comments
Labor	Total population in 2003 was 32.2 million.
Cost savings	IT professionals earn an average annual salary of C$79,1176, or US$56,599, compared to $80,286 in the United States.[1]
Language skills	English and French are the official languages of Canada, and many people speak both.
Technical skills	Technical skills are excellent. Microsoft hires more engineers from the University of Waterloo than anywhere else.
Education	The university system is one of the best in the world.
Cultural compatibility	Canada has a rich, shared culture with both the United States and the United Kingdom.
Quality	Canada had 12,371 ISO 9000 certifications as of 2002.

Table 11.3: Canadian Workforce's Attractiveness and Economics

Category	Comments
Infrastructure	Some infrastructure may be aging in major cities.
Stability	Canada has very little political and economic risk.
Legal environment	Strong legal system.
Regulatory environment	Federal and local governments are very supportive of foreign investment and outsourcing ventures. A member of NAFTA and the World Trade Organization (WTO).
Travel convenience	Toronto is a short, one-and-a-half-hour flight from New York. In some cases, outsourcing sites are near enough for U.S. company managers to drive to them.
Time zone	Canada has six time zones. Toronto and New York both follow eastern standard time (EST) and are five hours behind Greenwich mean time (GMT).

Table 11.4: Canada's Location Attractiveness and Risks

Challenges

Canada, while safe, may not satisfy some companies' hunger for cost savings. The country falls at the high end of the offshoring pack, comparable to Ireland. U.S. companies looking to run a 24x7 operation also should not consider Canada since it matches up roughly with U.S. time zones, although the minimized time difference allows U.S. managers to easily reach their Canadian partners during U.S. business hours.

Long-Term Outlook

Canada is becoming a popular nearshore destination. To remain competitive, it must promote itself more aggressively as a nearshore option for U.S. firms.

Destination: China

Since the late 1970s, China has been busy charting a course of economic reform. When the first Sino-foreign joint venture, the Beijing Aviation Food Company, was founded in 1980, no one was aware of the event's significance. Over the next two decades, approximately 220,000 businesses would follow Beijing Aviation Food's lead, bringing the previously isolated country welcome foreign investment, technology, and management expertise to nurture its growth.

Does history — or at least economic history — repeat itself? China has already proven itself adept at absorbing manufacturing jobs. Since 1992, more than 760,000 U.S. manufacturing jobs have moved to its shores according to the U.S.-China Security Review Commission. Now the question is whether China can position itself as an attractive destination for companies interested in business process offshoring. With its accession to the WTO, tapping its enormous, relatively inexpensive labor force should become easier.

Competitive Advantages

China's most obvious advantage is its cheap labor pool. While companies worry that the talent pool will be used up in smaller nearby countries, such as the Philippines, that possibility virtually does not exist for China. The country's educational system produces as many, if not more, scientists and engineers as there are in the United States, and universities have seen their enrollments more than double in a few short years.

Category	Comments
Labor	In 2003, China had the world's largest population, 1.3 billion.
Cost savings	High-tech workers earn an average yearly salary of $7,057, while an worker in Beijing earns a yearly salary of $2,314.[2]
Language skills	Students aged eight and nine years old attending school in major Chinese cities are required to learn English. In addition, to ready itself for the 2008 Olympics in Beijing, the country is leading an intense effort to increase the population's proficiency in English.[3]
Technical skills	China's universities graduate almost as many scientists and engineers as their U.S. counterparts do.
Education	University enrollment jumped from 7.8 million students in 1998 to 16 million in 2002.
Cultural compatibility	China is allowing the import of more Western books and films in an effort to show it is becoming more tolerant and to comply with WTO guidelines. However, the government continues to regularly censor all media.
Quality	Few companies have attained CMM Level 5 certification but several have reached CMM Level 3. At the end of 2002, China led the world with the most ISO 9001 certifications (40,997), and 75,755 ISO 9000 certifications in total.

Table 11.5: Chinese Workforce's Attractiveness and Economics

Not only is labor plentiful, it is inexpensive, although relative to many Asian countries, such as Malaysia, Thailand, Vietnam, Indonesia, and the Philippines, labor costs are higher and increasing steadily. The country's labor, environmental, and health and safety standards are also more relaxed than those of the United States.[4]

Challenges

The legal and business environments within China remain a challenge for many companies. Firms consistently cite "bureaucratic inertia, lack of transparency, inconsistent enforcement of the law, and strict regulatory control" as issues with which they regularly struggle.[5] Protection of intellectual property and enforcement of copyright laws are also serious problems in China. Many countries hope that China's accession to the WTO will lessen these obstacles.

Cultural compatibility is another issue businesses will face in China. For many years, the country's borders were effectively closed to outside influence, particularly Western influence, but recently more Western books, films, and music have been spotted on the shelves of China's stores. The pace of social change, however, continues to lag far behind the pace of economic change.

Category	Comments
Infrastructure	Infrastructure varies widely. It is best in the special economic zones that the country built to attract foreign investment.
Stability	China has been fighting pressure from the United States and the European Union to float its currency, the yuan, in an effort to make exports more attractive. Such a change could destabilize China and affect the world economy. Mainland China had 5,237 SARS cases in 2003, with 349 deaths. The country formed an anti-SARS task force to ensure that a similar outbreak would not happen again.
Legal environment	The Business Software Alliance estimates that China pirates, or installs without a license, 92% of its business software. It has the second-highest piracy rate in the world, following Vietnam, which has a 97% piracy rate. Microsoft battled China for three years over copyright infringement, and Cisco won a settlement from Huwaei, a Chinese communication equipment company, for wholesale infringement. Two recent amendments to copyright laws may signal China's willingness to take the issue more seriously.
Regulatory environment	WTO acceptance in December 2001 has led to China's relaxing many of its regulations. In addition, many foreign businesses situated in the special economic zones as well as in the economic and technological development zones enjoy national and local tax reductions, tax holidays, and other concessions afforded by local governments.
Travel convenience	Travelers flying from New York to Beijing arrive at their destination in about 19 hours (includes one stop).
Time zone	Despite its size, China operates on one time zone and is 13 hours ahead of EST and eight hours ahead of GMT.

Table 11.6: China's Location Attractiveness and Risks

Long-Term Outlook

China's status as a major world power means that its actions not only affect its citizens and communities but also the world's. Many multinationals view China as an integral part of their long-term strategy. A major disease outbreak, the collapse of China's banking industry, a change in its currency policy, or the growing gap between China's socioeconomic classes could have serious consequences for all, especially the companies that select China as an offshoring destination.

On the bright side, China's membership in the WTO should help to keep the country in line and eventually trickle down to reform the legal and business environment on a local level. The 2008 Olympics to be held in Beijing represents another positive for those considering China as an offshoring destination. Offshorers should see benefits in terms of better infrastructure and a greater number of English speakers.

Destination: India

Read any article on BPO, and chances are that India will be cited in the first few lines as one of the most common destinations for companies looking to outsource business processes. India is already recognized as a haven for software development. In recent times, India has become the preferred destination for BPO, too.

Offshoring in India began in 1985 when Texas Instruments established a captive R&D unit in Bangalore. And in 1992, many years before the current BPO craze, Swissair and Tata Consultancy Services teamed up to build a shared services center to complete revenue accounting services for airlines.

India developed its outsourcing foothold by sticking to certain core IT capabilities such as application maintenance, application development, database management, and packaged application customization. Sticking to the basics has paid off. In the decade following, offshoring exploded in India, with many Fortune 1000 companies electing to set up wholly owned offshoring centers in India or to outsource work to external service providers based in India. Citibank, Motorola, Oracle, Apple, and Microsoft are just a few of the bigger names that have set up shop in the country.

Currently, firms are focused on India-based, captive, back-office service centers for firms. These service centers are owned and managed by multinationals that have the process expertise, in-house demand, and patience to support major investments and multiyear transitions. These pioneers have seen cost savings of 40%–50% and quality that meets or beats industry benchmarks.

Competitive Advantages

India ranks high on several parameters such as quality, potential of talent pool, cost structure, overall process capability, educational systems, and major productivity gains. The country is home to the largest educated English-speaking population in the world.

Recent, rapid improvements in telecom infrastructure, favorable government and tax incentives, increased investments in technical education, along with an abundant supply of programmers, engineers, and accounting talent have made India a hot spot for offshore initiatives. Within the country, some of the leading cities are Bangalore, Hyderabad, Mumbai, Chennai, New Delhi, Gurgaon, and Pune.

Category	Comments
Labor	Total population in 2003 was 1 billion.
Cost savings	India offers significant opportunities for labor arbitrage with labor costs 50%–60% lower than those of other countries. An Indian IT professional earns an average annual salary of U.S. $8,593 (compared to $80,286 in the United States).[6]
Language skills	An estimated 250–300 million, or 25%–30%, of the total population speak English.
Technical skills	India's workforce offers an extremely large pool of technical skills. The country's universities add 180,000 engineering graduates to its ranks annually. At the end of 2002, NASSCOM estimated that there were approximately 522,000 Indian software and IT services professionals.
Education	At any given moment, more than 6 million people are enrolled in the 200 universities, 5,000 colleges, and 100,000 secondary schools.
Cultural compatibility	Despite training in pop culture, a cultural gap still exists between Indian agents and Western customers.
Quality	When it comes to software development and process methodologies, all top-tier vendors are certified at CMM Level 5. India had 8,110 ISO 9000 certifications as of 2002.

Table 11.7: Indian Workforce's Attractiveness and Economics

India has a 9–12 hour time difference with respect to U.S. and European markets. This time difference is useful in the case of BPO operations: It results in reduced turnaround times since processing services are performed during the night hours of developed countries. This means that a job submitted at 6 p.m. Pacific Standard Time (PST) reaches India at 6 a.m. (India's time) and is completed by 6 a.m. PST the following morning, enabling a 24x7 operation.

Challenges

Companies that select India as their offshoring destination will encounter challenges. The country's layers of bureaucracy and tricky regulatory environment are notorious. India's democracy is well-established, but religious and separatist violence does occur, and the possibility of war with Pakistan looms.

India also has resource challenges. Given the rapid growth of offshoring, there are very high attrition levels as companies poach each other's employees. Another problem is limited middle management strength. The resource pool consists of graduates excellent at first level jobs but with minimal skills for middle management.

Category	Comments
Infrastructure	Bottlenecks in telecommunications, transportation, and energy seriously limit the nation's economic growth and development. In some areas, electric power is erratic and the telephone systems unreliable.
Stability	Although it is currently safe to travel to India, tensions between Pakistan and India continue. In addition, major religious riots can disrupt BPO operations.
Legal environment	India has several rigorous laws designed to protect copyrights and intellectual property (IP) rights. Enforcement, however, of IP rights and patent protection is weak.
Regulatory environment	The Indian government allows total income tax exemption on export of BPO services under Sections 10A and 10B of the Income Tax Act. The current general corporate tax rate is 35% plus surcharge.
Travel convenience	Flying from New York to Bangalore, India, takes two days and includes two stops.
Time zone	India is 9 hours ahead of EST, which enables a U.S. firm to operate a 24x7 operation.

Table 11.8: India's Location Attractiveness and Risks

The Indian government is proactively addressing these issues. Government officials are serving as advocates and sponsors for offshore investment by undertaking a range of policy changes to encourage the development of infrastructure. Begun in 1991, India's government restructuring program includes the liberalization of trade restrictions and foreign investment regulations, commitments to protection of IP property rights, and a general loosening of state control over business practices.

Long-Term Outlook

India should remain an attractive option for companies desiring to outsource people-intensive processes, such as transaction processing or customer care. Its attractiveness may diminish somewhat as multinationals like IBM and smaller India-based vendors compete for the same talent pool, thereby driving labor rates upward and increasing employee turnover.

Destination: Ireland

Offshoring to Ireland is similar in many ways to outsourcing to Canada. Companies tend to select the two countries as offshoring destinations for similar reasons: increased stability and lowered risk.

Category	Comments
Labor	Ireland's total population in 2003 was 3.9 million.
Cost savings	Programmers are paid $25,000–$40,000 per year. Customer service representatives are paid an average salary of $31,466 annually.[7]
Language skills	English is the primary language, but many citizens learn other languages. Agents generally are fluent in two or more languages, which is critical for companies seeking to support European operations.
Technical skills	Ireland has invested in high-tech education but has fewer than 10,000 graduates in computer and software engineering each year.
Education	The educational system is strong but the number of graduates is limited. More than 38,000 students graduate each year, almost half of which are graduates with qualifications in engineering, computer science, business, and science.[8]
Cultural compatibility	As a developed country, Ireland's cultural compatibility with other members of the European Union and the United States is very high.
Quality	Ireland had 2,845 ISO 9000 certifications as of 2002.

Table 11.9: Irish Workforce's Attractiveness and Economics

Competitive Advantages

Ireland wisely invested in its educational system and is now reaping the rewards with an increasingly well-educated and growing workforce. However, the number of available technical graduates is limited to a few thousand annually, which can make the country more of an ideal destination for call center operations rather than software development. A solid infrastructure and educational system, increased cultural compatibility, and English proficiency also add to Ireland's attractiveness.

Challenges

Ireland is one of the oldest players in offshoring. According to IDA Ireland, the Irish government agency responsible for the industrial development and investment of overseas companies into Ireland, more than 1,100 overseas companies have established operations on the Emerald Isle. With its membership to the European Union, Ireland has watched its economy outpace the rest of Europe and its labor force and wage rates increase, while unemployment decreased.

Category	Comments
Infrastructure	Fully deregulated telecom market with more than 20 providers.
Stability	Low political risk.
Legal environment	The country joined the WTO on January 1995. Companies face little bureaucracy. Legal procedures are uncomplicated, inexpensive, and quick.
Regulatory environment	Ireland has a highly beneficial corporate tax environment. It offers a number of grants — for capital, R&D, training, and employment — to offset the costs of setting up operations. There is no local tax except on property.
Travel convenience	The nonstop flight from New York to Dublin measures six-and-a-half hours.
Time zone	All of Ireland follows GMT, which translates to Dublin being five hours ahead of EST.

Table 11.10: Ireland's Location Attractiveness and Risks

The Irish talent pool is quickly being used up by large companies such as Dell and Microsoft, while the cost savings advantage of offshoring diminishes. Ireland is not a very scalable offshoring location for back-office operations due to the lack of low-cost labor.

Long-Term Outlook

U.S. companies such as Dell, IBM, and Microsoft have development centers in Ireland, which are increasing competition for labor and thus driving the cost of labor up. The talent and maturity of services in Ireland are very good, but you will need to pay more for such skills.

Destination: Mexico

In the last decade or so, Mexico has undergone an enormous transformation, opening its closed economy, negotiating free trade agreements with more than 30 countries, and implementing more fiscally responsible policies since the peso imploded in 1994. Mexico's people are no longer dominated by one political party but instead live under a multiparty democracy. The government has tried to make its actions more transparent, publishing the financial statements of state and local governments in the newspaper and on the Internet. In addition, Mexican government officials have made an effort to apply policies more consistently and not to devise new ones with every administration change. All of these events have combined to give Mexico a presence in the offshoring market.

Category	Comments
Labor	Total population in 2003 was 104.9 million. Mexico has excellent employee retention.
Cost savings	A call center agent earns $4.25 per hour.[9]
Language skills	Has a large pool of English- and Spanish-speaking resources.
Technical skills	Only 2% of the population has university degrees, but several good technical universities do exist.
Education	Mexico has an extensive system of 240 institutions of higher education (colleges and vocational/technical schools) and 69 universities. In the Monterrey area, educational levels tend to be above the national norm.
Cultural compatibility	Many Mexicans have spent time in the United States and understand the U.S.-Hispanic market.
Quality	Mexico had 2,508 ISO 9000 certifications in 2002.

Table 11.11: Mexican Workforce's Attractiveness and Economics

Competitive Advantages

The most obvious advantage Mexico has as an offshoring destination is its location. For North American companies fearful of outsourcing processes to a provider located more than a day's flight away, Mexico is an interesting prospect. It appeals to companies that prefer not to rush to India but instead want to take advantage of a nearshore option.

The country also offers competitive labor rates — not as cheap as China, but not as expensive as Canada — and a wealth of Spanish-speaking resources. As Spanish is one of the most widely spoken languages in the world (ranked with English, Mandarin Chinese, and Hindi) and one of the dominant two in the United States, this advantage is not insignificant.

Category	Comments
Infrastructure	Infrastructure is poor outside of the country's three technology parks in Monterrey, Apodaca, and Guadalajara. The electricity system, which is state controlled, will require a $100-billion infusion within a decade in order to meet growing demand.[10]
Stability	The general political climate is relatively calm.
Legal environment	The Mexican legal system differs significantly from the U.S. system. For example, civil litigation is rare in Mexico because it's expensive and no punitive damages are awarded. Litigation in Mexico isn't practical unless a vital business objective is at stake.
Regulatory environment	Mexico is subject to the extensive guidelines of NAFTA, but Mexican customs regulations, product standards, and labor laws may offer pitfalls to unwary U.S. companies.
Travel convenience	Flying direct from New York to Mexico City takes five-and-a-half hours.
Time zone	Mexico takes up three different time zones. Mexico City is one hour behind EST and six hours behind GMT.

Table 11.12: Mexico's Location Attractiveness and Risks

Challenges

Mexico's mid-1990s currency crisis puts the country in a precarious position. The country has only implemented fiscally responsible policies in the last few years, which means that the government cannot begin spending freely on education and infrastructure without risking its newly attained investment-grade rating. Without massive investments in the two, however, Mexico will lose out as an offshoring destination and receive only low-level work, such as basic call center operations. The country has already watched the number of its manufacturing jobs dwindle as they were relocated to China. If Mexico doesn't secure outside funding to overhaul its educational system and infrastructure, the same fate could be in store for its jobs.

Mexico also faces challenges in the forms of crime. President Vincente Fox has begun to tackle the widespread problem of corruption.

Long-Term Outlook

Mexico has gained ground as a viable offshore market. If the country continues on its stable economic course, remains immune to the currency crises of its South American neighbors, and invests heavily in its infrastructure and educational system, it could emerge as a top destination for offshoring IT services and call center operations.

Destination: The Philippines

The Philippines is one of India's closest competitors in providing BPO services. Leading global companies such as Procter & Gamble, Sykes Enterprises, Accenture, and ChevronTexaco are using the Philippines as a base for supporting business processes. These processes include accounting and financial reporting, technical customer support, employee services, accounts payable, and travel management. Many companies have their Asia-Pacific shared services centers in the Philippines.

Competitive Advantages

A long U.S.-Philippine relationship has resulted in low language and cultural barriers between the two countries. Although Philippine BPO providers acknowledge India's head start in offshoring, they point out that Filipinos understand American consumers very well. In addition, for many in the workforce, "The English language in the Philippines is almost second nature to a lot of our countrymen. The medium of instruction in universities and in business is English," according to Charina Quizon of Ambergris Solutions, a Philippine-based provider of customer care, inbound sales, and technical support solutions.[11] As a result, the

Philippines is considered a good location for offshore call centers.

Philippine BPO activity is mainly concentrated in four locations: Manila, Cebu City, Makati City, and Pasig City. In these centers, there is a sizable Filipino workforce skilled in both technology and business processes. Average IT salaries range from $5,000 to $15,000 per year. Average BPO salaries range from $3,000 to $10,000 per year depending on experience.[12]

Category	Comments
Labor	Total population in 2003 was 84.6 million. Low employee turnover is an advantage.
Cost savings	Philippine call center workers start at $2.50 and may go as high as $5.00 (compared to U.S. rates of $8–$20).[13]
Language skills	The Philippines has two official languages: Filipino and English. English is widely spoken.
Technical skills	The universities generate more than 15,000 technical graduates each year.
Education	Universities are considered quite good. More than 400,000 students graduate every year.
Cultural compatibility	Close ties exist with the United States.
Quality	The Philippines had 766 ISO 9000 certifications in 2002.

Table 11.13: The Philippine Workforce's Attractiveness and Economics

Challenges

Political stability and corruption are the primary problems. Since the impeachment of former President Estrada on corruption charges, the country has devoted itself to attracting foreign investment, assigning several senior government officials to promote trade and foreign investment, and closely overseeing any disputes involving foreign investors to ensure they are treated fairly. In addition, President Arroyo has waged a campaign to rid the country of corruption, setting her sights on the customs and tax departments.[14]

The prospect of terrorism is a recurring problem. Four Muslim rebel groups advocating for an Islamic state in the southern Philippines have contributed to the country's instability by leading bombing attacks on civilians (although these attacks have been confined to a small region).

The country's attractiveness as an offshoring destination received a boost when U.S. President George W. Bush declared the Philippines a "major non-NATO ally" in May 2003.

Category	Comments
Infrastructure	High-quality telecom infrastructure in major cities.
Stability	The country faced economic problems in the early 1990s including inflation, rising unemployment, and complaints of official corruption. A more stable political and economic environment has emerged in the last few years.
Legal environment	A member of the WTO since January 1995.
Regulatory environment	In 1991, the Philippines created special economic zones. Companies that set up operations in these zones may receive a tax holiday for up to six years.
Travel convenience	Travel time from London to Manila is approximately 15 hours and includes one stop. Travel time from New York City to Manila is about 21 hours and includes at least one stop.
Time zone	The Philippines is located within one time zone that is eight hours ahead of GMT and 13 hours ahead of EST.

Table 11.14: The Philippines' Location Attractiveness and Risks

Long-Term Outlook

The Philippine government must deliver on its promise of economic reform in order to sustain the country's positive momentum. It also must overhaul the tax system to bolster government revenues and further deregulate and privatize the economy.

Companies have expressed concerns that the Philippines has limited offshoring manpower, but that concern appears unwarranted. Several years ago, call centers remained concentrated in the metro Manila district, but companies have realized that an attractive labor force exists outside the capital and have set up operations in Cebu City, Makati City, and Pasig City. As the Philippine population continues to grow along with university enrollment, the country remains an attractive offshoring destination.

Destination: Russia

With an economic growth rate of almost 7% in 2003[15] and investment-grade credit ratings from some of the international rating agencies, Russia has emerged from its economic upheaval of the late 1990s and made a reputation for itself as an attractive offshore market, particularly for software development.

Russia's strength is its engineering and scientific talent. It has about 3,500 engineers for every 1 million people, nearly the same ratio as the United States.[16] To take advantage of this talent, companies such as Boeing, IBM, Dell, and Citibank have established a presence there.

Category	Comments
Labor	Total population in 2003 of 144.5 million. Employee retention is considered a problem in Russia.
Cost savings	A software developer may earn $10–$40 per hour, which translates into a fully loaded cost of $40,000.
Language skills	Significant language barriers exist between Russian-speaking workers and English-speaking customers.
Technical skills	Russia has approximately 1 million technically trained employees, more than China, Japan, or the United States, and three times as many as India.[17]
Education	Worldwide, Russia has the third-largest pool of engineers, mathematicians, and scientists per capita. Many universities, mainly in the major cities — St. Petersburg, Moscow, and Novosibirsk — offer a steady stream of technical graduates.
Cultural compatibility	As a former communist country, the current generation of Russians does not have much cultural compatibility with Westerners.
Quality	Russia had 1,710 ISO 9000 certifications in 2002.

Table 11.15: Russian Workforce's Attractiveness and Economics

Competitive Advantages

The immense pool of technically trained Russian employees is a huge draw for companies interested in offshoring software development. The technical skills of the Russian workforce go beyond basic programming and extend to complex engineering tasks. In fact, more people work in R&D in Russia than in any other country in the world.[18]

Along with Canada, Ireland, and Mexico, Russia markets its proximity to Europe and the United States as a distinct advantage over other offshoring countries. An eight-hour difference between the East Coast of the United

States and Moscow means that firms can hand work off at the end of the business day to staff in Russia, who can have it ready the following morning. The advantage for European companies lies in being able to sync schedules with Russian workers.

Category	Comments
Infrastructure	Infrastructure is best in technology parks and major cities. Bandwidth costs are high.
Stability	Russia is a barely functional democracy.
Legal environment	The legal environment is weak and constantly in flux.
Regulatory environment	Russia is the only country of the top eight offshoring locations without membership in the WTO.
Travel convenience	A nonstop flight from New York to Moscow is nine hours.
Time zone	Russia spans 11 different time zones. The easternmost time zone is two hours ahead of GMT and the westernmost is 12 hours ahead of GMT.

Table 11.16: Russia's Location Attractiveness and Risks

Challenges

Critics of Russia argue that the bureaucracy needs to be downsized dramatically, regulations for banks need to be tightened, and reforms in the country's tax structure have to be completed. Skeptics point to the investigation of a major shareholder in one of the nation's top oil companies on fraud charges as evidence of the government's willingness to meddle when it suits its best interest.

Russia must reform its business practices to help make it a global offshore player. Russian business practices are not as transparent as U.S. businesses may be used to, even with the spate of business scandals concerning hidden deals. Russian businesses eventually must adopt U.S. GAAP or other accounting standards used in Western countries.

There also are security concerns regarding Russia, despite the government's assertions that the war in Chechnya is over. A wave of suicide bombings — several of which have occurred in the offshoring hub of Moscow — reinforce security as an issue.

Lastly, companies that consider establishing offshore operations outside of major Russian cities may sacrifice sound infrastructure.

Long-Term Outlook

Russia's eventual acceptance to the WTO, possibly in 2004, should enhance its attractiveness as an offshoring destination. Much rides on whether Putin or his successor continues an agenda of opening up the Russian economy to foreign investment.

Destination: South Africa

South Africa has come a long way from its troubled past and is fast becoming known as an attractive offshoring destination. The country has embraced foreign investment by opening all business sectors to investors and by placing limited restrictions on the extent or form of foreign investment.

Competitive Advantages

Some U.K. and German companies view South Africa favorably because its time zone (two hours ahead of GMT) allows them to keep their offshoring operations in sync with their local operations. While the flight to South Africa from the United Kingdom is long, the lack of a significant time zone difference allows better coordination of offshore operations.

Companies also cite a diminished cultural gap between South Africans and U.K. or U.S. citizens. Alison Jones, director of sales and operations Europe with Source One Communications, a global offshore contact center solutions provider, explained her company's decision to open a contact center in South Africa this way: "Very often…when I phone an Indian call center there are accent problems. It is very scripted and false…. Whereas in South Africa, it's a lot more natural. The conversation flows better, and people are able to engage in conversations much easier, much more naturally."[19]

The favorable exchange rate is another advantage of offshoring in South Africa, although the rand has been gaining ground steadily on the U.S. dollar and the euro. In 2002, the average rand per dollar was 10.53, while in 2003 the average rand per dollar was 7.81.[20] The euro has fared slightly better. In 2002, the average rand per euro was 9.91, while in 2003 the average rand per euro was 8.68.

Challenges

South Africa began a privatization push of its state-owned enterprises in the late 1990s in an effort to secure much-needed outside funds. Although the telecommunications fixed-line monopoly in South Africa ended, rates are still not competitive, which drives costs up for businesses interested in setting up call center operations.

Category	Comments
Labor	In 2003, South Africa's total population was 42.8 million.
Cost savings	IT professionals in South Africa earn an average annual salary of U.S. $30,055 (compared to $80,286 in the United States).[21]
Language skills	South Africa has 11 official languages. Many South Africans speak English, and it is often used in business and in government.
Technical skills	South Africa has 15 *technikons* — universities of technology that offer degree programs up to the doctoral level — that specialize in technical education.
Education	The South African university system consists of 21 universities graduating some 400,000 students. The quality of education is considered good.
Cultural compatibility	South Africa's British and German heritage makes it highly compatible with European companies. English is understood and spoken by most people.
Quality	South Africa had 2,625 ISO 9000 certifications in 2002.

Table 11.17: South African Workforce's Attractiveness and Economics

The country faces an uphill battle socially and medically. The AIDS virus has taken a severe toll on South Africa, with an estimated 11% of the population infected.[22] A 2003 World Bank study warned that the nation could face a "complete economic collapse" if it does not take steps to combat the disease, although government officials have called that claim unfounded and point to the steps they have taken to decrease the infection rate. In addition, South Africa has an extremely high crime rate. Both of these problems could translate to increased costs for employers in the form of healthcare and security.

Lastly, South Africa must confront its shortage of skilled employees, many of whom have left South Africa and sought work in other countries, such as the United Kingdom.

Category	Comments
Infrastructure	Roads, rail, air, and shipping are improving steadily. Gauteng province is the high-tech hub with 70% of the high-tech workforce of South Africa.
Stability	South Africa has been a multiparty democracy since the lifting of apartheid. Although the transition from Nelson Mandela's to Thabo Mbeki's presidency was stable, Mbeki's political judgments on several key policy issues such as race, HIV/AIDS, and Zimbabwe have been questioned.
Legal environment	The Competition Act of 1998 was developed to end anticompetitive practices and dominance. Companies have complained that South Africa enforces intellectual property right and copyright law loosely.
Regulatory environment	The taxation system is in a state of transition. Packages for investors in strategic industrial projects are available and entail tax allowances for approved investments.
Travel convenience	Direct flights to South Africa leaving from New York's JFK and arriving in Johannesburg take 15 hours. More than fifty foreign air carriers serve South Africa, including most European, Asian, and African airlines.
Time zone	South Africa operates on one time zone — two hours ahead of GMT and seven hours ahead of EST.

Table 11.18: South Africa's Location Attractiveness and Risks

Long-Term Outlook

South Africa is a middle-income, developing country. It has an abundant supply of natural resources, well-developed financial, legal, communications, energy, and transport sectors.

Growth, however, has not been strong enough to cut into high unemployment, and daunting economic and social problems remain from the apartheid era, especially the problems of poverty and the lack of economic empowerment among the disadvantaged groups.

Honorable Mentions: Countries on the Verge

As the number of companies considering offshoring grows, so do the number of countries competing for their business. While India holds the largest market share and should continue to do so for years, several countries are looking to give India a run for its money. In Eastern Europe,

Hungary, Poland, and the Czech Republic are steadily signing contracts for offshoring work. In Asia, Singapore, Malaysia, and Vietnam pose the biggest threat to the top offshore locations. In South America, Brazil is emerging as a contender in offshoring. Let's look at each of these up-and-coming offshore destinations.

Brazil. Brazil could topple one of the top eight offshore locations with its enormous population if President da Silva and his team are successful in their agenda of maintaining economic stability by fighting inflation, instituting tax and pension reform, and maintaining strict fiscal discipline. However, Brazil's struggle to pay off its massive amount of debt means that the government has little funding to reinvest in the country's educational system or infrastructure.

The Caribbean. The Caribbean could emerge as a competitive offshoring force if call centers continue to crop up in Jamaica, the Dominican Republic, Puerto Rico, and other locations. The main obstacle to the Caribbean's success as an offshoring destination is the high cost of connectivity and access. The Caribbean's primary benefits are its nearness to the United States, as well the long trading history between the region and the United States.

Eastern Europe. Eastern European countries such as Hungary, Poland, Romania, and the Czech Republic merit honorable mention because they possess some or all of the following: skilled software engineers; up-to-date infrastructure; increased ease of travel from Western Europe or the United States in comparison to India, China, or the Philippines; and decreased cultural gaps with Western European customers.

Israel. Israel was one of the primary destinations for offshore outsourcing until the prolonged conflict with the Palestinians began. The country's labor pool, though small in comparison to players such as India or China, is quite technologically savvy. In particular, Israel has shown a talent for developing high-end systems, security software, and learning systems.

Malaysia. Malaysia's status as a choice offshore location is backed by a strong pro IT government, which has led to the development of the famous Multimedia Super Corridor (MSC). The MSC occupies a 15-kilometer by 50-kilometer corridor governed by innovative cyberlaws, policies, and practices to provide companies an ideal multimedia environment. Other positive factors include a largely English-speaking workforce and low real estate and labor costs. Malaysia has very sophisticated communications and IT infrastructure.

Singapore. Due to a government that encourages foreign investment by offering businesses big tax incentives, excellent telecom and IT infrastructure, and a culture heavily influenced by the West, Singapore has teetered on the edge of becoming a major offshore destination. A shortage of skilled IT workers and a lack of sufficient low-cost labor are the reasons why it hasn't become one of the top offshoring destinations.

Vietnam. Vietnam is emerging as an offshore destination for software development and architecture. The country is politically and economically stable and, although poor, has invested heavily in educating its population. Typical pay is about $6,000 a year, high by local standards (Vietnam's gross domestic product is about $400 per capita). The cost of IT development in Vietnam is estimated to be 15% less than doing the work in India.[23]

Summary

Managers considering offshore outsourcing in a new country or geographic region must evaluate macroeconomic, demographic, and political issues of long-term significance. They must carefully weigh international trade issues, such as currency exchange risks, import-export quotas, and taxes. The availability of skilled labor; infrastructure support services; political, cultural, and legal concerns; and quality-of-life issues — all must be addressed before a significant investment in a new country is made.

Companies tend to learn from their experiences in site selection. Often, two or three sites that seem to have identical location profiles yield vastly different operational results. After looking at several existing sites, managers begin to see what makes a location good for their specific purposes. They find that a good location for a call center is not necessarily a good location for a software development center.

The best approach to location selection is to analyze the demographic and performance characteristics of the firm's existing sites and select sites based on those factors most closely associated with superior operational results.

Chapter Twelve

Final Thoughts on Offshore Outsourcing

King Louis XVI: "Is it a revolt?"
Duc de la Rochefoucauld-Liancourt: "No, Sire, it is a revolution."

Over the past decade, offshore outsourcing activity has accelerated at a rapid pace. Large, global companies have recognized the importance of "leasing or buying" versus "building" capabilities when striving to meet corporate cost reduction and growth objectives.

Corporate boards and senior management are beginning to understand the economic impact offshore outsourcing is having and are starting to ask: "What are our competitors doing in this area? What should our offshore outsourcing strategy be?" We addressed both of these topics in this succinct but detailed guide to offshore outsourcing. We hope it is now clear to our readers that offshore outsourcing is not a "nice-to-have" strategy but a "need-to-have" strategy.

Some key points that we emphasize throughout this book follow.

Offshore outsourcing is becoming a "need-to-have" competency. As the global capacity for delivering remote services develops, many business processes currently being performed internally will be outsourced. Whichever business process you choose to offshore, successful implementation will demand considerable front-end investment and long-term strategic planning.

Offshore outsourcing is a tactical business decision with long-term implications. Companies must achieve two milestones through offshoring to compete successfully: 1) cost reduction, which is realized by transforming cost structures, and 2) competitive differentiation, which requires companies to actively define innovative operating models and process capabilities to satisfy the changing needs of the market place.

Offshore outsourcing is no longer an unproven model. Numerous firms have demonstrated that offshore outsourcing, if executed well, can be a powerful tool for reducing operating costs. It has become clear in recent years that leading companies can utilize offshore outsourcing to benefit and enhance a variety of business processes from IT application development to customer care. However, it is imperative that the strategic goals and expected results are predetermined.

The Internet is transforming offshore outsourcing. The Internet's vast power and unique economics underpin the future of offshore outsourcing. Internet-enabled offshore outsourcing has matured considerably over the past five years and offers significant advantages to companies that know how to do it right. Creative firms such as Dell, IBM, HP, and GE have already seized this model to create new value propositions.

We are in uncharted territory. New rules. New tools. New business models. This means new management techniques have to be created to effectively manage offshore outsourcing.

Management strategies tend to come and go, but we are convinced offshore outsourcing is not just another fad. It is a powerful idea, albeit a difficult one to implement. This book doesn't give a magic formula for success but demonstrates that sensible strategies can produce substantial rewards.

Whether you are exploring a pilot project or ramping up an established offshoring project, it is critical that you work through these questions:

- Do you have a compelling business case for offshoring that will win stakeholder commitment and approval?

- Which business processes are candidates for offshoring?

- What evaluation criteria are important to your company when selecting offshore providers?

- What should the primary location selection criteria be? What is the best location for your business needs?

- What risks need to be mitigated when shifting business operations offshore?

- How do you effectively transfer knowledge to the offshore center? How do you maintain business continuity throughout the transition?

- What service level agreement metrics are necessary?

- What change management and governance issues have to be addressed?

The key to success is a disciplined plan that minimizes risks. The market leaders that have been successful at offshoring do not view outsourcing as a short-term fix for saving money and "getting rid" of some noncore functions. They are building a long-term foundation that can help lower operating costs, improve customer service, and generate top-line growth.

Firms that ignore the offshoring outsourcing phenomenon are reminded of an obvious risk: If they cannot reduce their cost structures quickly, they may be heading for trouble. The facts bear out the implications of this remark. Of the companies appearing on the original Fortune 500 list in 1954, well over 400 companies were gone from the list almost 50 years later.[1]

We close this book with some advice. If you want your company to be successful, make sure you plan its innovation and cost containment strategies well. Include offshore outsourcing as a part of the tactical mix, and keep this book handy. You never know when you may need it.

Endnotes

Chapter One

1. Pete Engardio, Aaron Bernstein, and Manjeet Kripalani, "The New Global Job Shift," *BusinessWeek*, February 3, 2003.

2. Manjeet Kripalani and Pete Engardio, "The Rise of India," *BusinessWeek*, December 8, 2003.

3. John Ribeiro, "Accenture to double India staff to 10,000," IDG News Service (as posted on InfoWorld), December 3, 2003.

4. Stella M. Hopkins, "State's Contracts Ship Work to India," *Charlotte Observer* (North Carolina), August 10, 2003.

5. The leader of this school of thought, Oliver Williamson, developed the concept of asset specificity and built a theory of the firm based around the need for firms to economize on transaction costs.

6. If you are interested in learning more about diffusion, see Everett Rogers's *Diffusion of Innovations* (New York: Free Press, 1995).

7. The source was a presentation given by William Strauss, senior business economist and advisor, Federal Reserve Bank of Chicago, titled "Manufacturing in Long-Term Perspective," at a workshop held on September 30, 2003.

8. Geoff Moore in his book *Crossing the Chasm* (New York: HarperBusiness, 1991) popularized the concept of the technology adoption lifecycle. His model is based on the diffusion work of Everett Rogers.

9. These percentages are based on the classic normal distribution or bell curve, which means statistically that a random sample of any given population of companies must contain: 2.5% innovators, 13.5% early adopters, 33.4% early majority, 33.4% late majority, and 16.0% laggards.

Chapter Two

1. This information was originally released on one of GE's many Web sites, www.gecapitalindia.com/gecapital/factsheet.pdf.

2. Mr. Scott Bayman, president and CEO, GE India, included this information in a presentation titled "Return of the Big Bet: U.S. Business in India" given to the U.S.-India Business Council at its 27th annual meeting in Washington, D.C., on June 17, 2002.

3. This information was contained within the NASSCOM (India's National Association of Software and Services Companies) and McKinsey 2002 report the two organizations coauthored.

4. EDS released this information during its 2003 annual shareholders meeting held on May 20, 2003.

5. See note 2 above.

6. The source for this information was a 2003 LUXOFT white paper. See the LUXOFT Web site, www.luxoft.com, for more information.

7. December 3, 2003, Accenture press release titled "Accenture Set To Ramp Up India Headcount To 10,000," posted on the Financial Express Web site, www.financialexpress.com.

8. See note 1 above.

Chapter Three

1. Spencer E. Ante, "Savings Tip: Don't Do It Yourself," *BusinessWeek*, June 23, 2003.

2. E-Business Strategies conducted an interview with Richard Swanson, director of BPO Services, Patni Computer Systems, on September 19, 2003.

3. For more information, read Dell's press release, "Dell Launches International Services in India," June 14, 2001.

4. Chitra Phadnis, "Dell Forays into Software — On Hiring Spree," *The Hindu Business Line* (Internet edition), June 14, 2002.

5. Associated Press, "Dell Cancels Indian Tech Support," as released on the CNN Web site on November 25, 2003.

6. J.R. Carter originally stated this in the June 19, 2002, LUXOFT press release, "DELL and LUXOFT Set up a Dedicated Software Development Center."

7. David Tzeng and Chou Hua-hsin, "Wistron Lands 1.1 Million PDA Contract from Dell, Due out for Christmas," Digitimes.com (www.digitimes.com) July 31, 2002.

8. Andrew Park, Faith Keenan, and Cliff Edwards, "Whose Lunch Will Dell Eat Next?" BusinessWeek Online, August 12, 2002.

9. Knowledge@Wharton, "What Works, What Doesn't: Lessons From Two Companies that Outsource Back-Office Tasks," publication date unknown.

10. This information originated from a presentation given by American Express at the NASSCOM India Leadership Forum, held on February 12, 2003.

11. See note 9 above.

12. Knowledge@Wharton, "Anatomy of an India Success Story," as released on CNET News.com on June 7, 2003.

Chapter Four

1. Kerry Massaro, "Managing the Offshore Relationship," *Wall Street & Technology*, October 3, 2003.

2. Ibid.

3. Ibid.

4. Larry Greenemeier, "Offshore Outsourcing Grows to Global Proportions," *InformationWeek*, February 11, 2002.

5. Source: Gartner Dataquest.

6. Tata Infotech, "Tata Infotech wins World Book contract," May 9, 2001, press release.

7. Tata Infotech provides more information in its company profile, which can be found on the company's Web site, www.tatainfotech.com.

8. This Coors case study written by EDS was posted on the EDS Web site, www.eds.com, as of December 9, 2003.

9. Eric Wahlgren, "Cognizant: Riding the Outsourcing Wave," *BusinessWeek*, October 10, 2003. Also see the case study posted on the company's Web site www.cognizant.com/customers/customers_case_fdms.htm, as of October 18, 2003.

10. Mylene Mangalindan, "Google to Open Center in India," *The Wall Street Journal*, December 11, 2003.

11. Julie Gallagher, "CIOs Turn Their Attention to BPO," Insurance and Technology Online (www.insurancetech.com), October 23, 2002.

12. E-Business Strategies conducted an interview with Venu G. Vaishya, the vice president of application maintenance and development and offshore solutions for Covansys Corporation, on October 20, 2003.

13. Ibid.

14. Stephanie Overby, "The Guardian View," *CIO*, June 1, 2003.

15. Lori Chordas, "Eyes on India," *Best's Review*, May 1, 2003.

16. E-Business Strategies conducted an interview with the Aztec Software Vice President of Marketing, Shirish Netke, on December 11, 2003.

17. Julia King, "IT's Global Itinerary: Offshore Outsourcing Is Inevitable," *Computerworld*, September 15, 2003.

18. E-Business Strategies conducted an interview with Bob Evans, CEO of Symphony Services Corporation, on September 8, 2003.

19. This quote originated from a questionnaire that NIIT SmartServe completed for E-Business Strategies on October 30, 2003.

20. See note 16 above.

Chapter Five

1. Michael Goldstein, "Customer call center jobs exported from U.S. to India," *New York Daily News*, January 20, 2003.

2. Sykes Enterprises, "Sykes Enterprises, Incorporated Selected by Procter & Gamble for 5-Year, $70 Million Global Customer Care Contract," June 30, 2003, press release.

3. E-Business Strategies conducted an interview with Derek Holley, president of eTelecare, on October 10, 2003.

4. E -Business Strategies conducted an interview with Ashish Kumar, AVP marketing, 24/7 Customer, on September 23, 2003.

5. This information was released in Sykes Enterprises' 2002 annual report.

6. B. Cleveland, president of the Incoming Calls Management Institute (ICMI) as posted on the Outsource World Web site, www.outsourceworld.org, on May 5, 2003.

7. Nadji Tehrani, "19 Years of Call Center/CRM Evolution and the Incredible Growth Continues! What Next?" *Call Center Solutions*, July 1, 2000.

8. The source for this information was an overview presentation written by Ambergris Solutions released to E-Business Strategies on November 10, 2003.

9. Greg Paeth, "Convergys sending jobs overseas," *The Cincinnati Post*, November 15, 2003.

10. CNET News.com, "AOL adds 400 jobs in India," released on CNET News.com Web site (http://news.com.com) on July 16, 2003.

11. For more information, refer to Source One's Web site, www.sourceoneglobal.com.

12. Mary Hayes, "Outsourcing Call Centers Pays Off for Delta," *InformationWeek*, June 17, 2003.

13. Paul McDougall, "Opportunity on the Line," *InformationWeek*, October 20, 2003.

14. Same as note 12.

15. The source for this information was Wipro's case study on Delta posted on the company Web site (www.wipro.com/spectramind) as of December 10, 2003.

16. Arielle Emmett, "Outsourcing Overseas: Asian 'Hot Spots' Flare," *Customer Interface*, April 1, 2002.

17. Carol Borghesi, director of BT Retail's Next Generation Contact Centers, released this information during a BT CRM event titled "The Cultural Implications of CRM," held on November 14, 2002.

18. Nick Wyke, "Cool centres welcome call of excellence," posted on the Times Online Web site, www.timesonline.co.uk, on April 25, 2002.

19. See BT's 2003 annual report.

20. BT Retail, "BT Retail Announces Extra Investment in UK Contact Centres and Confirms Plans for Two Centres in India," March 7, 2003, press release.

21. BT Retail and HCL Technologies, "HCL secures $160 million contract from BT," April 7, 2003, press release.

22. Infosys Technologies released this information during its fourth-quarter 2003 earnings call held during April 2003.

23. This information originated from an eWorld (a division of The Hindu Business Line) interview with Ian Rippin of BT Retail and Sujit Baksi of HCL BPO conducted by Rukmini Priyardarshini on June 25, 2003.

24. E-Business Strategies conducted an interview with Sanjay Kumar, founder and CEO of vCustomer Corp., on September 22, 2003.

25. E-Business Strategies conducted an interview with Eric Paljug, vice president of marketing, vCustomer Corp., on September 19, 2003.

26. E-Business Strategies conducted an interview with Somshankar Das, chief executive officer and president of e4e, on October 23, 2003.

Chapter Six

1. This information was originally released in Accenture's case study on Rhodia titled, "Cause Celebre: Outsourcing...Changing the Way the Cookie Crumbles," available on the Accenture Web site as of December 10, 2003.

2. British Airways, "A new BA for the new millennium," September 18, 1996, press release.

3. "British Airways opts to follow Indian trail," *The Corporate Accountant*, January 1997.

4. "British Airways to cut 600 accounting jobs," *Aviation Daily*, November 8, 1996.

5. "BA sets up subsidiary to source software from India," *Aviation Daily*, November 5, 1996.

6. "BA 'Business Efficiency Program' said vital to competing," *World Airline News*, October 7, 1996.

7. IBM "Offshore resourcing: Once adventurous, now essential for financial services firms," IBM Business Consulting Services white paper.

8. WNS Global Services, "British Airways: Making Customer and Profit Connections with WNS," WNS Global Services case study available through the *CIO* Web site, www.cio.com.

9. Ibid.

10. The information contained in this case study was based on a client profile that Ephinay Corporation sent to E-Business Strategies on October 3, 2003. We disguised the name of the firm for confidentiality reasons.

11. E-Business Strategies conducted an interview with Michael D. Gantt, the CEO and president of Ephinay Corporation, on September 25, 2003.

12. E-Business Strategies conducted an interview with Andy Kankan, founder and executive vice president of Ephinay Corporation, on October 10, 2003.

13. Ibid.

14. eFunds Corporation, "Risk Management Alternatives signs contract with eFunds," July 26, 2001, press release.

Chapter Seven

1. IBM and Procter & Gamble, "P&G and IBM Sign $400 Million Employee Services Outsourcing Agreement," September 9, 2003, press release.

2. This information was released in the BT Outsourcing Case Study, "Outsourcing gives BT focus and adds value to bottom line," written by BT and available on the company's Web site, www.btglobalservices.com, as of December 11, 2003.

3. Accenture originally included this information in its case study "BT—Human Resources Outsourcing" available on the company's Web site, www.accenture.com, as of December 11, 2003.

4. This data was released at the 2002 annual conference of the Society for Human Resource Management.

5. Motorola and Affiliated Computer Services, "ACS and Motorola Sign 10-Year Contract for Human Resources Services Valued at $650 Million," December 19, 2002, press release.

6. Shari Caudron, "HR is Dead…Long Live HR." *Workforce*, December 23, 2002.

7. Sarah Lunday and Rick Rothacker, "BofA to Send Tech Jobs Overseas; Bank Says It Will Outsource Less Than 5% of Tech Operations," *Charlotte Observer* (North Carolina), March 6, 2002.

8. Indo-Asian News Service, "$2 Million Global Technology Centre Coming Up in Hyderabad," June 25, 2003.

9. General Motors and Arthur Andersen, "General Motors And Arthur Andersen Extend Financial Transactions Processing Agreement To Europe," May 16, 2000, press release.

10. Affiliated Computer Services and General Motors, "ACS Announces New Human Resources Servicing Contract with General Motors for European Operation," November 4, 2003, press release.

Chapter Eight

1. This quote originated from a questionnaire that TransWorks completed for E-Business Strategies on October 27, 2003.

2. eOriginal, "Electronic Signature Legislation to Streamline Business Process and Enable 'Complete' E-Commerce," June 16, 2000, press release.

3. This information was based on a case study that TransWorks sent to E-Business Strategies on October 27, 2003.

4. Joshua Weinberger, "Voice of Experience: S.A. Ibrahim - The Down Payment," *Baseline* magazine (www.baselinemag.com), June 1, 2003.

5. Infosys, "Infosys subsidiary, Progeon, to provide Business Process Management services to GreenPoint Mortgage," press release, June 4, 2002.

6. Aviva, "Aviva announces offshoring plans for 2004," December 2, 2003, press release.

7. This information originated in an overview presentation that ICICI OneSource sent to E-Business Strategies on November 23, 2003.

8. John Harney, "Staking a Claim to Excellence with an Offshore Component," published on www.outsourcing-offshore.com, March 2003.

9. This information was originally listed on the ACS Web site under the client testimonials section, www.acs-inc.com/bpo/fa/ourclients.html.

10. Monica Tadak and Caroline Rader, "Outsourcing Hospital Medical Transcription Services with CBay Systems," (publication data unknown).

11. CBay Systems lists this information as one of the reasons companies should consider it for offshore medical transcription on its Web site, http://www.cbayscribe.com/cbaysystems/why.htm.

12. The information related to LexisNexis was pieced together from several sources. Two primary sources were the LexisNexis case study written by Datamatics and LexisNexis case study published by Microsoft.

13. Andrew Pollack, "Who's Reading Your X-Ray?" *The New York Times*, November 16, 2003.

14. James Brice, "Globalization comes to radiology," *Diagnostic Imaging*, November 1, 2003.

Chapter Nine

1.   E-Business Strategies conducted an interview with Phaneesh Murthy, CEO, iGATE Global Solutions, on December 3, 2003.

2.   E-Business Strategies conducted an interview with Sanjay Kumar, founder and CEO, vCustomer Corp., on September 22, 2003.

3.   E-Business Strategies conducted an interview with Somshankar Das, the chief executive officer and president of e4e, on October 23, 2003.

4.   Businesswire (via ClariNet news services, www.clari.net), "ICICI OneSource 4th Q Forecast: Financial Services Offshore Outsourcing Will Grow by 20%," September 24, 2003.

5.   Jack McCarthy, "Redefining offshore outsourcing," *InfoWorld*, November 29, 2002.

6.   E-Business Strategies conducted an interview with Richard Swanson, director of BPO services, Patni Computer Systems, on September 19, 2003.

7.   This quotes originated from an interview that E-Business Strategies conducted with Tim Barry, vice president of outsourcing at Keane Inc., on October 14, 2003.

8.   E-Business Strategies conducted an interview with Tim Lavin, senior vice president for operations, Ambergris Solutions, on November 21, 2003.

9.   Stephanie Overby, "Inside Outsourcing in India," *CIO*, June 1, 2003.

10. Mary Hayes, "Doing Offshore Right" *InformationWeek*, August 4, 2003.

11. See note 5 above.

12. E-Business Strategies conducted an interview with Ilya Billig, vice president of marketing at LUXOFT, on November 11, 2003.

13. Paul McDougall "Opportunity on the Line," *InformationWeek*, October 20, 2003.

14. Ibid.

15. See note 2 above.

16. See note 5 above.

17. Stephanie Overby, "The Hidden Costs of Offshore Outsourcing," *CIO*, September 1, 2003.

Chapter Ten

1.   E-Business Strategies conducted an interview with Vellayan Subbiah, vice president of sales and marketing at 24/7 Customer, on September 23, 2003.

2.   Stephanie Overby, "The Hidden Costs of Offshore Outsourcing," *CIO*, September 1, 2003.

3.   David Lazarus, "Lazarus At Large: A politician who reads the papers," *San Francisco Chronicle* (column), October 26, 2003.

4.   E-Business Strategies conducted an interview with Tim Lavin, senior vice president for operations, Ambergris Solutions, on November 21, 2003.

5.   E-Business Strategies conducted an interview with Derek Holley, president of eTelecare, on October 10, 2003.

6.   E-Business Strategies conducted an interview with Krishnaswamy Subrahmaniam, president and CEO of Covansys India and Asia, during November 2003.

7.   Many Indian companies opt to have their fiscal year end on March 31, rather than December 31, as the majority of U.S. and European companies do.

Chapter Eleven

1. The 2003 Information Technology Toolbox, Inc (ITtoolbox) Salary Survey.

2. CNETAsia, "High-Tech Salaries in China Climbing: Survey," August 21, 2003. See also the Chinese Web site, www.china.org.cn.

3. "Chinese Lamas Learning to Speak English," *People's Daily* (www.english.peopledaily.com.cn), January 2, 2003.

4. Elizabeth C. Economy, "Asia Expert Says U.S.-China Relations Booming," interview by Bernard Gwertzman, posted on the Council on Foreign Relations Web site (www.cfr.org) September 12, 2003.

5. This information was originally released in a 2002 white paper written by the American Chamber of Commerce in the People's Republic of China.

6. See note 1 above.

7. This information came from the following Web site: www.offshoreitoutsourcing.com.

8. See the Web site of IDA Ireland, the Irish government agency responsible for the industrial development and investment of overseas companies Ireland, at www.ida.ie.

9. Brendan B. Read "'Gracias por Llamar' (Thank You for Calling)" *CallCenter Magazine*, October 10, 2003.

10. Christian Stracke, "Mexico—The Sick Man of NAFTA" *World Policy Journal* 20 no. 2 (2003).

11. E-Business Strategies conducted an interview with Charina Quizon, marketing manager, Ambergris Solutions, on September 19, 2003.

12. neoIT's "Mapping Offshore Markets" white paper published in April 2003.

13. ePerformax, a company that specializes in offering contact center solutions from the Philippines or the United States, released this information on its Web site, www.eperformax.com.

14. Stuart Grudgings, "Corruption Dogs Philippines as Elections Near," Reuters, September 26, 2003.

15. Geri Smith "Emerging Might; Champion in China, Russia, and Elsewhere Lure Investors," BusinessWeek online, July 14, 2003.

16. The source was the Russian Web site www.outsourcing-russia.com

17. Source: the World Bank.

18. "Whitepaper on Offshore Software Development in Russia" published by the American Chamber of Commerce in Russia, last modified February 21, 2003.

19. E-Business Strategies conducted an interview with Alison Jones, director of sales and operations Europe for Source One Communications, on September 10, 2003.

20. As of October 9, 2003.

21. See note 1 above.

22. The Washington Post News Services "World in Brief: One-Fifth of S. African Military Has Aids Virus," October 8, 2003.

23. Andrew Bibby, "Outsourcing to Vietnam," *Financial Times*, August 20, 2003.

Chapter Twelve

1. For an old but detailed analysis of the changes in the Fortune 500 see "Forty Years of the 500" by Carol J. Loomis, *FORTUNE*, May 15, 1995.

Index